Consuming Korean Tradition
in Early and Late Modernity

Consuming Korean Tradition in Early and Late Modernity

Commodification, Tourism, and Performance

edited by Laurel Kendall

University of Hawai'i Press | Honolulu

Library of Congress Cataloging-in-Publication Data
Consuming Korean tradition in early and late modernity :
commodification, tourism, and performance /
edited by Laurel Kendall.
     p. cm.
Includes bibliographical references and index.
ISBN 978-0-8248-3393-0 (hardcover : alk. paper)
     1. Korea — Civilization — 20th century — Congresses.
2. Korea (South) — Civilization — 20th century — Congresses.
3. Korea — Social life and customs — 20th century —
Congresses.   4. Korea (South) — Social life and customs —
20th century — Congresses.   5. National characteristics,
Korean — Congresses.   6. Culture and tourism — Korea
(South) — Congresses.   I. Kendall, Laurel.
DS916.27.C66 2011
951.904—dc22   2010023992

Designed by April Leidig-Higgins

Printed by Edwards Brothers, Inc.

Contents

Laurel Kendall
Preface and Acknowledgments vii

Laurel Kendall
Introduction:
Material Modernity, Consumable Tradition 1

Part I. Modernity as Spectacle/Spectacular Korea 19

1 **Katarzyna J. Cwiertka**
Dining Out in the Land of Desire:
Colonial Seoul and the Korean Culture of Consumption 21

2 **Timothy R. Tangherlini**
Shrinking Culture:
Lotte World and the Logic of Miniaturization 39

Part II. Korea as Itinerary 65

3 **Hyung Il Pai**
Travel Guides to the Empire:
The Production of Tourist Images in Colonial Korea 67

4 **Okpyo Moon**
Guests of Lineage Houses:
Tourist Commoditization of Confucian
Cultural Heritage in Korea 88

5 **Robert Oppenheim**
Crafting the Consumability of Place:
Tapsa and *Paenang Yŏhaeng* as Travel Goods 105

Part III. Korean Things 127

6   Laurel Kendall
The *Changsŭng* Defanged:
The Curious Recent History of a Korean Cultural Symbol 129

7   Kyung-Koo Han
The "Kimchi Wars" in Globalizing East Asia:
Consuming Class, Gender, Health, and National Identity 149

Part IV. Korea Performed 167

8   Judy Van Zile
Blurring Tradition and Modernity:
The Impact of Japanese Colonization and Ch'oe Sŭng-hŭi
on Dance in South Korea Today 169

9   Keith Howard
Kugak Fusion and the Politics of Korean
Musical Consumption 195

Bibliography 217

Contributors 245

Index 247

Preface and Acknowledgments

Consuming Korean Tradition in Early and Late Modernity explores "traditions" that are produced and consumed in recognizably modern ways. Beyond the now common recognition that self-conscious "tradition" is a sign of the modern, we are concerned with the specific processes that enable the recognition, appreciation, marketing, and consumption of emotionally resonant Korean things. We consider the birth of these processes in early modern Korea as well as their contemporary realization in theme parks, performances, handicrafts, cuisine, and tourism.

This volume had its origin in a conference held at the Center for Korean Studies at the University of Hawai'i October 13–15, 2006 and funded by the Korea Foundation and the Northeast Asian Area Council, Association for Asian Studies. We are grateful to the Center and its Director, Homin Sohn for hospitality. Special thanks go to Edward J. Shultz, former CKS Director and now Dean of the School of Pacific and Asian Studies, for encouraging this project from its inception, fundraising, and hosting us in the best sense of aloha. Thanks to Ned's thoughtfulness and extraordinary organizational abilities, neither an earthquake nor a major power blackout in the city of Honolulu deterred us from our schedule and a jolly celebration at the end.

Geoffrey White and Judy Van Zile served as discussants. Although Sangmee Bak, John Finch, Eun Mee Kim, Jennifer Jung-Kim, Seungkyung Kim, and Roald Maliangkay were not able to complete papers for this volume, their enthusiastic participation in the conference deepened our understanding of the topic. Kristen Olson, in the Anthropology Division of the American Museum of Natural History, assisted in the preparation of the final manuscript. Patricia Crosby, at the University of Hawai'i Press, provided valuable advice and encouragement throughout the process of editing.

Korean terms are romanized according to the McCune-Reischauer system and Japanese terms according to Hepburn, with the exception of words that have conventional spellings in English (Park Chung-hee) or in cases where an author has a preferred name romanization. Names are given in Korean and Japanese order, surname first, unless a cited author has published in English using English name order. Authors writing on the colonial period give then-contemporary place-names in Japanese with the Korean equivalent in parentheses following the first use (Keijō [Seoul]).

Consuming Korean Tradition
in Early and Late Modernity

Laurel Kendall

Introduction
Material Modernity, Consumable Tradition

When Taebok turned the knob of the radio on the little table beside Master
Yun's bed, traditional music poured out instantly, as if it had been waiting:
"Tta-ang-tchi-tchi, chŭ-ŭng-chung-ji. Ta-ang-chŭng-ŭng-ta-ang . . ."
— Ch'ae Man-sik, *Peace under Heaven*, 1938

I passed a stone lion at the entrance to the tearoom and stepped inside to the
slow rhythm of a folk song from one of the northwestern provinces. A wedding
costume from long ago mounted on the wall caught my eye. Kites ornamented
the ceiling — a unique sight. With its wooden chests serving as tables, its candle-
stick holders shaped like butterflies, its framed folk paintings and such, the tearoom was cozy and classic. — Kang Sŏk-kyŏng, "A Room in the Woods," 1986

The relics of early Korean modernity appear in museum displays of vintage radios — like the one described in Ch'ae Man-
sik's period novel — gramophones, old photographs, magazines, and postcards; their contemporary equivalents, in the high-tech
gadgetry that South Korea so adroitly produces for global and domestic
markets. Seoul subway cars reverberate to cell-phone renderings of sym-
phonies, Christian hymns, and rock tunes from the Korean wave. Anthropologist Daniel Miller argues that "consumption represents, at the very
least, one possible idiom for these larger problems of modernity," a conscious coming to terms with things not of one's own making (1995a, 2). But
if, as Baudrillard (2001) asserts, the objects of consumption are primarily
"simulacra," copies or citations in infinite replay of something else, some
contemporary South Korean simulacra are conscious citations of "tradition": the nearly inevitable portrait of the bride and groom posed in traditional costume, the CD of traditional or traditionalist-fusion music, the
folk village theme park or staged folk festival as a site of both foreign and
domestic tourism, the elegant riffs on traditional ceramics, textiles, and
woodcraft on sale in Seoul's Insadong District. The traditional motif tea-

room in Kang Sŏk-kyŏng's story of alienated South Korean youth traffics in the notion that replicas of old furniture and folk paintings and herbal teas served in rough earthen bowls are in some basic sense "traditionally Korean" and therefore the customer's own things — a pleasurable eliding of their other identity as reproductions and commodities. At the same time, the traditionalist tearoom décor provides pleasant background to the quintessentially modern possibility of two college-educated women meeting for conversation in a commercial tearoom even as their grandmothers might have imbibed modernity in the roof garden of an early twentieth-century Seoul department store. Dean MacCannell offers the apt observation that "the best indication of the final victory of modernity over other socio-cultural arrangements is not the disappearance of the non-modern world, but its artificial preservation and reconstruction in modern society" (1999, 7).

As an ideological position, modernity suggests receptivity to social and technological innovation and a repudiation of the past, but modernity also implies encounters with new material environments and new ways of regarding and engaging the world (Baudrillard 1987; Bennet 1988; Mitchell 1989). Arjun Appadurai writes of how, growing up in Bombay, he "saw and smelled modernity reading *Life* and American college catalogs at the United States Information Service library, [and] seeing B-grade films (and some A-grade ones) from Hollywood at the Eros Theatre, five hundred yards from my apartment building" (1996, 1).

This material, sensate, and embodied experience of modernity, and how such a modernity comes to define, package, and selectively present "tradition" as its own shadow image, concerns us here. Modernities are seldom complete and far from uniform. The radio, a luxury in 1930s Seoul, contained within itself the slow rhythm of a Korean folk song, an image Ch'ae Man-sik uses to suggest the conservative Korean patriarch contained within Master Yun's modern veneer. Decades later, the influx of consumer goods from a global marketplace breeds South Korean anxieties over a perceived loss of cultural traction (Cho Hae-joang 1998; Nelson 2000, 2006), a local variation of what Ulf Hannerz (1992) has dubbed "Cocacolonization." Miller (1995c), David Howes (1996), and James Watson (1997) argue to the contrary that even despite the relentless flood of new commodities, local cultures have sufficient resilience to appropriate new forms into local meanings and uses, as described for South Korea's experience of McDonald's (Bak 1997), Starbucks (Bak 2005), and globalized consumption more generally (Bak 2004; Moon 1997a). *Consuming Korean Tradition* looks at the other side of the mirror, exploring the ironic space where contemporary South Koreans consume a traditional "us" that, like the music lurking inside Master Yun's radio, comes packaged in such modern commodity forms as recorded music; commercial venues for food, tea, and alcohol; ticketed performances; shopping mall entertainments; gallery art; and alternative tourist itineraries. In other words, tradition becomes a commodity enabled by updated iterations of some common apparatuses of modernity that Koreans first encountered in the early twentieth century, including the staged performances, department stores, reproducible images, and early tourism discussed in this volume.

Consuming Korean Tradition, like the conference that preceded it, sustains a dialogue between historians of early modern Korea and scholars of contemporary South Korean life. We describe how experiences of new "modernity" in the colonial period and of "traditional Korea/Korean tradition" in late modernity have been constructed, experienced, and reinforced through and around the consumption of distinctive goods and services. Broadly speaking, the chapters on the colonial period describe Japanese gazing a quaintly historicized Korea while Koreans in colonial cities gazed a modernity constructed to showcase Japanese accomplishments (G. Shin and Robinson 1999b; Robinson 2007). Se-Mi Oh has described colonial Seoul's spectacular modernity, replete with electric lights, streetcars, impressive architecture, and a fashionable promenade, as an instrument for the creation of desiring colonial subjects (2008). In Oh's recounting, the colonial city was a place of doubled mimicry, its most fashionable Honmachi District evoked Tokyo's Ginza, itself an approximation of Western urban spectacle. In this setting Koreans' early encounters with new forms of commoditized goods and services incubated the experiences and apparatuses of a modern consumer society to come, but through circumstances that would retrospectively link the loss of an imagined rural authenticity to the loss of Korea itself.

South Korea in the late twentieth and early twenty-first centuries is a fundamentally different place, a strong nation-state and techno-giant that has mastered all manner of modern forms from one of the world's largest megamalls to the hugely successful production of pop culture for a global market. At the same time, and in a manner everywhere conducive to nostalgia, South Koreans express anxiety over the corrupting influence of new wealth (Abelmann 2002, 2003; Nelson 2000, 2006; Kendall 2008). On such ground, traditional things become desirable commodities, and a nostalgic embrace of tradition — in modern commodity form — constitutes one South Korean response to the flux and contradiction associated with a postmodern condition (cf. Jameson 1984).

About tradition and consumption

Traditions serve national, local, or ethnic communities' self-imagining as the claimed link to a common past experience, to that which is invoked as a common "culture." A quarter century ago, Eric Hobsbawm and Terence Ranger (1983) put forth the then radical claim that many seemingly venerable traditions were the conscious products of modern state formation and were not very old at all. At the same time, modernities have produced within themselves the idea of vanishing and consequently precious "traditions" as the primordial stuff of us-ness newly recognized in theretofore quotidian acts of celebration, veneration, dress, cuisine, handicraft, or features of a rural landscape (de Certeau 1984; Handler and Linnekin 1984; Handler 1988; Ivy 1995). Kosaku Yoshino suggests that consumption, broadly defined as a meaningful engagement with the material world, becomes handmaiden to this process via objects, landscapes, museums, and monuments (1999). As "heritage," tradition has a positive global currency that now includes the complex cultural politics attending UNESCO's World Heritage designation of a given nation's natural and historic sites and the "intangible heritage" of its festivals and performing arts (Kirshenblatt-Gimblett 2006). The evocation of tradition assumes both nostalgic conjurings of lost worlds and the possibility of selective nonremembering (e.g., Anagnost 1994, 231; Pemberton 1994; Robertson 1988, 503).

What then do we mean by "tradition" in the context of contemporary South Korea? If the consumption of "Korean tradition" takes place in infinitely replicable commodity form, does "commodity" necessarily mean "artifice"? Are invented traditions necessarily hollow, void of meaning? Is the "simulacrum" always a fake; can it sometimes be regarded as a significant work of cultural production in its own right? Can commodified encounters with artful simulacra be meaningful and culturally resonant, as Joy Hendry suggests for Japanese theme parks (Hendry 2000b)? Our own debt to Hobsbawm may seem obvious but requires some positioning. In the quarter century since the publication of *The Invention of Tradition*, its critics have highlighted the difficulty of distinguishing the living and potentially mutable stuff of grassroots custom from the "traditions" Hobsbawm characterized as recent and artificial. While both the patriotic traditions fostered by elites and the counterhegemonic practices of popular resistance were arguably "invented," they have borrowed an aura of legitimacy from prior custom at least as often as they were cut from whole cloth (Chakrabarty 1998; Comaroff 1985; Vlastos 1998). South Korea offers abundant examples of resonant invention, from President Park Chung-hee's annual photo op — planting of the year's first rice shoot and sharing cups of rice wine with the farmers — to the drums, gongs, and shamanic protest theater of the Popular Culture Movement. As Stephen Vlastos argues, "the primary value of the invention of tradition to the critical study of culture is heuristic rather than theoretical; it raises new and important historical questions" (1998, 5). Hobsbawm's formulation thus encourages us to consider when and why specific traditions become visible and important, to be cognizant of their particular historical, social, political, and economic contexts. This kind of analysis, often identified with cultural studies, is now widely used across the social sciences. Vlastos further surmises that invented tradition may have as much to do with the emergence of capitalism as with the rise of the nation-state (p. 9), a tacit acknowledgment of the link between tradition and consumption that we will be exploring in this volume.

Some citations of tradition arrive bearing powerful sensate associations in visual images, sounds, tastes, or fragrances (E. Edwards, Gosden, and Phillips, et al. 2006a, 2006b) and as embodied memory experienced in performance (Connerton 1989) — consider the enlivening percussion of drum and gong in *samul nori* music, the pungent odor and spicy tang of kimchi, or the nostalgia induced by the country breakfast that Okpyo Moon describes (in this volume). Others are hollow memorializations devoid of significant memory (cf. Nora 1989), as described in Keith Howard's discussion of how limited the market really is for "authentic" classical Korean music (in this volume). Tradition becomes most valued when it is seen to be both rare and endangered, but as the government-subsidized perpetuation of classical Korean music suggests, such value does not necessarily create a mass market appeal.

Anthropologists of Japan have described a late twentieth-century middle-class nostalgia for a vanished village world as desire for an imagined cultural authenticity in the face of seemingly pervasive Westernization. They relate how such anxieties have been addressed through the merchandising and mass-marketing of the lost home village (*furusato*) as tourism, cultural performances, media, mass-marketed local products, folklore, music, and handicrafts (Creighton 1997; Robertson 1988, 1998; Ivy 1988, 1995; Kelly 1986; Moeran 1984, 1997; Moon 1997b; Yano 2002). At a basic level of comparison, South Korea offers ready parallels in its rapid industrial transformation and accompanying loss of rural bearings in the 1960s and 1970s,[1] followed, a generation later, by a nostalgic consumption of those foods, drink, goods, performances, and experiences associated with a vanished rural way of life. Government patronage enabled the restoration of rural sites (Kwang-ok Kim 1988) and the revival of folk performances and festivals (Howard 1989; J. Yang 2003), projects that took commodity form as tourist draws that begat subsidiary service industries or became ticketed, broadcast, or recorded performances. The nostalgia market makes a felicitous meeting of popular and entrepreneurial imagination in "traditional" restaurants and drinking establishments, the adaptation of traditional Korean clothing for contemporary wear (Ruhlen 2003), the Korean Folk Village theme park (Tangherlini 2008; Hendry 2000b, 97–98), and a market in popular books on Korean folklore. As in Japan, a new middle class has become potential consumers of tradition on the basis of their disposable incomes, leisure, automobile mobility, and appetites for both family entertainment and artistic connoisseurship, but they consume Korean tradition in a distinctive South Korean flavor.

There is a critical difference between South Korea and Japan. Korea experienced early modernity as colonial modernity crafted in and through the Japanese Empire. An independent South Korea subsequently industrialized under a cold-war military dictatorship with a draconian transformation of urban and rural life that critics now describe as slavish Westernization. In South Korean nostalgia talk, the rural past was not so much "lost" as taken away by someone else, and an undercurrent of patriotism ripples through the conversation. Consider the runaway success of Im Kwon-taek's 1993 film, *Sŏp'yŏnje*, the story of a vagabond family of *p'ansori* singers, performers of traditional ballad opera, who wander a decaying but still picturesque countryside accompanied by Kim Soochul's fusion rendering of traditional music. The little band struggles against a dwindling audience for their art, undermined by the popular Japanese *enka* music of the colonial period and, in the postwar, by Western pop tunes. While the daughter sings her heart out in the marketplace, her spectators are seduced and literally carried away by a brass band belting out the 1940s hit song "Bésame Mucho." Even despite its controversial plot premise — the father blinds his daughter to better preserve her tragic and innately Korean sense of song — the film inspired a revival of popular interest in *p'ansori,* already subsidized as intangible heritage. *Sŏp'yŏnje* was widely praised as evoking a joyful sense of self-recovery, a lost Koreanness (Cho Hae-joang 1998, 81–84).

If the consumption of Korean tradition aims at shoring up an "authentic" national identity, it does so in relation to significant Others. Colonial products — postcards, souvenirs, tourist sites — exoticized Koreans (Pai in this volume; Gwon 2005, 2007), as colonial regimes so often shape an inventory of traditional objects, sites, and images of the colonized (Cohn 1996). The idea that the colonial period nearly erased indigenous Korean traditions adds a particular luster to the traditionalist revival of performing arts, rituals, and village festivals (C. Choi 1995, 111).

The global marketplace brings its own ironies to the production of consumable tradition. Many "traditional" Korean handicrafts, from souvenir cell-phone dangles of Korean macramé to hempen funeral shrouds and miniaturized *changsŭng* (village guardian poles), are now made with cheaper Chinese materials and produced with less expensive Chinese labor. Korea's recent "kimchi wars" disputed Japanese and Chinese claims to produce authentically Korean-tasting pickled cabbage, even as Chinese-made kimchi and kimchi ingredients dominated the South Korean market (Han in this volume). Moon (in this volume) relates how a tradition-oriented Andong lineage, at pains to lure daughters-in-law into rural households, looks to offshore production for a bride from China's Korean minority.

Gazing the spectacular

Rather than presenting our work in two chronologically designated bundles — the very recent past and the more distant modern past — the chapters in this volume are organized into four topical sections around the themes of spectacle, tourism, material objects, and performance. Modern forms and practices introduced into colonial Korea become apparatuses for the consumption of tradition in more recent times. Modernity has been described as a quintessentially visual experience, an experience of spectacle, the theme of the first section (Berman 1983; Debord 1983). In "Dining Out in the Land of Desire: Colonial Seoul and the Korean Culture of Consumption," Katarzyna J. Cwiertka illuminates the role of the colonial-era department store in the construction of a novel urban environment, an intensely visual site where modernity could be gazed upon, experienced, and enacted, if sometimes only through the fantasies engendered by commercial display. Here one could buy, or imagine buying, the accoutrements of a stylish embodied modernity of corsets and haberdashery and the furnishings of a modern domestic environment. While a relatively small proportion of the colonial Korean population lived in cities, and even fewer could freely indulge in the fashionable goods and services provided by the department store, entrance was free and, unlike traditional Korean social space, relatively unrestricted by age, class, or gender (although overtly ragged and rural gawkers would probably have been intimidated at the threshold). It was a space where colonized and colonizers mingled, sharing in the common practice of modern consumption and desire. Without compromising their reputations, women promenaded in this public space, gazed the enticing displays of luxury goods inside elegant and well-lit store interiors, ascended in vertigo-inducing elevators (like Virginia Woolf's Orlando), and dined in chic department store cafés. Dining out in the modern and consequently neutral space of a fashionable department store restaurant or café offered the possibility of new forms of leisure activity contingent upon modern forms of socialization, friendship, and, just possibly, flirtation, courtship, or seduction. The Korean department store, like the early department stores of Paris, Tokyo (their immediate model), and Shanghai, inculcated modernity as an experience of consumption.

In contemporary South Korea, the once spectacular department stores have yielded pride of place to the megamall. Lotte World, the subject of Timothy R. Tangherlini's chapter, bills itself as the world's largest indoor amusement park and shopping mall. That at least two other sites contest this claim suggests that the Lotte complex offers not mere mimicry but mastery of a global form offering what Tangherlini describes as "certain extreme visions of both shopping and entertainment." As the fabulously bloated grandchild of the old colonial department store, the Lotte complex offers a site of fantasy and consumption, a place for the enactment of leisure-time social bonding, but where Cwiertka describes the department store as a common public space, reducing social differences, Tangherlini emphasizes the commercially calibrated specialized uses of different spaces inside Lotte World: "scary" rides in the amusement park for teens, the pool for moms and kids, big-box-type shopping in the discount store for families, the high-end department store for elegant women. As Tangherlini suggests, the ability to sustain such diversity testifies to the size, buying power, and extensive capacity for leisure consumption of the South Korean middle class. Indeed, he argues that the middle class uses places like Lotte World to enact its social relationships.

Like the radio that contained the possibility of traditional music, the third floor of Lotte World contains a Minsokch'on, or Folk Village, that presents in condensed space the history of Korea from the age of the dinosaurs through the colonial period, replicating in miniature the visual inventories of the National Folk Museum and the Korean Folk Village theme park. The penultimate gallery offers the visitor a panoptic vision of Korean village life in some nineteenth-century never-never land where all manner of cultural activity is performed simultaneously by a multitude of dolls. In Tangherlini's analysis, this Folk Village claims no more "authenticity" than the rest of the complex, and the visitor, complicit in the artifice, accepts Lotte World's miniaturization of Korean history as another consumable. Even so, the Lotte Group chairman's recognition that the existence of some area devoted to "culture" inside the complex would garner positive publicity suggests that a familiar iconography of Korean tradition confers an aura of legitimacy that it is good to gaze upon.

The tourist gaze

In "Travel Guides to the Empire: The Production of Tourist Images in Colonial Korea," Hyung Il Pai describes how Japanese interests mimicked the already well-established devices of late nineteenth-century European tourism to market the Korean peninsula as a destination for both Japanese and European travelers. Facilitated by the Chōsen Government Railway's links to China and Europe, tourism in the Korean colony generated familiar amenities in the form of hotels, restaurants, excursion tour packages, guidebooks, souvenirs, maps, brochures, and postcards. Pai describes how tourist promotion followed a predictable iconography of exotic women, picturesque ruins and landscapes, and quaint natives. Tourism had an imperial subtext where ancient sites were appropriated into a (spurious) narrative of early Japanese hegemony on the peninsula, and promotion material placed an iconic emphasis on modern colonial buildings and institutions — banks, post offices, steel bridges — as testimony to the positive transformation wrought by the empire upon the otherwise exotically bedraggled "Hermit Kingdom."

By the end of the twentieth century, tourism had become a global and mass phenomenon, and South Koreans, once the subjects of colonial gazing, were now among the groups of middle-class Asian tourists who descended from air-conditioned tour buses all over the world, Korean-language tour patter competing with Japanese and Taiwan-accented Chinese (Graburn 1997). In his study of *The Tourist,* Dean MacCannell (1999) describes how, by this period, in a manner equivalent to the drabness attending many formerly magnificent department stores, the term "tourist" had taken on a derisive quality among those seeking more "authentic" experiences in their travels. John Urry (1990) describes such quests as markers of class distinction to which global and domestic tourist industries have readily responded, as they have for the Korean middle-class traveler. But unlike MacCannell's hypothetical authenticity-seeker who craves backstage encounters with "the natives," and having more in common with the middle-class urban Japanese seeker of a nostalgic rural *furusato,* or "old home village," experience, the domestic tourists in the chapters by Okpyo Moon and Robert Oppenheim seek time-machine encounters with Korean us-ness.

In "Guests of Lineage Houses: Tourist Commoditization of Confucian Cultural Heritage in Korea," Moon describes a seemingly fortuitous encounter between the heirs of venerable lineages of the former *yangban* nobility, strapped for cash to maintain their ancestral homes as heritage sites, and the domestic and overseas Korean visitors who seek connection with Confucian tradition. The promotion of these sites and the tourists' own understanding of their experiences conflate an essential "Korea" with the traditions of a historical social class and a particular region. As Moon aptly demonstrates, such encounters also require significant compromises with some fundamental principles of *yangban* behavior. Lineage heirs become innkeepers, taking strangers into their homes for a fee, whereas the *yangban* of old famously shunned commerce. When an entrepreneurial *yangban* heir invites outsiders to observe and learn from his family's ancestral rites, he allows his visitors to breach a proprietary boundary that excludes women and non-kin. Rites become tourist performance in which, as Moon notes, this same heir choreographs his ritual with pauses for the benefit of the spectators' cameras. In the end, authenticity in the conservative Andong countryside proves as chimerical as authenticity in the quests of MacCannell's European and American tourists, but visitors describe a meaningful connection to Confucian tradition even so.

In "Crafting the Consumability of Place," Robert Oppenheim considers two seemingly contradictory middle-class South Korean travel genres that gained popularity in the 1990s. *Tapsa*, or *tapsa yŏhaeng* — field-study travel — is a sort of domestic heritage tourism that purports to "survey" or "study" historic monuments in the Korean landscape, an enterprise of scholars, amateur antiquarians, and folklore buffs but now offered to a broader market through organized tours. *Paenang yŏhaeng* describes foreign backpack travel by an individual or small group seeking meaningful encounters "off the beaten track." At face value, *tapsa* suggests a self-conscious consumer nationalist return to "Korean things" while *paenang yŏhaeng* embraces the global and foreign, but Oppenheim's analysis suggests significant points of commonality, drawing on debates within economic anthropology to suggest that the *tapsa* aficionado and the international backpacker share a common transactional frame such that the traveler invests in an experience without undue encumbrance or commitment.

Oppenheim's argument reinforces a central theme of this volume; "tradition" gets consumed in modern, often globally recognizable commodity forms and is restructured by them. Tourists who overnight in the tile-roofed houses of the former *yangban* elite, hobbyists who comb Kyŏngju's historic landscape on *tapsa* day-trips, and Korean backpack travelers in Europe all share in MacCannell's characterization of the alternative tourist, motivated to see and experience deeply, beyond the artifice of the package tour (1999, 94), and as Urry would expect, their needs are being met through specialized tour opportunities and a proliferation of websites and publications. At the same time, as Oppenheim here and Moon in another context (1997b) affirm, any but a superficial understanding of these otherwise broadly recognizable experiences enjoyed by broadly recognizable middle-class people begs cognizance of South Korean nuance.

Both Moon and Oppenheim cite the 1990s media encouragement for domestic South Korean tourism as a counterweight to globalization. These activities might also be understood as a midlife and more temperate extension of the populist nationalist enthusiasms of students in the 1980s. In particular, Moon and Oppenheim cite the popularity of history professor Yu Hong-jun, whose early 1990s publications describing rambling odysseys to then little-known Korean sites encouraged South Koreans to look at the remnants of their ancient past with fresh eyes, to seek "the presence of ordinary and innocent truth and beauty" that had been washed out of the museum presentations and school trips through which South Koreans normally encountered the material remains of their history (quoted in Oppenheim 2008b, 90, 84). Some cognoscenti subsequently claimed that Yu's best-selling books "ruined" formerly isolated sites by encouraging hordes of tourists and attendant concessions on an itinerary that had once been the distinction of scholars and art connoisseurs. Such criticism evidences the willingness of many ordinary South Koreans to at least give lip service to Yu's message, to seek out Korean things and engage them with newly awakened Korean eyes through distinctive modes of travel.

Korean icons

The runaway success of Yu's publications suggests a particularly receptive 1990s moment, with South Koreans perceiving Korea in new ways. It also represents the successful fruition of other, equally idealistic projects from twenty years earlier that similarly encouraged South Koreans to make emotional as well as intellectual contact with their own living history by viewing its material fragments. Alain Delissen (2001) has described how architect Kim Sugun used the journal *Konggan* (Space) to create a visual repertory of "Korean things," training the reader's eye to recognize an innately Korean sensibility or aesthetic in an array of cultural fragments from roof shapes and tile patterns to shamanic ritual and mask dance. The 1970s literary journal *Ppurigip'ŭn namu* (Deep-rooted tree) and its 1980s successor volume *Saemigip'ŭn mul* (Water from a deep spring) embraced a similar visual repertory in their illustrations. Also in the 1970s, the passionate collector Zozayong (Cho Cha-yong) encouraged Koreans to see their own spirit in the tigers and magpies of a theretofore unappreciated folk art, images that now, like the work of French expressionist painters, appear on T-shirts, coffee mugs, and drink coasters.

These renderings of quotidian or once little-valued things into visual icons of Koreanness occurred through the work of mechanical reproduction in the publication of books, glossy magazines, art books, postcards, and illustrated magazines and the manufacture of kitsch (cf. Benjamin 1969). Likewise, in the colonial period, similar technologies had been deployed to mass-produce visual images of Korean quaintness in postcards and souvenirs (Gwon 2005, 2007; Pai in this volume). A reinvigorated anthropology of material culture encourages us to examine how things take on new representational forms and meanings (Appadurai 1986a, 1986b; Kopytoff 1986; Miller 1995a) and how they construct social identities and communicate cultural differences between individuals and groups (Myers 2001a, 2001b; Weiner 1992). Commodity consumption is very much a part of this conversation (Appadurai 1986a; Miller 1994, 1998, 2002a), which we join, with two Korean examples, in Part III.

In "The *Changsŭng* Defanged: The Curious Recent History of a Korean Cultural Symbol," I focus on a single iconic Korean image embodied in a work of handicraft and follow it across a century of Korean modernity. The village guardian pole has been read through multiple gazes over the course of the twentieth century and has had cameo roles in some of the other stories told in this volume. Roughly carved out of tree trunks or hewn of stone, *changsŭng* with bulging eyes and fanged grins once guarded the entrances to Korean villages from malevolent forces. Japanese photographers reproduced them as ethnographic curiosities in books and on postcards for the developing tourist market. Miniaturized *changsŭng* were sold as tourist souvenirs. Since the 1980s, the *changsŭng* has been reinvested as a "Korean thing," erected in folk village theme parks, including Lotte World, made the subject of *tapsa* excursions, given photographic representation in nostalgia-inducing rural settings, and produced as high-end handicraft and gallery art and is said to be best appreciated by a discerning Korean eye.

The notion of a "Korean eye" can itself be considered a modernist notion, insofar as modernity privileges sight over other senses (E. Edwards, Gosden, and Phillips 2006a). Nostalgia, however, is multisensate, as suggested in Moon's evocation of sleeping on the heated floor of an old *yangban* house, waking to the rural cries of birds and chickens, and savoring an abundant Korean country breakfast. Kyung-Koo Han's discussion of kimchi, the spicy fermented vegetables that constitute an inevitable item of Korean cuisine, brings taste and odor into the mix. As a staple of Korean cuisine, kimchi is more widely and literally consumed than are *changsŭng*, but in common with the *changsŭng*, kimchi has been an object of multiple and shifting value.

While Koreans commonly describe kimchi as essential to nearly any meal consumed with chopsticks and to some others besides, they do so in cognizance that many non-Koreans consider kimchi smelly and unhygienic. Han observes how, in the era of underdevelopment, Koreans were themselves encouraged to regard kimchi and other traditional foods as nonnutritious, perceptions that have made a 180-degree turn as experts extol the healthful properties of traditional cuisine over the rich Western foods South Koreans now widely consume. As a repository of sentiment, kimchi carries associations of mother love, family kitchens, and networks of female kin and neighbors working together to produce a winter supply. In other words, the kimchi of memory is anything but a commodity; its investments are familial and emotionally resonant. Not so the kimchi most South Koreans eat today; the lifestyle of a modern housewife, apartment living, and the social isolation of urban households opt against its laborious preparation and make kimchi talk simultaneously nostalgia talk.

Han argues that while domestic kimchi production has been shrinking and South Koreans now eat less kimchi than in the past, discursive valuations of kimchi as the quintessential national food have been increasing. This ironic situation provides essential background for two incidents that the South Korean press dubbed the "Kimchi Wars" *(kimchi chŏnjaeng)*. In 2004, Japanese manufacturers aggressively pursued the international kimchi market and registered traditional organisms used in the fermentation process as their own, stoking vehement protest. In the fall of 2005, reports of parasite eggs in Chinese-produced kimchi fueled awareness that much of the kimchi consumed in Korea was a Chinese import or otherwise factory produced, sparking emotional reflections on the decline of home-made kimchi, a measure of how much South Korean life had changed in a few short decades.

Performing tradition

There are those who regard kimchi making and *changsŭng* carving as endangered national heritage (although they are not officially designated as such). The two chapters in this final section concern another domain of precarious cultural practice, Korean performing arts. In the 1960s, when all manner of traditional handicraft, music, song, dance, and theater appeared to be melting into air, committed folklore scholars encouraged the government to establish a system for designating a growing inventory of "intangible heritage," to be perpetuated by carefully vetted exemplars who trained promising students (J. Yang 2003). There are those who argue that such interventions are innately artificial; some critics characterize staged performances of folkloric ritual and dance as "taxidermy" (C. Choi 1991,

54). Arguments over the authenticity of performance forms and disputes between purists and those who would adapt their art to a changing performance milieu long predate the South Korean intangible heritage system. Judy Van Zile profiles the work of Ch'oe Sŭng-hŭi, who began her dance career and quickly escalated to stardom during colonial times. Initially inspired to study Western-style modern dance by Japanese modern dancer Ishii Baku, Ch'oe was subsequently encouraged to return to her Korean roots. Her brief study with a Korean dance master led to an interest in developing a new kind of dance that drew on older and recognizably Korean forms. Ch'oe was controversial in her day. She had a successful career in Korea and Japan and toured internationally, but she was also criticized, initially because her dance was more "exotic" than recognizably "Korean," and later because her choreographing of Korean dance forms was judged "inauthentic." Ironically, Ch'oe's creative work inspired what is performed today as a standard stage repertoire of "traditional Korean dance."

Keith Howard explores a contemporary contestation between performing arts purists and innovators and the mixed blessing of official patronage. Howard argues that *kugak,* traditional Korean music, sustained by the National Center for Korean Traditional Performing Arts, abides as a hermetic circular network of students who form the core audience for recitals by their teachers, graduates who populate ensembles and orchestras, performers who commission composers, and composers who are university teachers. *Kugak* has failed to create a mass audience, for lack of any necessity to do so, and most Koreans who have not been trained in the form are not attracted to it. Kugak fusion, on the other hand, appeals to a broader audience by combining elements of the *kugak* tradition and instrumentation with elements of jazz, pop, rap, hip-hop, or Western classical music and, predictably, incurs the enmity of *kugak* purists for not being sufficiently Korean. More accessible than traditional *kugak,* some kugak fusion experiments have been hugely successful. Kim Soochul's soundtrack for the film *Sŏp'yŏnje,* which framed traditional Korean flute melodies and *p'ansori* songs with synthesizer harmonies, sold a million copies. At the same time, Howard observes, Korean music is a precarious enterprise, competing for a domestic share in a global music market. Kugak fusion, as a flexible and evolving genre, has managed to create a broad South Korean audience for artists who play *kugak* instruments or sing *kugak* songs.

Conclusion

As a central premise of this volume, traditions, so named, become accessible through a variety of modern forms that enable their contemporary consumption. Chapters on the colonial period help us understand the early Korean histories of the forms themselves. Traditions assume value as a consequence of contemporary concerns, needs, and imaginings. The traditions we describe for South Korea today have as their recent history perceptions of near loss during the rapid industrialization and urban transformation of the 1960s and 1970s, the various official and individual preservationist projects that took shape in response to this specter of vanishing, and the popularization of vernacular cultural forms in association with political protest in the 1980s. By the 1990s, South Korea had gained political stability, and a broad middle class enjoyed new forms of consumption and leisure, but South Koreans also expressed anxiety about what it meant to be Korean in a country replete with foreign commodities and cultural imports. The sum of these experiences valorized an inventory of tradition as broadly recognizable Korean ways of being, seeing, listening, and eating distinct from a "Western" or "Japanese" habitus. These self-conscious traditions are now widely apprehended, accessed, and consumed through modern commercial forms, many of which can be traced to the early twentieth century.

Tradition in commodity form distills the local and the particular into something more broadly embraced as "Korean." The lineage houses in Andong and the Silla ruins in Kyŏngju come to stand for a broadly Korean cultural experience, regionally distinctive *changsŭng* become national icons, kimchi flavors particular to individual kitchens meld in the commercial production of a uniform kimchi taste, Lotte World miniaturizes a traditional inventory of local and ritual practices in near entirety. To retain an aura of legitimacy, producers of consumable tradition necessarily assert that what they have to offer is more than "just a commodity." Advertisements describe processed kimchi as an expression of mother love, producers of *changsŭng* guardian posts explicitly deny their product's commodity status by reasserting its spiritual and artistic meaning, lineage households that accommodate tourists take pains to distinguish themselves from commercial inns, and participants in organized *tapsa* tours of the Kyŏngju countryside see themselves as engaged in a form of culture work and therefore superior to conventional tourists on the standard Kyŏngju tour course.

If the traditions we describe here have been selectively adapted to modern forms of consumption, then we might also speculate as to the mutability of these same contemporary arrangements. If the valorization of tradition in South Korea appeals to a sense of loss, part nostalgia, part anxiety over the fate of a distinctive Korean identity, is this the particular impasse of a particular moment in time? In her conference paper, Eun Mee Kim described South Korean responses to the Korean wave *(hallyu)* phenomenon, the unprecedented international popularity of Korean pop music and soap operas. She described South Koreans who had chafed under their self-perception as the sometimes reluctant consumers of other people's culture and who are now encouraged by both government and media to see themselves as major producers in a global culture industry. Will this experience afford sufficient national self-confidence to overcome fears of a vanishing Korean identity? Will the consumption of tradition, in some of the forms described here, lose its motivating sense of urgency? Will South Korean anxieties over an influx of guest workers and foreign spouses and the relentless risks of global capitalism foster a more strident nativist response than the innocent pleasures we have been describing? Alternatively, will the idea of "Korea" admit ethnic and cultural diversity to its notion of "our things"? Our accounts of South Korean life in the years immediately before and after the turn of the millennium encourage another look, a decade or so hence.

Note

1. A now aging cohort's nostalgia for its own youth in those same difficult years is manifest in such things as soap operas recalling the period (Abelmann 2002, 2003), the unexpected success of the War Museum's re-creation of an urban squatter village in its 2005 exhibition "Oh! Mother" (Ah! Ŏmŏni), and the designation of Seoul's Pukch'on neighborhood as a historic site. This gritty urban nostalgia is worthy of its own volume.

Part I

Modernity as Spectacle/Spectacular Korea

The spectacle is not a collection of images, but a social relation among people, mediated by images. — Guy Debord, *The Society of the Spectacle*

Modernity has been described as a quintessentially visual experience that invites its subject to gaze a series of organized and orchestrated images and, by so doing, to experience a new sense of self in relation to known and unknown worlds (Berman 1983; Debord 1983). Modern visual experiences include the department store, the motion picture, the museum, the World's Fair, the flaneur's journey through the city, the tourist itinerary, and conventions of landscape and portrait photography (Bennet 1988; E. Edwards, Gosden, and Phillips 2006b; Mitchell 1989; Urry 1990). Katarzyna Cwiertka's chapter on the colonial department store describes Korean encounters with this spectacular urban space. At Lotte World in contemporary Seoul, South Koreans have mastered and transcended the spectacular form. Timothy Tangherlini shows us that this constellation not only embraces the department store, the megamall, and the theme park but also permits the visitor to gaze at both playful and sober representations of the Korean past, never far from the recognition that all is simulation.

Dining Out in the Land of Desire
Colonial Seoul and the Korean Culture of Consumption

Avoiding the speeding motor cars to save my life, I managed to come to the Railroad Station. I wanted to drink a cup of very hot coffee to take away the bitter taste in my mouth. A cup of coffee, hot coffee! Yes, it would be good. As I went into the coffee shop, I recalled I had not a penny. I was dazed. Not knowing what to do, I walked on aimlessly for a long time.

   I can't remember where I wandered before I found myself in the roof garden of a down-town department store. I sat on a bench to recall the twenty-six years of life I've lived on earth. — Yi Sang, *Wings,* 1936

This chapter examines the culture of consumption of colonial Korea, illuminating the role of the department store as the key icon of a modern urban space where new practices, attitudes, and dreams were being born. Focusing on the dining facilities operated by the department stores, this study aims to uncover the multiple meanings of the "department store experience" and to grasp the rationale behind the immense popularity of the stores during the 1930s and the early 1940s.

This analysis of the culture of consumption that thrived in Keijō (Seoul) and major Korean cities at the time significantly enhances our understanding of urban life in the colonial context. In the interwar period the Korean urban landscape was transformed through Japanese intervention. The new urban infrastructure, including electric streetcars, grand architecture, and new forms of public entertainment, significantly altered the experience of urban living (Kim J. 1999; Shin M. 2003; Yŏnse taehakkyo kukhak yŏn'guwŏn 2004). Inevitably, this newly emerging colonial setting was perceived differently by the Japanese and Korean residents. Generally speaking, the former enjoyed a higher standard of living and had already been accustomed to the conveniences and trappings of the modern city. To the latter, apart from a handful of Koreans who had had an opportunity to travel abroad, the hybrid Japanese-Western urban land-scape that was being recreated in colonial Korea was entirely unfamiliar. With the exception of domestic help employed in Japanese households, the colonized and the colonizers led separate lives, rarely interacting with each other (N. Cohen 2006; Uchida 2005). However, the growing public space of the modern city increasingly provided a setting for an encounter, if not interaction. In the "dream world" created on the department stores' premises, boundaries of the colonial framework could be temporarily transcended.

Dining out in Keijō

According to the 1939 records of the Keijō Chamber of Commerce, over 250 establishments serving food and drink operated in the capital at the time (Keijō shōkō kaigisho 1939, 252–269). The records divided these establishments into several categories, the largest being Japanese-style restaurants (73), followed by cafés (55), so-called *shokudō*, or cafeterias (34), bars (30), Japanese restaurants specializing in a specific dish, such as *sukiyaki, sushi,* or *udon* noodles (23), Korean-style eateries and pubs (22), tearooms (9), Korean-style restaurants (8), Western-style restaurants (5), and Chinese-style restaurants (4). The list compiled by the chamber of commerce was far from complete, as is evident from the much larger membership of restaurant guilds active in the capital at exactly the same time (Keijō shōkō kaigisho 1939, supplement 18–19). For example, the Restaurant Business Association of Keijō (Keijō ryōriya eigyō kumiai) counted 44 members, the Association of Keijō Cafeterias (Keijō shokudō kumiai) 250 members, the Japanese and Western Food Association of Chongno (Keijō shōro wayōshoku kumiai) 70 members, the Western Food Business Association of Keijō (Keijō seiyō ryōrigyō kumiai) 80 members, the Japanese and Western Food Business Association of Eastern Keijō (Keijō tōbu wayō ryōrigyō kumiai) 41 members, the Chongno Association of Korean-Owned Restaurants (Keijō shōro chōjin inshokuten kumiai) 270 members, the Restaurant Association of Western Keijō (Keijō seibu inshokuten kumiai) 107 members, and the Restaurant Association of Southern Keijō (Keijō seibu inshokuten kumiai) 140 members. Moreover, the figures included neither food peddlers who sold a variety of snacks throughout the city nor the restaurants and eating houses run by Chinese immigrants (Kwang-ok Kim 2001, 202–203; Yang Y. 2005, 64).

These inaccuracies notwithstanding, the chamber of commerce's records abundantly demonstrate that, by the late 1930s, not only did Keijō offer its citizens a wide range of options for dining out, but the city's gastronomic scene had also acquired a highly multicultural character. Dining establishments that served foreign food — Japanese, Chinese, or Western — became part of the daily life of thousands of Koreans.[1] This ubiquitous presence of cafés, bars, eateries, and department store restaurants is reflected in colonial-period fiction. For example, the narrative of the novel *Three Generations* includes dialogues staged in Japanese noodle shops, Western-style restaurants, and hybrid Western-Japanese bars and cafés (Yŏm 2005, 45, 56, 77–78, 132–133, 136, 346). The cafeteria at the Seoul Railroad Station features in Yi Sang's celebrated novel *Wings* (1970, 211–212), and unemployed intellectual P— the protagonist of Ch'ae Man-Sik's novel *A Ready-made Life* — "depending on the amount of money in hand, . . . might have Chinese pancakes, beef-and-rice soup, or even a Western-style lunch in a department store" (1998, 64). As Janet Poole astutely observes, the conspicuous appearance of such establishments, along with other kinds of modern urban infrastructure, as a context for modernist Korean fiction highlights their very novelty (2004, 41). Nonetheless, their presence throughout the city and, more importantly, their popularity among Korean clientele reveal the transformative impact of Japanese consumer culture on the Korean colonial society.

The popularization of Japanese-style eateries in Korea is closely related to the Japanese penetration of the country since the late nineteenth century. A steady flow of Japanese migrants, and later colonists, resulted in the spread of facilities and services, including those related to food, that were considered essential for maintaining a Japanese lifestyle (Duus 1995, 324–328). Restaurants, inns, and brothels were among the first enterprises that sprang up in the Japanese residential areas to cater to the needs of the clientele, which at the time was overwhelmingly male. As early as 1888, Seoul counted five Japanese liquor shops, ten Japanese-style confectioners, and fourteen Japanese restaurants (Chŏng H. and Yi 1996, 96). Japanese residents in Korean cities experienced no impediments in recreating the gastronomic scene of the homeland, which had already been transformed by rapid Westernization (Cwiertka 2006, 42–55). A characteristic feature of the twentieth-century Japanese urban gastronomy was its three-tiered Japanese/Western/Chinese structure. This structure implied that, along with traditional Japanese establishments, Western-style and Chinese-style restaurants were ubiquitous and available at various price ranges. Modern, large-scale eateries, such as the ones operating at train terminals and at department store, customarily served all three cuisines (ibid.).

Generally speaking, the spread of Western-style gastronomy in Korea was only marginally related to direct influences from Europe and the United States. Like other aspects of Korean modernity (G. Shin and Robinson 1999b), the construction of modern gastronomy in Korea was mediated by a Japanese filter. The incipient Western-style restaurants, though, were an exception. They emerged in the early years of the twentieth century in hotels managed and patronized by European and American nationals. The pioneering establishment was Sontag Hotel, run by a Russian woman of German origin, Antoinette Sontag (1854–1925). Sontag had arrived in Korea in the 1880s, accompanying her sister, who was married to Karl Weber (1841–?), the first Russian envoy to Seoul (Lankov 2007, 90). In 1902 she secured permission from King Kojong (1852–1919) to establish a hotel that was to accommodate foreign guests of the Imperial Korean Household. For this purpose the court gave her a three-story brick building that had initially served as a Western-style reception hall for foreign diplomats.

Sontag Hotel was modeled on similar establishments that provided lodging for genteel travelers from Europe and the United States throughout Asia (Cwiertka 2006, 39–41). Following the conventions of the time, the hotel operated a restaurant that served French-style meals (Kim W. 1996, 208). In 1909, Sontag left Korea and the hotel was taken over by a Frenchman, J. Boher, who was already the proprietor of two other Western-style hotels in Seoul, Central Hotel and Palace Hotel. At that time, Sontag Hotel was advertised in the *Seoul Press* as "the largest and most convenient hotel in Korea," offering "every home comfort for family and tourist visitors and finest French cuisine" (Kim W. 1996, 219).[2] However, within only a few years, in concert with the colonial encroachment on the Peninsula, the Japanese-owned Chōsen Hotel stripped the Sontag of its reputation as Seoul's best hotel, in culinary terms as well as in other amenities. This new grand hotel, erected in 1914, became a showcase of the Japanese "civilizing mission," the epitome of Western-style convenience and sophistication in the Far East. Along with such modern conveniences as electric lights and fans and steam-heated bedrooms with attached bathrooms, the hotel offered outstanding dining facilities (Japan Tourist Bureau n.d., ca. 1930s, 1–2). The Regular Dining Room had the capacity to serve breakfast, lunch, and dinner simultaneously to as many as ninety customers, and the hotel also operated a Private Dining Room for smaller parties and a large Banqueting and Ball Room that could accommodate up to three hundred guests (Editorial 1934b, 87).

The Japanese and Korean elites were regular guests of the hotel's restaurant. For example, the Regular Dining Room is reported to have been a favorite spot for posh ladies to gather for afternoon tea, sandwiches, confectionery, and ice cream (Editorial 1934b, 87). In the winter months (between November and February), the Banqueting Room was usually fully booked for wedding parties, and during the rest of the year it frequently hosted official banquets organized for the leading members of the colonial establishment, such as the office of the governor-general and the Seoul Chamber of Commerce (ibid.).

While the Chōsen Hotel undoubtedly outshined its competitors in terms of exclusiveness and elegance, the trendiest spots for dining out in Keijō were located elsewhere — in the department stores a short walk down south (Yano K. and Morikawa 1936, 207–208). Several factors were responsible for the popularity of department store restaurants in the colonial capital during the 1930s and 1940s. First, a much broader segment of the population could afford them than could dine at top-end establishments like the Chōsen Hotel. In the mid-1930s, for example, the hotel charged 2 yen for a table d'hôte lunch and 2.5 yen for a table d'hôte dinner. In comparison, the restaurant inside the Keijō Railway Station, an establishment equivalent to a department store restaurant, served Western-style lunch and dinner for half that price. Cafeteria Aokidō was famous for its economical 0.5-yen lunch, while a budget eatery inside the Keijō city hall charged mere 0.2 to 0.35 yen for a Western-style meal and 0.22 yen for a Japanese-style one (Editorial 1934b).

The three-tiered structure of early twentieth-century Japanese gastronomy — in other words, Japanese-, Western-, and Chinese-style food functioning as the three standard choices for a restaurant meal — was successfully transplanted to the colonial department stores, which served dishes in the three styles.[3] Department stores usually outsourced the cooking itself to professional restaurateurs who dispatched their cooking staff to the department stores' kitchens. For example, at the Mitsukoshi department store only Western-style dishes and drinks were prepared by its staff. The restaurant Kikuya (in Nanzan-machi) took charge of Japanese-style dishes and noodles; the restaurant Kawachŏ (in Asahi-machi) was responsible for Chinese cuisine and tempura and eel specialties; sushi came from the renowned Sushikyū in Meiji-machi. In the case of Minakai department store, Japanese and Western dishes were outsourced to Hanatsuki restaurant, and Chinese food and noodles to the restaurant Benke (Editorial 1934a, 86). The prices of meals oscillated around 1 yen, depending on the item — a fee comparable to those charged by other establishments that operated throughout the city.

The appeal of multicultural menus notwithstanding, it seems unlikely that the food was the sole or even the most important factor behind the tremendous popularity of department store restaurants in the colonial capital. It seems more plausible that their splendid interiors, superb service, and modern ambience constituted their chief added value. First of all, they were much grander than comparable eateries elsewhere in the city (Figure 1.1). For example, the restaurant of the Mitsukoshi department store was able to serve 130 to 150 customers simultaneously, and its competitors — the Chōjiya and Minakai department stores — as many as 180 to 200 (Editorial 1934a, 86–87). An additional attraction was that the restaurants were usually situated on the top floors of multistory modern buildings. The restaurant of the Minakai department store, constructed in 1933, for example, was famous for its magnificent view. It was located on the sixth floor, the highest dining site in the entire city. Customers were transported to these unusual locations by elevators — in itself a fascinating experience for most diners. Waitresses dressed in Western-style uniforms — all eighteen years old or younger — completed the bewildering picture (Editorial 1934a).

The turnout at department store restaurants was relatively high. In Keijō, on average, approximately one thousand customers dined at each of the restaurants on weekdays, and the number often doubled on Sundays and holidays (Editorial 1934a, 87). For comparison, Selfridge's, a leading department store in early twentieth-century London, operated a restaurant that served between two and three thousand patrons a day (Rappaport 1995, 144). In the United States, Field's department store in Chicago had a large tearoom, "seating five hundred for afternoon tea, from three to five in the afternoon on the fourth floor" (Leach 1993, 137). As was the case in Europe, the United States, and Japan, the popularity of the department store restaurants in colonial Korea seems to have only partly been related to their gustatory pleasure. Since comparable food was served in other restaurants throughout the city, it seems that what appealed most to

Figure 1.1. A typical department store restaurant interior, ca. 1930s. Courtesy of Mitsukoshi.

the Japanese and Korean crowds who frequented department store dining halls was an opportunity to enter the "dream world" of commodities. Labeled by contemporaries as "palaces of consumption" and "lands of desire," the department stores used their restaurants to lure customers onto the premises of the store itself.

From Mitsukoshi to Hwasin: The department store as a vanguard of mass consumption

Chandra Makerji traces the beginnings of modern materialism in early modern Europe to its booming trade in silks, spices, and other exotic commodities and thriving circulation of consumer goods, arguing that these circumstances provided a critical impetus for the rise of the capitalist mode of production (1983, 1–15). Reminding us that such a Eurocentric approach to materialism is not without dangers, Craig Clunas demonstrates patterns of consumption in sixteenth-century China that paralleled, if not surpassed, those in Europe (1991, 170–172). Identifying the roots of a contemporary culture of mass consumption appears less problematic. There seems to be a general consensus among scholars concerning the role of the department store — originating in Paris and soon recreated in other European countries, North America, and Western colonial enclaves — as the vanguard of consumer culture (e.g., MacPherson 1998; Tamilia 2005). The department store provoked desires and feelings toward things, becoming a place where customers went to be entertained by commodities, where selling was mingled with amusement. The chief validation behind its phenomenal influence was the simple fact that it allowed consumers to "indulge temporarily in the fantasy of wealth" (Williams 1982, 91).

Lower prices and a large selection of commodities displayed under one roof only partly explain the success of the new stores that began to thrive in Europe and North America toward the end of the nineteenth century. Much more significant was that each item on sale was marked with a fixed price and that the customers were encouraged to inspect the merchandise even if they did not intend to make a purchase. It was a revolutionary idea indeed, since prices in retail shops had thus far been subject to negotiation and it was difficult for a buyer to back out once the negotiations began. In other words, the department store introduced an entirely new dimension to shopping by providing the customer with the freedom to browse, "the liberty to indulge in dreams without being obliged to buy" (Williams 1982, 67). But the new consumer culture nurtured inside the department stores entailed much more than changing practices related to purchasing commodities. The marketing strategies of the nineteenth-century large-scale retailers — aimed in the first place at elevating profit — cultivated an entirely new consciousness among their customers by inflaming a continuing desire for the new (Campbell 1992) and creating an entirely new public space in which shopping functioned as a new form of entertainment. A defining principle in designing this new space was the emphasis on its distance from the ordinary. By using cutting-edge technology and modernist architecture, department stores became surreal visions of utopian modern life. On the other hand, through the use of exotic décor they could temporarily be transformed into one or another Oriental fantasy world. In the United States, Leach explains, "depending on the fashion of the month or year, each particular subtheme might be Islamic, Indian, Japanese, or Chinese, with stores decorated as mosques, temples or desert oases" (1993, 104). Along with the emphasis on the distance from the ordinary, Turkish rugs, Oriental silks, and Venetian lanterns conveyed a sense of lavishness and had a highly seductive effect, which in turn underscored the department store's imagery as a "dream world" or a "land of desire" (Williams 1982, 71).

As the department stores began to be transplanted into Asia, their imagery as a surreal fantasy world became even more pronounced, without any need for such "Orientalizing" strategies. In early twentieth-century China or Japan, the unfamiliar-looking grand multistory buildings themselves, with their escalators, elevators, and revolving doors, epitomized exoticism, far removed from the everyday reality of the population (MacPherson 1998). In Japan, along with introducing the population to the world of fashion, brands, and good taste, department stores performed the additional role of an educator that informed the public about Western architecture, technology, and culture. Furthermore, as Louise Young explains, they also "promoted themselves as sites for novel urban entertainment and created recreational spaces that celebrated a notion of leisure built around consumption" (1999, 62). In their quest for a new concept of recreational space, Japanese department stores devoted large amounts of floor space and lavish resources to creating lounges, restaurants, exhibition galleries, roof gardens, roller-skating rinks, children's playgrounds, and even miniature zoos. "Such spaces," Young argues, "enunciated an idea of leisure that incorporated recreation into a daily ritual of consumption" (ibid., 63). As symbols of the West and triumphant visions of the modern, Japanese department stores functioned also as tourist attractions — becoming themselves "sites of consumption" in every sense of the word (Moeran 1998, 159).

These characteristics of the Japanese department store were recreated, down to the minute details, in colonial Korea. The first retailer to proclaim itself a department store, or *paekhwajŏm*, was Mitsukoshi, already a pioneer of the department store business in Japan (Moeran 1998, 145–151). It opened a sales office *(shutchōjo)* in Keijō in 1916 that, twelve years later, was transformed into a branch store *(shiten)*. In October 1930, Mitsukoshi moved into a splendid new building opposite the Keijō Post Office, the current Shinsege department store (Hayashi 2003, 99; see Figure 1.2). The sales of the new Keijō *shiten* were comparable to those of the branch in Osaka, the second-largest city in Japan (Matsuda 1972, 26).

Mitsukoshi was the only Japan-based department store that operated in Korea, and the Keijō branch was its only store in the colony. Other Japanese department stores in Korea were all local enterprises that managed

Figure 1.2. Main hall of the main Mitsukoshi department store in Tokyo, ca. 1930s. Author's collection.

a network of branch stores in major Korean cities and later expanded to Manchuria and China. Similar to the pioneering department stores in Europe and Japan, they originated from dry-goods enterprises. Chōjiya, which had since 1904 been a chief supplier of uniforms for the Japanese and Korean government and the Korean railway, was first to follow in the footsteps of Mitsukoshi and proclaim itself a department store, in 1921. Five years later, the Hirata department store opened its doors to the public. It was a low-profile store that capitalized mainly on bulk sales of low-priced commodities and did not invest in the sorts of monumental interior and amenities that became representative of the department store experience in colonial Korea as elsewhere (Hayashi 2003, 48–50). In 1929, Minakai joined the business and soon became the largest chain of department stores in the colony. It operated full-fledged stores in P'yŏngyang and Taegu (both opened in 1933) and in Pusan (opened in 1937), as well as smaller branch stores in Poju, Kwangju, Mokp'o, Kunsan, Taejŏn, Wŏnsan, Hamhŭng, and Hŭngnam.

Keijō of the 1930s saw the heyday of department store culture in colonial Korea. One by one the stores moved to the magnificent new multistory buildings — Chōjiya in 1929, Mitsukoshi in 1930, and Minakai in 1933. The last retailer that proclaimed itself a department store in the capital was Tonga department store, which opened in 1932 and was later renamed the Hwasin department store. Hwasin was a proud creation of the Korean entrepreneur Pak Hŭng-sik and an amalgamation of the two Korean retail enterprises — Hwasin Sanghwe and Tonga Puin Sanghwe — that emerged in the 1920s in reaction to the encroachment of the Japanese merchants in the colony (Oh J. 2004, 130–133). The store vanished in the flames of an accidental fire in January 1935 but reopened in an even grander seven-story form two and a half years later. The total floor space of the new Hwasin was the largest in Korea, outshining even the Mitsukoshi store (Hayashi 2003, 175).

The phenomenal growth in popularity of department stores in 1930s Keijō can be best illustrated by the stores' tax records (see Table 1.1). Between 1931 and 1942, the sales tax paid by all the department stores (including the discount store Hirata) increased more than fivefold — from 9,465 to 56,319 yen. Under the economic boom generated by the Sino-Japanese War (1937–1945), sales skyrocketed, doubling revenues during the period 1939–1942. The important role that the department stores played in the construction of consumer culture of colonial Korea is customarily downplayed as a chiefly "Japanese for Japanese" phenomenon, implying that the Japanese retailing business was patronized mainly by Japanese customers. In reality, the situation seems to have been the reverse. Based on the stores' records, business historian Hiroshige Hayashi argues that the Japanese department store businesses in Keijō (and elsewhere in colonial Korea for that matter) were 60 to 70 percent dependent on their Korean clientele (2003, 19, 105). In his view, patronage by the Japanese population alone would not have sustained three full-fledged Japanese department stores. A similar conclusion had been reached by a 1930s contemporary who described the ongoing "department store war" in Keijō for the journal *Chōsen oyobi Manshū*. Based on comparison with the United States, which ranked in the early twentieth century as the country with the highest concentration of department stores in the world, he calculated that the

Table 1.1. Sales Tax Records of the Department Stores in Keijō, 1931–1942

Store	Sales Tax Collected (in Yen) by Year							
	1931	1933	1935	1936	1937	1938	1939	1942
Mitsukoshi	2,465	3,853	4,313	4,651	5,359	6,261	7,841	16,686
Chōjiya	3,038	3,460	4,379	4,628	4,657	4,935	5,614	14,302
Minakai	1,439	1,164	2,757	3,878	3,957	4,239	4,500	9,551
Hirata	1,853	1,732	2,012	2,329	2,319	2,653	2,830	4,850
Hwasin	670	1,314	2,388	2,001	2,457	2,990	4,069	10,930
Total	9,465	11,523	15,849	17,487	18,749	21,078	24,854	56,319

Source: Oh Jin-sŏk 2004, 137.

Japanese department stores of Keijō could never survive without Korean consumers (Inoue 1933, 81).

What were the main reasons for the Korean customers to patronize department stores? In November 1934, *Chosŏn ilbo* evaluated a department store shopping experience based on an opinion poll conducted among its readers. Respondents cited the abundance and variety of goods on sale, as well as a feeling of security and trust, as the chief advantages of department store shopping, along with convenience of home delivery and agreeable service.

Various attempts by Korean retailers to win back their customers from the Japanese merchant houses, confirms that even in the 1920s a strict segregation along ethnic lines was not the defining principle of the consumer culture of colonial Korea (Oh J. 2004, 129–130; Poole 2004, 50). This does not necessarily mean that the ethnic factor was entirely irrelevant. Hwasin clearly capitalized on its Korean identity and cultivated the notion that shopping at the Korean department store was a patriotic deed. The store was strategically situated in the Chongno District, the precolonial heart of the capital, thus distancing itself from the "Japanese" part of the city south of the Ch'ŏngge Stream, where the other three major department stores were clustered. However, Pak Hŭng-sik did not create a new market but capitalized on the already existing one. Most products on sale at Hwasin were brand commodities manufactured in Japan, the majority of Hwasin's managerial staff were Japanese, and the entire business formula was an exact copy of the Japanese model (Hayashi 2003, 149, 174–176). Even despite Hwasin's explicitly Korean identity, many Korean customers still chose to patronize Mitsukoshi because of its greater variety of goods and better facilities (Editorial 1935; Poole 2004, 50).

Women and the culture of consumption in colonial Korea

As Rosalind Williams and other historians of consumption have pointed out, shopping and consumption had already been established as a pleasurable social activity among the upper classes in the West before the rise of the department store (Williams 1982, 19–57). For example, an early nineteenth-century British contemporary observed, "When persons of distinction are in town, the usual employment of the ladies is to go a-shopping. This they do without actually wanting to purchase anything" (Nava 1996, 46). If not the inventor of the idea of shopping as entertainment, the department store was responsible for democratizing the experience. Mass production of nonessential consumer goods and ready-to-wear clothing, paired with the development of cheap and reliable means of transportation, played a critical role in this retail revolution. However, this transformation would not have been possible without the chief actors on the scene of "dream worlds": women.

As elsewhere, a key secret behind the commercial success of the department store in colonial Korea was that it created comfortable, exciting, yet socially acceptable ways for Korean women to actively participate in modern urban life. Still, this innovation did not unfold without consequences. As elsewhere, the new culture of consumption introduced by the department store had a transformative, emancipating effect on women (Leach 1984, 320), an effect that did not escape the attention of the Korean media. The July 19, 1930, edition of *Chosŏn ilbo,* for instance, lamented the selfish behavior of female students in the capital. Immediately after passing the first exams — the report explained — they rushed to Mitsukoshi or Chōjiya to buy makeup, without even giving a thought to the hardships that the family in the provinces endured to pay their tuition fees. A September 22, 1933, column of the same newspaper criticized the young generation of Korean housewives, who neglected kimchi making and other household chores and instead dragged their husbands and children to department store restaurants, unnecessarily straining the family budget.

Such criticism expressed in the Korean media during the 1930s echoes concerns voiced in London a few decades earlier. Public opinion feared that participation of women in urban commercial culture encouraged sexual, moral, and social disorder (Rappaport 1996, 70). Interestingly, the idea of women taking refreshments on the premises of the department store assumed a central place in the censure. Operating a restaurant as part of a retail store was a new idea that first emerged in nineteenth-century Paris, when the very concept of the department store took shape (M. B. Miller 1981). Whiteley's was the first store in London, which, following the Paris example, began to serve food and drink in its small refreshment room. This innovation, introduced in 1872, inspired a heated public debate over acceptable feminine spaces and behaviors outside the private home and family circle. When accused of encouraging moral and social decline by luring women outside the respectable boundaries of the home, the store's management argued the opposite — that its facilities protected women from entering "places of ill-repute such as [a] public house to have a drink or other refreshment" (Rappaport 1996, 71).

During the following decades, the idea of the department store as an extension of the drawing room, a safe refuge in the modern city where genteel women could socialize with other genteel women, became increasingly pronounced. As Erika Rappaport explains, "English department stores, like those in other countries, boasted extensive and elaborate dining facilities, lavatories, reading and writing rooms, and other services. Luxurious interiors and numerous amenities encouraged customers to spend an entire day shopping within these large comfortable retail palaces" (1996, 66). In the late 1930s, Hwasin and other department stores of Keijō offered its customers a range of services that one could expect from a reputable department store abroad. Near the entrance, one could find an information stand that handled inquiries about the location of the departments, as well as selling tickets for public transport and coupons for use in the in-house restaurant. Nearby was a cloakroom where one could deposit luggage for the duration of the visit to the store. Resting areas and elevators made traveling between the departments less tiring. Other facilities included dressing rooms, restrooms, powder rooms, telephone booths, a beauty parlor, a photo studio, a hothouse, and a space where one could admire small birds (Oh J. 2004, 142–143). Spaces for taking refreshments completed the picture. Contrary to the premodern Korean gastronomy that was exclusively male oriented (Yi Sŏng-u 1980), the store restaurants were targeted specifically at women and "happy families" (*Chŏson chungang ilbo*, August 4, 1934, cited in Poole 2004, 52). Thus, for many Korean women a visit to a department store entailed a rather rare opportunity to dine out.

The first department store restaurant in the United States was installed at Macy's in New York in 1878. It was located on the second floor, and the menu was limited to cold food prepared off the premises, supplemented by hot tea, coffee, and chocolate —"a cheerless offering by modern standards, perhaps," comments Ralph Hower in a monograph on Macy's history, "but a boon to the tired shopper of 1870's and '80's whom progress had not yet supplied with convenient and inexpensive restaurants" (1946, 161). Along with providing weary shoppers with refreshments, the store restaurants had in time acquired an additional function. They were to attract customers to enter the store and were usually subsidized, providing the food, the service, and the ambience at a lower cost than if they had not been part of the stores' marketing strategies. In the United States, department stores competed with each other for customers by installing ever more extravagant dining settings, not infrequently causing financial liabilities for the store owners (Leach 1993, 137).

While the furnishing of those restaurants was definitely more luxurious than that of the dining rooms of the majority of their customers, it was by no means strikingly different. For Korean and Japanese women, however, the restaurant interior was a far stretch from their traditional domestic setting. The same holds true for the served food. With the exception of the dining room at Hwasin, which also served Korean cuisine, the menus of department store restaurants in colonial Korea were overwhelmingly foreign. Soups, cutlets, omelets, macaroni, and fritters on the menus of European and American department stores did not differ much from the daily fare of the shoppers, but pork cutlets, vegetable salads, and curries on rice were entirely unfamiliar to Koreans, unless they belonged to the exclusive circle of cosmopolitan elite (Kim T'ae-su 2005, 257–258).

In sum, the department store restaurants in colonial Korea were designed, as elsewhere, with a double purpose in mind: to lure potential shoppers into the store and to keep them on the premises longer. Korean women ardently embraced department store restaurants for the same reasons their counterparts in Europe and the United States did, but Korean women had additional reasons for excitement, similar to those experienced by Japanese women (Hatsuda 1993; Young 1999). First, the food on the menu included dishes that they hardly had an opportunity to sample elsewhere; foreign food remained in the domain of restaurants and professional caterers throughout the colonial period, practically never being prepared at home. Furthermore, the sleek and modern appeal of the Western-style buildings of the Korean department stores, and the interior of their dining halls, stood in strong contrast with the familiar surroundings of the Korean home. These differences underlined the juxtaposition of the multiple temporalities of colonial Korea, a relatively traditional Korean life at home and the dazzling speed of change in the Japanese/Western public life in the city.

Department stores and colonial modernity in Korea

The innovative retailers behind the facades of the department stores sought to create new sets of social relationships, perception and roles that would permit the adaptation of themselves, their work force, their clientele, and the bourgeois public to the changing society that the department store represented and was itself helping to bring about. (M. B. Miller 1981, 6)

As elsewhere, the department store played a crucial role in the construction of the modern culture of consumption in Korea. It was ardently embraced by Korean urbanites despite its association with Japanese colonial oppression. By 1941, for example, the sales of the Keijō branch of the Mitsukoshi department store were twice those of the comparably sized store in Sapporo (Mitsukoshi honsha 2005, 160). In principle, Korean subjects of the Japanese Empire did not differ from shoppers elsewhere; all fell under the seductive spells of modern retailing (see Figure 1.3).

Buying commodities was not the main inducement that drew crowds to the department stores that flourished in Korea during the 1930s and 1940s. Rather, the "retail palaces" provided an opportunity for the urban masses to participate in the public culture of spectacle that came to characterize the modern city. Dining out in these locations was part and parcel of the experience of being modern. The department store allowed ordinary people to escape from everyday reality and indulge temporarily in the fantasy of wealth. This was particularly true for women who had few reputable and justifiable ways to escape from the confinement of the domestic sphere.

Terms such as "ordinary people," "urban masses," and "crowds" must be clarified in the context of department store customers, however. These

Figure 1.3. A 1930s cartoon from *Chosŏn ilbo*, illustrating a crowd of women rushing to a department store. *Source:* Shin Myŏng-jik (2003).

terms refer to the bourgeois class of landowners, entrepreneurs, and urban professionals, rather than to disowned farmers, coolies, and factory girls. The department store was a bourgeois-class destination for going out, a destination that, as *Chosŏn ilbo* advised its readers on December 1, 1934, required of female visitors proper attire, hairstyle, and makeup. In 1936 a department store meal was worth a day's wages of unskilled labor, a ten-day supply of firewood for his family of five, or a two-day supply of rice to feed them; it was more expensive than a pair of rubber-soled shoes (Grajdanzev 1944, 180, 204). When seen from this perspective, department store dining reveals a class dimension that vividly differentiates the *crowds* of department store customers from the rest of the Korean population.

Nevertheless, these experiences, like many other aspects of colonial modernity, reveal the ambiguity of the colonizer assuming the position of a trendsetter in colonial Korea. Moreover, as indicated above, the ambiguity was two-dimensional, since the very survival of the trendsetter — the Japanese department stores — depended on the patronage of their Korean clientele. The department stores in colonial Korea provided a site for Japanese and Koreans — the colonized and the colonizers — to share the same experience of being modern consumers seduced by things and fashions. The Japanese and Koreans dined together in the grand dining halls of the department stores, the latter not infrequently outnumbering the former (Yi Kyŏng-hun 2001, 118).

Considering that the overwhelming majority of the Korean population lived in rural rather than urban areas, one might dismiss these experiences as marginal, since only a small fraction of Koreans were able to familiarize themselves with the new culture of consumption. However, the importance of this incipient phase derives from the prominent role it acquired later. The major innovation of the department store was the creation of an entirely new environment for public leisure centered around shopping — a fundamental principle of the contemporary shopping mall. Recognizing the department store as an embryo of Lotte World (see Tangherlini in this volume) adds contemporary significance to the exploration of colonial Korea's consumer culture.

Notes

1. The use of the term "Western food" (*yangsik*) in Korea has been largely influenced by the Japanese category of *yōshoku,* with its twofold meaning. On the one hand, it is a neutral term referring generally to European and American cuisines, with a strong emphasis on the Anglo-Saxon culinary tradition due to the overwhelming British and American presence in East Asia during the mid- and late nineteenth century. On the other hand, the term came to signify domesticated versions of selected British and American dishes featured on the menus of cheap Western-style restaurants that began to operate in Japan after the late nineteenth century (Cwiertka 2006, 49).

2. Lankov reports that Sontag served homemade Russian meals rather than French cuisine in her hotel and that some of her guests perceived the establishment as lacking in sophistication (2007, 90). It is possible, therefore, that it is Boher who should be credited for the culinary erudition of Sontag Hotel, not Sontag.

3. The only accommodation to Korean circumstances took place at the Korean-owned Hwasin department store, which served Korean-style meals along with Japanese-style and Western-style dishes (Oh J. 2004, 170; Kim T'ae-su 2005, 253).

Shrinking Culture
Lotte World and the Logic of Miniaturization

His eyes tell him he is in a different world — a dream world, perhaps a nightmare world — where all is bizarre and fantastic — crazier than the craziest part of Paris — qayer and more different from the everyday world, . . . [H]e is prepared to accept all sorts of extravagances — things that elsewhere would be impossible — in perfect good faith for the time being. — Frederic Thompson, "The Summer Show," 1907

Lotte World squats on its huge haunches like a concrete hippopotamus near the southern banks of the Han River in a neighborhood known as Chamsil.[1] Kang Nae-hŭi suggests that "in Seoul . . . all . . . roads lead to Lotte World," and he is not far off the mark (1995). Major thoroughfares and a large expressway bring thousands of visitors each day by bus and car to its entrances and labyrinthine underground parking lots, while Seoul's subway lines 2 and 8 intersect at a busy transfer station that opens to a subterranean shopping arcade, which in turn feeds effortlessly into Lotte World itself (ibid.). Inside and around the massive structure is an overwhelming array of stores, services, and amusements: clothing, souvenir, and department stores; opticians; pharmacies; restaurants; snack vendors; plazas; a "traditional market"; two theme parks — one indoors and one outdoors; performance stages; a multiplex cinema; a full-service health spa; a massive water park that could best be likened to an artificial lake; an artificial lake that makes the water park seem diminutive; a luxurious hotel, with all of the accoutrements befitting its four-star rating; an art gallery; a concert hall; and a medical clinic that not only offers plastic surgery and dentistry but also includes an ob-gyn practice, thereby affirming the hermetic nature of this world (see Figure 2.1). At the very top of the complex is a folklore museum, while at the very bottom, in an odd and probably accidental homage to Dante's Inferno, an enormous ice-skating rink. Taken as a whole, Lotte World could be seen as a nightmarish example of what Frederic Jameson has labeled "a

Figure 2.1. A view toward Magic Island at Lotte World. Photograph by author.

mutation in built space itself" (Jameson 1991, 38). However, the majority of Lotte World's visitors see it as a considerable achievement that brings the fantasy worlds of shopping malls, amusement parks, sports halls, and museums together in one convenient package, making the "other," the "exotic," and the "adventurous-yet-safe" easily accessible to a massive urban population.[2]

Lotte World is billed by its giant parent conglomerate as the world's largest indoor amusement park and shopping mall, a claim that is echoed almost verbatim by the Mall of America outside of Minneapolis, Minnesota, and the West Edmonton Mall in Canada. These complexes share certain extreme visions of both shopping and entertainment, at the same time as they significantly refigure the ways in which people come together to form fleeting communities, the manner in which class and age distinctions become inscribed on the lived urban environment, and the ways in which things — including space — are consumed. What sets all of these places apart from either their shopping mall forebears or their theme park cousins is the combination of a themed amusement park with the choreographed space of the shopping mall. In exploring this development in design, Rodrigo Salcedo mentions, "For mall developers and managers, the mall is a dreamland aimed at rescuing citizens from the problems of everyday life. Thus, 'West Edmonton Mall' promotes itself as a 'shoppers' dream and a world of excitement and adventure'" (2003, 1087–1088). Similar motivations can be ascribed to the designers of Lotte World, who consciously shifted away from solely offering themed amusements toward the synergy of the amusement park and shopping.

In an introduction to a volume considering the design aesthetics of both shopping malls and theme parks, Sarah Chaplin and Eric Holding observe, "Contrary to modernist arguments about authenticity, these places are where authentic experiences of modern life now occur, places where people meet, make friends and deal with their sense of alienation generated by the kind of sensory urban overload which Georg Simmel noted in his 1906 essay, *The Metropolis and Mental Life*" (1998, 8). To suggest that the denizens of Seoul suffer from "urban overload" and its attendant sense of alienation may be an understatement. Numerous critical studies have highlighted the shift in networks and communities presaged by the huge apartment complexes that now dominate Seoul's residential landscape (Gelezeau 1999, 2003). Similarly, other studies have traced the rise of youth subcultures starting in the early 1990s that specifically address aspects of alienation and urban overload among the middle class (Epstein 2000; Epstein and Tangherlini 2002). Because of these rapid changes in the man-made environment and the simultaneous urbanization of the population, community structures were profoundly altered. Consequently, patterns of socialization and interaction have been adapted to this urban environment, and sites of leisure, such as Lotte World, have taken on an important function beyond their obvious role as places where things are bought and sold. At Lotte World, for instance, middle school and high school students reaffirm important peer relationships while waiting in line for the flume ride, parents bond with young children while watching the Lotty and Lorry parade, grandparents interact informally with their grandchildren while tossing wooden sticks in a traditional game of *yutnori* at the folklore museum, colleagues solidify work relationships while fine-tuning their golf swings at the indoor driving range, and friends discuss everyday concerns while bargain hunting on the subterranean "Trevi Fountain" plaza. All of these activities highlight connectedness and are integral to aspects of urban socialization, community formation, and enculturation. They also constitute important "authentic" experiences of the urban middle class, even if the surroundings are decidedly "inauthentic." People enjoy the replicas — of buildings, of places, of historical times, and of experiences — but are not for a minute fooled by them; the kids on the flume ride are well aware they are riding a flume ride in Lotte World, and not coursing down a tributary to the Amazon in a dugout canoe.

This abandonment of an overarching concern with an external authentic referent is a crucial development. Earlier themed spaces stretching back to Skansen and Maihaugen in Scandinavia and the cultural exhibitions of the world's fairs often strove for mimetic representation of foreign places or the past (Bendix 1997; Kirshenblatt-Gimblett 1998; Sandberg 2003; Tangherlini 2008). By rejecting these earlier forms of authenticity, the mall and the theme park now emphasize consumption and efficiency. An interesting aspect of this shift away from the external logic of authenticity is the increasing role that consumption plays as a backdrop for activities such as family bonding or other types of community formation. Rather than casting a wistful eye away to the "foreign" or back in time toward the older and therefore more "authentic," as implicit in earlier theme parks and museum displays, the current parks — and shopping malls for that matter — embrace the notion that all experiences are authentic. Susan Davis notes, "Unlike the rock concert, and more like the shopping mall, the theme park depends on the construction of a landscape and the careful planning of human movement through space. The spatial rationale of the theme park is to cluster commercial opportunities — from hot dog stands to designer boutiques — around attractions which can range from rides to human or animal or robotic performances" (1996, 403). Mark Gottdiener continues, observing that these "themed environments work not only because they are connected to the universe of commodities and are spaces of consumption, but because they offer consumers a spatial experience that is an attraction by itself; that is, they promote the consumption of space" (1998, 15). I can think of few places where this is more apparent than at Lotte World.

The shopping mall–cum–theme park and the theme park–cum–shopping mall are clearly related phenomena, not only in their physical design but also as products of similar historical processes. Both are loci of interrelated consumption, and both offer an important window onto how the middle class lives. Although the lifestyles of the Korean middle class have become an object of increasing academic interest (Hart 2001; Kendall 2002; Moon 1997a; Nelson 2000), the majority of the scholarly study of theme parks and shopping malls has been directed at North American examples or, in some limited cases, on Western European analogs (Backes 1997; Bloch, Ridgway, and Dawson 1994; Kowinski 1985; Sandicki and Holt 1998; Sherry 1998; Vester 1996). Joy Hendry's work exploring the wide range of theme parks that have cropped up in Japan marks a welcome departure from this theoretical homogeneity (2000a). She proposes that "contextualized cultural description" might be a better approach than "de-contextualized grand theory," since she worries that Western analytical models may not be able to explain East Asian cultural phenomena (ibid.). Yet processes of globalization and capital development, as well as the lively two-way street that now exists between nodes of capital, such as Seoul and Los Angeles, all mean that an exclusion of Western interpretive models would be equally irresponsible. Writing about the advent of enormous shopping mall/theme park complexes in Southeast Asia, Alyson Brody observes that "in the space-restricted, hot, polluted city" these megalithic complexes serve "as all-encompassing leisure spaces, places where families and young couples alike can spend the day eating in restaurants, drinking coffee, seeing movies, and even go ice-skating or bowling. They are, in other words, hyper-modern expressions of new . . . middle-class lifestyles and mentalities" (Brody 2006, 541). This observation also holds true for Lotte World. Indeed, many informants emphasized the "convenience" offered by Lotte World, and the fact that, irrespective of weather, it is a place where they can entertain children and guests, shop for staples, and even take care of a sore tooth.

It is not terribly interesting, from a theoretical perspective, to see how things are the same at shopping malls and theme parks around the world. Such a study would simply confirm that global consumerism has penetrated the middle class of many different countries, and that marketers and designers appropriate things from other malls and parks that seem to work. A focus on difference and particularization not only is more interesting but also can tell us more about the local aspects of culture that make a themed space such as Lotte World so compelling. The folklorist C. W. von Sydow's concept of the oikotype, borrowed from botany, may be a useful theoretical concept in this context. Just as biological organisms are influenced by their physical environment, cultural expressions are influenced by the social, economic, and cultural milieu from which they emerge and which they in turn influence (Sydow [1932] 1948). In this context, Lotte World can be seen as a Korean oikotype of the melding of the shopping mall and the theme park. Its development and its subsequent use reflect local Korean historical processes and consumer practices (Crawford 1992; Nelson 2000; Uzzell 1999). Salcedo suggests that "when malls in other countries are examined, it becomes clear that they are the outcome of glocalization processes that combine the post-Fordist capitalist logic of mass production and consumption with local political, social and cultural influences that introduce significant variation" (2003, 1085). Lotte World is clearly recognizable as an example of this international type of consumer space. At the same time, discussions with visitors reveal a specificity that is not solely Korean but rather related to Seoul itself. If the newer version of Lotte World ever opens in Pusan — currently slated for 2012 — accompanied by a self-indulgent 107-story skyscraper, it too will undoubtedly become a highly localized expression of consumer practice, reflective of the people who live in Pusan. Just as with the Seoul Lotte World, the historical trajectory of urbanization and patterns of residential and commercial development — as well as the ways in which people navigate that city — will influence the manner in which Pusan Lotte World develops and the ways in which people engage it. Of course, skeptics such as Lee Doo-jae, senior executive managing director of Lotte World, scoff at the notion of a Pusan Lotte World: "It will never get built," he says.

What is Lotte World?

Unlike well-known American parks such as Disneyland and Busch Gardens, or large outdoor Korean parks such as Seoul Land and Everland, Lotte World is decidedly not a themed amusement park–cum–shopping mall (Davis 1996; Hendry 2000a; Weinstein 1992). In contrast to these parks, Lotte World does not present a unified experience with a consistent cast of characters and related thrill rides. To be sure, its two amusement parks, Adventureland and Magic Island, do have their themed rides, including the famous balloon ride and an Egyptian river adventure ride. The two parks also share their own recognizable mascots — Lotty and Lorry. But the mascots are better known for their role on children's cookies than at the parks, and the themed attractions are neither related to the mascots nor to one another. The two parks accordingly lack a consistency of representation that informs many other amusement parks. Indeed, when compared with the centrality of Snow White's castle and Mickey at Disneyland, Lotty and Lorry seem to be afterthoughts. Contributing to this lack of unity, many of the attractions are little more than simple copies of attractions from other parks, as are park uniforms, logos, benches, and even trash receptacles. As such, Lotte World is a pastiche of various other pastiches. Yet unlike the larger, better-known parks they imitate, the Lotte World parks do not dominate smaller, dedicated retailing endeavors such as the Downtown Disney mall at the much larger Disneyland. In other words, the Lotte World parks gesture at being theme parks while simultaneously resisting the totalizing nature of such a characterization.

Inverting the equation helps little: Lotte World is not a shopping mall–cum–amusement park. That characterization obtains more readily for its American counterpart, the Mall of America. Even though visitors to Lotte World have a comprehensive array of stores and services at their disposal and can buy almost anything they might conceivably want or need, the complex resists categorization as simply a very large shopping mall. The majority of visitors do not go to the amusement parks at Lotte World with the idea that they will split their time between the parks and the shopping mall. Similarly, most people who go shopping at the various stores have no intention of going to the amusement parks. Although one can see into the parks from windows in the mall, few people cross over between the two; on weekdays the gates between the two spaces are closed, and during the weekend the gates are little used. Visitors to Adventureland and Magic Island do not come primarily to shop, and retail shopping is not the focal point of their Lotte World experience on that particular day; indeed, nearby malls such as the newly erected Lotte Castle would undoubtedly provide a more focused and, according to one informant, more "modern" shopping experience. By way of contrast, the theme parks at the West Edmonton Mall, despite their considerable size, are there to offer a diversion from the main act of shopping. Margaret Crawford writes, "The WEM's nonstop proliferation of attractions, activities, and images proclaims its uniqueness; but, beneath its myriad distractions, the mall is easily recognizable as an elephantine version of a generic type — the regional shopping mall" (1992, 6). The hierarchy of consumer priorities at malls is clear, just as the hierarchy of consumer priorities at theme parks is clear: people go to the mall to shop (and for entertainment), and people go to the theme park for entertainment (and to shop).

One would be hard-pressed to prioritize activities at Lotte World, since the "components" of the world are not inextricably linked. This lack of integration is an important facet of Lotte World. Despite what Kang says about the difficulty of getting around Lotte World, one can in fact visit only one part of the world quite easily — be it the sports hall, the swimming center, the amusement parks, the discount store, the department store, the skating rink, the food court, the shooting range, or the shopping mall. Indeed, at times it is quite difficult to navigate from one space to the other, because of the clear differentiation of spaces in the world. One of the most noteworthy elements of Lotte World is how clear this differentiation of space results in a similarly clear differentiation of visitors. Visitors self-select into various groups based on age, gender, and class. This last category is, of course, problematic, since most visitors to Lotte World fall into the ever-growing category of middle class. Yet a form of microdifferentiation becomes abundantly clear as one navigates the spaces of the world.

The Lotte World hotel clearly caters to the upper reaches of the middle class, the majority of guests being either well-heeled Korean families, overseas Koreans returning for a visit, or Japanese tourists, who make up the majority of non-Korean visitors to Lotte World. The proximity of the department store — known as one of the most luxurious in Seoul — and the easy physical flow from the hotel lobby to the first floor of the department store confirm a relationship based on class. The clientele of the department store, in turn, tend to self-select, with many more women visitors than men. By way of contrast, the discount store that anchors the other end of the shopping complex caters to families and other middle-class consumers, in much the same way that Target or Costco captures a similar American demographic. Interestingly, the shopping mall that runs the length of the north side of the complex is decidedly less popular than either the department store or the discount store, and far less popular than the ever-crowded underground arcade and discount plaza — areas that both teem with middle-aged women who, as one informant put it, are engaged in an energetic hunt for "good stuff cheap."

The differentiation of space continues at the theme parks, where young children between two and eight are most attracted by the indoor Lotte Adventure and its tamer rides, while teenagers and young adults congregate across the footbridge on Magic Island, where the rides are "scarier." The ice rink attracts both school-age children taking instruction in short-course speed skating and teenagers and young adults using Lotte World as part of a "date course." The swimming pool attracts parents — primarily mothers — with young children and teenagers (but probably not the same teenagers who are either at Magic Island or skating that day), while the sports complex caters to a more affluent and largely middle-aged or older crowd who segregate themselves along gender lines. The folklore museum almost exclusively draws mothers with school-age children, grandparents with their grandchildren, and foreign tourists, most of whom are Japanese. The areas that have the most overlap are the hotel and the department store, and the amusement parks and the folklore museum; all of the other spaces function as destinations unto themselves, and few people move between the spaces during any given visit. In contrast, there is no such use-differentiation at more traditional shopping malls or amusement parks. Similarly, it is not difficult to recognize priorities at either: the former emphasize "retail experiences" and the latter emphasize "themed entertainment." Such priorities are missing from Lotte World. When asked what they do there, informants would hesitate, mention that it depended on whom they had along, and then launch into an agglomerative list describing all of the things that they have done, at one time or another, at Lotte World.

Coincidentally, the lack of prioritization of experiences among visitors at Lotte World mirrors the diversified nature of the Lotte conglomerate itself. The Lotte Group is Korea's eighth-largest *chaebŏl* (conglomerate) and is a major player in the department store, fast food, beverages, candy, publishing, entertainment, and hotel industries in Korea. Like most *chaebŏl*, it also has divisions that work in financial services, heavy industry, petrochemicals, and construction, but for the Lotte group these are lesser concerns. Lotte was originally founded in Tokyo in 1948, in the aftermath of the war, by Sin Kyuk-ho, a Korean national living in Japan. Sin named the conglomerate after Charlotte, the love interest in Goethe's *Die Leiden des jungen Werthers* (1774), a gesture to both a Romantic spirit and his own cosmopolitanism. It is no doubt this vague Romanticism that also informs the frantic representations of European villages nestled up against Egyptian pyramids in Adventureland and architectonic glosses on both Bavarian castles and traditional Korean houses *(hanok)* on the outdoor Magic Island. While the Japanese origins of the Lotte Group surprises many contemporary Koreans, given both the penetration of nationalistic rhetoric informing the history of modern Korean economic development and the ubiquity of Lotte's products in Korean pantries, those origins confirm the role of Japan in the development of Korean capitalism during the colonial period as traced by Carter Eckert (1991). Lotte World is also an offspring of empire.

In the immediate postwar period, the main product of the Lotte Confectionary Company was chewing gum. Because of geopolitical concerns, the company did not penetrate the Korean market until the normalization of diplomatic relations between Japan and Korea in 1965. It finally began Korean operations in 1967, introducing one of the main staples of the Korean junk-food landscape, the Chocopie, a gloss on the American Mallomar and Scooter Pie, and thereby guaranteeing widespread recognition of its name and all its products. By that point, Korea was on a rapid trajectory toward industrialization and urbanization, and Japan had emerged as a budding global economic powerhouse. Equally importantly, Japanese consumers and, by the early 1970s, Korean consumers found themselves with increasing disposable income and leisure time, preconditions for the explosion of domestic tourism that Joy Hendry traces in her studies of Japanese theme parks (2000a, 2000b; see also MacCannell 1999). Coupled to the modernizing agenda of Park Chung-hee, Lotte found excellent economic conditions for its development of snack foods and urban shopping centers (Nelson 2000). By the 1980s, Lotte had emerged as a dominant player in retailing, entertainment, and foodstuffs. In 1989, Lotte World became the jewel in the crown of this burgeoning empire and soon developed into an important draw in the local consumer and tourist markets.

Built in the late 1980s, Lotte World was not completed in time to capture the crowds who came to Seoul for the Olympics in September 1988. With various construction delays, the complex opened in July of 1989. Although Lotte missed the Olympic opportunity, it did catch the rising tide of Korean affluence and successfully captured a huge and hitherto untapped domestic market; the rapid emergence of the Korean middle class during the 1980s and early 1990s, up through the IMF Crisis, provided a nearly endless stream of visitors. Lotte World continues to have a remarkable hold on Seoul's increasingly affluent middle class, registering a visitor tally in 2002 of nine million (in comparison, the Mall of America had an annual tally of forty-two million visitors; and Disneyland, thirteen million).[3] Intriguingly, and according to Lotte World's own statistics, only 10 percent of its visitors are foreign, most of them Japanese.

One of the main reasons for Lotte World's middle-class success is its proximity to Seoul itself. MacCannell and other, more recent scholars have explored the concept of "destination tourism," a process related to the development of many American theme parks in the exurbs. Davis writes, "The theme park became an 'away' place, separated from the everyday life of the city by distance as much as by imagistic control" (1996, 404). But this notion of the "separate" does not apply to Lotte World. Roman Cybriwsky notes that theme parks and shopping malls "are often designed to figuratively transport users to distant places or different times," a figurative transport that often coincides with a literal transport to outside of the city space (1999, 228). But Lotte World relies on just the opposite — a physical proximity that makes the visit to this "exotic landscape" within the easy reach of the entire population of Seoul through a single subway ride. Indeed, many teenaged informants emphasized the importance of proximity in their choice of visiting Lotte World. Since Lotte World is perceived as being nearby, they can easily incorporate it into their everyday life in the city.

There are several other theme parks in and around Seoul, including Everland in Suwŏn and Seoul Land in the city itself. Other smaller parks exist in Korea and more are being built, but few are as well known as these three. Visiting Everland — the most frequently mentioned other theme park in interviews — by contrast requires a long train ride followed by an even longer bus ride, or parent willing to brave the freeways. Visiting Seoul Land is not really an option, according to these kids; the rides are "no good" or "lame." Lotte World, by contrast, "has good rides" and "is easy to get to." Convenience may well be the biggest key to Lotte World's success.

Its success may also be due to its representation of excess — an excess that has been embraced and valorized by the expanding Korean middle class. This excess is reflected in the designs for the "supertall" Lotte World skyscraper proposed for an adjacent lot, and the comically horrifying designs for Pusan Lotte World. Kangnam, where Lotte World squats, has for the past two decades been the focal point of conspicuous consumption in Korea, at once creating an image of the modern Korean and spawning tales of the wretched excess of the "Orange tribe" (Nelson 2000). Lotte World itself mimics this concept of excess, spilling over in quite dramatic fashion into the surrounding environment. Indeed, its simultaneous incorporation of as much of the outside as possible, as well as its insistence on breaking out of its physical shell, are both part of its totalizing project. Echoing Sorkin, Davis points out that "as cities restructure themselves along touristic principals, the theme park extends outward, undermining older city forms and recasting urban areas as 'variations on a theme park'" (Sorkin 1992; Davis 1996, 417). Paradoxically, this totalizing gesture whereby Lotte World breaks out of its concrete shell to embrace the immediate neighborhood, although massive in scale, necessarily relies on miniaturization for its success.

Miniaturization is not unique to Lotte World. Indeed, the whole premise of the "mini-golf" course, an early version of the theme park, relies precisely on this concept. Susan Stewart writes, "Miniature golf, the fantasy land, the children's zoos and storybook countries realize the exotic and the fantastic on a miniaturized scale. The image that is produced not only bears the tangible qualities of material reality but also serves as a representation, an image, of a reality which does not exist" (1984, 60). Miniaturization can also be considered the enabling logic of both the shopping mall and the amusement park, even while the goal of both institutions is to indulge consumers in fantasies of excess while divorcing them from their money (ibid.). What makes Lotte World intriguing is the extent of the penetration of this logic of miniaturization into its constructed "world," and the cultural implications of that miniaturization situated in the specific geographic and historical context of Korea. What gets miniaturized at Lotte World? How does it get miniaturized? What are the implications of this miniaturization? As the name implies, Lotte World is intended to be a "world" for its visitors and, quite possibly, for the people who work there. Accordingly it requires a shift in scale — a miniaturization — to achieve that aim. Lotte World executes this shift surprisingly well, even if the implications of that success are somewhat unsettling.

Lotte World and the logic of miniaturization

Granted, "miniature" is not the first word that springs to mind when one arrives at Lotte World. All of the architectural gestures are grand, challenging normal scale and expectations of the "inside" — waterfalls cascade down walls five stories high, glass elevators zip up and down the interior on illuminated tracks, indoor plants that look like transplants from *Jurassic Park* reach upward, and the curved glass roof stretches off into the distance high up overhead. Crowds of people flock up and down staircases, gather in expansive indoor plaza areas, and flood the halls that branch out and around the complex; seemingly endless banks of escalators ferry their charges up and down past each other, while in other parts of the sprawling complex, throngs of swimmers splash across the expanses of the aquatics center, clusters of brightly clad skaters crowd the ice rink, and lines of up-turned faces wait expectantly alongside the amusement rides. Up across the top floors of the galleria, one can glimpse the rooftops of caricature-like buildings; a Dutch windmill, German half-timbered houses, a giant tree, and pyramids vie for space along this crowded horizon. After visitors step through the turnstiles of the amusement park, pathways branch off in all directions. Up above, a hot-air balloon/monorail twists and turns in serpentine fashion just below the expansive glass roof, while its passengers dangle below, staring down at the ice skaters who glide about in the very lowest ring of Lotte's World. Shouts and screams from the nearby rides echo through the enormous space — Lotte World is really loud. As pas-sengers leave the glass-roofed mall by monorail, Magic Island theme park looms ahead, dominating the skyline with its manic gloss on the Bavarian Mad King Ludwig's Neuschwanstein Castle. On first encounter, the place seems almost limitless in scope.

Initially, navigating Lotte World's labyrinthine pathways confirms this sense of limitless space and overwhelming scale. Kang mentions that Lotte World "draws people in and, if possible, holds them there for a long time. [It] moves its 'trapped customers' around busily. Its passageways are extensive, but no matter what direction they go, they never extend beyond the interior. After spending some time inside, people often begin to think, 'I don't know where I am; I can't find my way out'" (Kang N. 1995, 46). Kang misstates the case: rather than not knowing where they are, visitors know quite well where they are. How could they not? They are in Lotte World. One can always leave one part of the world for another, and indeed a visit to some parts, such as the swimming pool, more or less require a trip outside. Similarly, while finding one's car in the underground parking lot can prove challenging, leaving the complex by subway or bus, as the vast majority of visitors do, is a trivial exercise. What is more disconcert-ing than the sense of no exit is the creeping realization of constantly cross-ing one's own tracks. This realization strips away the first impressions of immensity and confirms the processes of miniaturization that inform not only the theme parks but every other aspect of the complex as well. The more time one spends there, the more aware one becomes that, despite the initial sense of limitless size, all of the ersatz foreign buildings, all of the amusement park rides, and all of the vistas are remarkably constrained. Moving through the space, one cannot help but realize that size does matter and that Lotte World is rather small — at least in comparison with the outside world, or the outside city, or even the outside theme parks from which it borrows so readily. At the same time, it is this reassuring shrinkage in scale that enables Seoulites to manage it and consume it time and again.

At Lotte World, the shrinking of physical distance (Spain is next to France is next to Germany, all in the shadow of Egypt and all under one large glass roof) and the shrinking of scale (a pyramid towers over a German village that looks serenely out on its near mirror image save for a windmill) effect this shift away from the real, a shift that visitors generally embrace, if they notice it at all. Concomitant to these physical shifts that enact the displacement of the real to fantasy (all the while enabling authentic experiences) is a temporal shift. Stewart writes:

> The miniature does not attach itself to lived historical time. . . . The reduction in scale which the miniature presents skews the time and space relations of the everyday life world, and as an object consumed, the miniature finds its "use value" transformed into the infinite time of reverie. This capacity of the miniature to create an "other" time, a type of transcendent time which negates change and the flux of lived reality might be seen at work in such projects as the Museum of the Miniature (1948). (1984, 65)

The same holds true for Lotte World.

This logic of miniaturization informs nearly every aspect of Lotte World. Despite all of its contradictory gestures toward being all-inclusive, toward being gigantic, toward being a totality — physically, culturally, architectonically, historically — the only way any of these gestures can succeed in the context of consumption is through miniaturization. Physical size is reduced, so that vistas, while grand, are still easily contained, either in one's own line of sight or in the camera's viewfinder. The distance between the fantasy world of television — such as the Korean series *Stairway to Heaven,* filmed in part at Lotte World — and that of the visitor is equally reduced, an acrobatic maneuver of dizzying cultural proportions that validates the fictional places of television as "real" at the same time as it allows visitors to insert themselves into the "fantasy world" of television (Crawford 1992). Similarly, the foreign is reduced in scope and impact through what can best be described as architectonic caricature, a form of miniaturization that exaggerates certain elements but, through that exaggeration, renders them no bigger than a mere amusement. History, whether local or global, is shrunk down as well to a manageable size. Here at Lotte World, all cultural, geographic, environmental, and historical processes are captured and tamed, and then made small, compact, and consumable.

The (mini) Folklore Museum at the top of the world

Nowhere is the logic of miniaturization more apparent than at Lotte World's Minsok Pangmulgwan (Folklore Museum). The entrance to the folk museum, on the third floor of the Lotte World galleria, mimics the entrance to Minsokch'on (Folk Village) in Suwŏn, with its angled eaves and tiled roofs, and announces through this design that here is something Korean and traditional. But instead of opening onto a painstakingly reconstructed vision of an imagined rural landscape, the Folklore Museum instead takes its organizational cues from the far more serious Kungnip Minsok Pangmulgwan (National Folklore Museum) on the grounds of Kyŏngbok Palace. After a short movement through a hall of multimedia videos, and a short jaunt through the evolution of mankind, visitors enter a room detailing life in the earliest Korean kingdoms. Mannequins populate tableaux from everyday life. In earlier work, I have shown how these principles of display are borrowed from early Nordic folk museums, translated through Japan and nascent South Korean nationalism (Tangherlini 2008). Yet even in the execution of this standard folkloric display, Lotte World shrinks things: Lee Doo-jae points out (and it is confirmed by the signage) that even these displays are only 80 percent of actual size. Nevertheless, Lotte World's Folklore Museum does a credible job of duplicating the efforts of the national museum, though, once again, on a much smaller scale. Whereas the Folk Village collapses most of the nineteenth century into one normative still life of rural Korea, while allowing for some distinctions between classes and regions, here the Folklore Museum collapses all of Korean history into one homogeneous vision of Korea, from the Cretaceous period to the recent past, making little provision for regional or class differences. The underlying implication is that Lotte World is the natural outcome of these events.

Part of what makes this collapsing possible is the museum's reliance on a preexisting index of Korean folklife. Through repeated and pervasive visual representations of traditional Korean expressions in the popular media, in educational institutions, and in the built environment, most Koreans — and even many visitors to Korea — have been made aware of a general "cultural inventory" of traditional Korea (Laurel Kendall, private correspondence, 2007). Because of these frequent references to this cultural inventory throughout Korea, traditional expressions have been reduced to a visual cliché. In turn, it is these visual clichés that inform Lotte World's miniature representation of Korean folklife.

The museum becomes far more interesting when one leaves the various rooms displaying life-size tableaux and enters the coronation hall. The miniature representation of a massive coronation at Kyŏngbok Palace is dramatic — the darkened hall is illuminated by spotlights that bathe the ceremony in stark, intersecting beams of light. It would all be quite awesome if it did not seem like an odd cross between a child's train set and Legoland. Here imperial pomp and circumstance are reduced to the scale of toys. Of course, there is something brilliant about this — children become quickly engrossed by something that, at other museums, is easily dismissed as being grown-up or boring. Stewart notes another effect of this "shrinkage"; it also erases history and, consequently, enables the nostalgic:

> For the function of the miniature here is to bring historical events "to life," to immediacy, and thereby to erase their history, to lose us within their presentness. The transcendence presented by the miniature is a spatial transcendence, a transcendence which erases the productive possibilities of understanding through time. Its locus is thereby the nostalgic. The miniature here erases not only labor but causality and effect. Understanding is sacrificed to being in context. Hence the miniature is often a material allusion to a text which is no longer available to us, or which, because of its fictiveness, never was available to us except through a second-order fictive world. (1984, 60)

The nostalgia invoked by the Folklore Museum is, of course, quite particular and relates to the relatively recent experiences of rapid urbanization, industrialization, and modernization and the attendant changes in the physical and social environments. The scale of the coronation — perhaps to compensate for the difficulty of feeling nostalgic for the reign of the earliest Chosŏn kings — is considerably larger than the scale in the next room.

The next room — a cavernous hall — is plunged into complete darkness save for individual spotlights trained on small displays. It is here that the museum's reliance on the visual clichés that stand in for all of Korean culture becomes most apparent. The displays in this hall illustrate various life-cycle celebrations and calendrical festivals from late Chosŏn rural Korea. The time frame is, not surprisingly, exactly the same as at Minsokch'on — namely, the late nineteenth century. But everything is tiny and artificial; the tallest buildings are no more than a foot from foundation to roof beam, and physical features such as lakes or the ocean are small blotches of blue covered with cellophane. There is no attempt at mimesis; rather, caricature appears to be the underlying ideology. All of the displays are wildly overpopulated and convey a sense of hyperactivity that echoes up from theme park floors below. The visitor can see everything that is "customary" in all of rural Korea all at once. Over there is a ceremony honoring Confucius, over here is a family *chesa* (ancestor rite). Look to the right to see a *tol* (first birthday celebration) and, further on, a *hwan'gap* (sixty-first birthday celebration). "Hey, look, aren't those shamans performing a ritual *kut*?" the visitor might want to shout, but then her eyes fall on the Cheju Island divers and she thinks back to the romanticized view of these women who populate tourist brochures and television specials (see Figure 2.2). All of the country's rural regional stereotypes are concatenated in one very small display.

The centerpiece of this room is a frenetic representation of a rural village market. All of the figures in the display, given their clear level of unrestrained energy, appear to have spent the morning at one of the new espresso bars cropping up around Seoul. Mini-mimesis is the underlying rhetorical stance of the display and enables a sense of caricature. Small, easily viewed, readily understood parts of Korean tradition — indeed the very best known examples of Korean tradition and rural life drawn from the iconic, clichéd of a traditional cultural inventory — are made to stand for the whole of rural experience, irrespective of region, historical period, or class status. But the caricature is not of the humorous sort of amusement park touts, or of the slightly dark vision of jaded European artists coaxing reluctant tourists to be caricatured in front of the Trevi Fountain in Rome. The figurines populating this display are a caricature of a different order.

"Caricature" may be the wrong word, as caricature can easily carry over into the grotesque. The miniaturization in the doll village, by contrast, invites a flight of fancy similar to that inspired by the amusement parks

Figure 2.2. A hyperkinetic *kut* in the doll village at Lotte World's Folklore Museum. Photograph by author.

below. Lee Choon-ho, chief curator of the museum and one of the people with the longest connection to, mentions in an interview:

> After the project had gotten under way, the decision was made to make things smaller. If we had decided to try to show things as they are in life-size . . . there wouldn't have been enough room to show all the things we wanted to show. At the same time, it wouldn't have worked if we tried to show everything with just one miniature village. From prehistoric times to the Three Kingdoms period is quite a long time. And of course the Chosŏn era is a more recent past, and so there are many more things to show from that time. We decided to give half the space to the Chosŏn era, so that's why that period is shown in miniature. Actually, the life-size houses from the other times are reduced in scale a little too, due to the size of the Lotte World building and the space given to the museum. The building was built first and the exhibits were designed afterwards, and so the exhibits were made to fit the building. It was designed to be an easy place for citizens and foreign visitors to

see various cultural aspects of Korea.... Since there are so many things to show from the Chosŏn era, we decided to put the dolls in place, and so that's how the museum came to be the way it is now.

Despite giving half of the exhibit space to the Chosŏn era, numerous aspects of folk culture are necessarily elided. The erasure of regional differences that marks the Chosŏn as an undifferentiated, national past is certainly recognized by the museum staff. In that regard, Lee Doo-jae laments, "We cannot show the various different cultures of the different regions of Korea, although we would like to. It's a very idealistic goal and a good thing to point out." Of course, many of the decisions regarding the museum were constrained by the Lotte boardroom, the building size, and the cost of launching a museum. Lee Choon-ho continues, "The original plan was not to design the museum in this way. The original idea was that it would be a place to display cultural treasures. However, there was not enough time to excavate such items, and since there was only a short time and it was not easy to purchase all the artifacts and items, there was a slight dilemma." The end result is quite remarkable. Instead of a museum that offers a totalizing narrative, the miniature village that comprises half of the museum space focuses primarily on contextualization at the same time as it puts the visitor into a position of visual control, towering over all of late Chosŏn's rural experience.

The dolls that populate the Chosŏn village were designed and installed by the duo of Yi Sŭng-ŭn and Hŏ Hŏn-sŏn. One of the most striking features of the doll display is its extraordinary attention to detail — a squid vendor, for instance, has scores of tiny dried squid on his cart, while a shoe vendor has several dozen pairs of shoes for sale, all in different sizes and different styles. As Gaston Bachelard observes, "because these descriptions tell things in tiny detail, they are automatically verbose" (cited in Stewart 1984, 47). This emphasis on minutiae has a secondary effect as well, as the single instance moves to the forefront. Stewart proposes: "The depiction of the miniature moves away from hierarchy and narrative in that it is caught in an infinity of descriptive gestures. It is difficult for much to happen in such depiction, since each scene of action multiplies in spatial significance in such a way as to fill the page with contextual information" (ibid.).

The two artists have also had recent success with another installation of small historical dolls, entitled "Ŏmma ŏryŏssŭl chŏken . . ." (When

Mommy was young . . .), which also relied on a series of miniature tableaux. Rather than representing a normative view of late Chosŏn rural culture, it captured specific moments in the lives of children and their parents (predominantly mothers) during the early years of Park Chung-hee's regime. The tableaux are vividly reminiscent of the early urban experience of the poor and activate a readily accessible nostalgia — nostalgia of *han,* historically engendered pain and grievance. Unlike the longing for a time that never was that informs Lotte World's miniature Chosŏn display, the "Ŏmma" display resists a desire for a return to what were clearly uncomfortable, deprived conditions (Appadurai 1996).

The potential for nostalgia of *han* emerges in the final exhibit hall of the Folklore Museum, a display of urban artifacts from the Japanese colonial period. The display mimics a movie set and depicts a surprisingly mundane street scene. Instead of using dolls, the exhibit relies on the visitors to populate the otherwise deserted streets. Here, the city has been shrunk to a handful of shops selling everyday essentials; several pristine examples of period cars fill out the hall. What is most notable about this display is the incredible normalness that pervades it — save for a few small posters, there is nothing that suggests that times were bad. Apart from the requisite depiction of a bloody interrogation that duplicates similar scenes from other Korean museums, the emphasis on suffering and subjugation that has become the normative mode for colonial-era displays is absent from the Lotte World exhibit. Nevertheless, the colonial-era room is still a bit of a jolt, given its intertextual connotations. Despite its seeming innocuousness, the exhibit indexes other displays that are far more accusatory. Because of this intertextuality, the display has the potential to alienate a large number of Lotte World's visitors. Lee Doo-jae mentions the odd tension underlying the colonial-era exhibit:

> Japan is actually a very close country . . . and to us they are customers as well. Making an exhibit of the colonial era is basically showing the bad things that Japan did to Korea during that time. That can be a real burden to the Japanese visitors, and if we focus too much on criticizing Japan for the deeds that they did during that era, it could evoke negative feelings. . . . The colonial period was the most miserable period in Korean history, and so it is a difficult era to emphasize and make big. We have many Japanese customers, so it is difficult to keep criticizing

them and blaming them. It is enough to just show them and make them feel bad.

Lee's point is clear. The exhibit is geared in large part to the Japanese visitors; by making it innocuous, the sense of accusation shifts from the overt to the implicit. For Koreans, the intertextual reading of the exhibit is always available: children can marvel at the "old" artifacts yet readily access grandparents' and teachers' accounts of the misery of the colonial period, while their parents immediately recognize the period and all its implications. Japanese visitors are instantly confronted with a well-known but often ignored period in their history. The exhibit thus serves two simultaneous purposes. On the one hand, it confirms the Koreanness of the Lotte conglomerate (if that was ever in question), despite its Japanese roots, by establishing a collaborative nostalgia of *han* with the Korean visitors. On the other hand, it gently elicits uneasy feelings of shame in Japanese visitors. It is no small wonder that the pathway through the exhibit feeds directly into the souvenir shop. Perhaps a Korean fan for fifteen thousand won can assuage some of that colonial-era guilt?

Interestingly, few visitors to Lotte World are aware of the folklore museum's existence. Normative visions of Korea's rural past have a hard time competing with fantastic visions of no one's future and really fast water rides. One Lotte World executive's own view on why the Folklore Museum is even there is somewhat confusing. Kim Sang-sook mentions, "It was the Lotte group chairman who thought of it, having a museum. This whole place, including the hotel, department store, and theme park. . . . There's only those kinds of things here, so he decided there should be some kind of cultural spot in the place. Also, the best newspaper reporters cautioned that there should be some sort of a cultural space, so this museum was built."

Discussing the goals of the museum, Lee Doo-jae says: "Because this is a private museum, it is not focused on some scholarly aspect of Korea, but it is geared to the students and the average people. All those events described here are not done in an overtly scholarly fashion. It's for students to see and learn, 'Oh, we were like that in the past.' That's the focus." His comments are echoed in English-language materials that describe the museum as "a cultural space for natural enjoying and understanding of the history and traditional culture of Korea rather than learning." Although the Korean catalog copy is linguistically more sophisticated, the disarming English characterization is probably more to the point: Lotte World's Folklore Museum does not attempt to compete with educational or national institutions; it is to be consumed just as the rest of the complex is.

Conclusion

In an earlier examination of themed spaces in Korea, I mentioned that the Folklore Museum at Lotte World was in many ways more "honest" than its larger-scale and more "official" counterparts (Tangherlini 2008). The miniaturization of historical experience at the Lotte World museum strips away the pretenses of authenticity and mimesis that inform the other museums (Hendry 2000a; Sandberg 2003). Similarly, the small scale of the displays at the Lotte World Folklore Museum allows the visitor to view the entire nineteenth-century Korean rural experience all at once — a bolus of Korean folklife. This representation relies on a normative cultural inventory for its successful portrayal of Korean traditional culture and allows the visitor to easily control the limits of the implied historical and cultural narrative. Coupled with the abbreviated tableaux and the large-scale reenactment of a coronation, the visitor to the Lotte World museum is offered a clear, uncomplicated, and remarkably brief narrative of life on the Korean peninsula, one that easily spans the vast reach of time from the dinosaurs to the present. In other words, at the museum all of the historical developments — as well as all of the consumer experiences — that eventually led to the construction of Lotte World can be seen in but a few glances. History is infinitely reducible at the Folklore Museum. Consequently, despite its seeming size, Lotte World shows that history and, for that matter, the world are containable. Both are purely surface-level phenomena.

At other museums, parks, and even shopping malls, there is a nagging sense that beyond the surface is an underlying, perhaps hidden framework that needs to be explored and critiqued. At Lotte World, in contrast, everything is on the surface. Oddly, this makes Lotte World a refreshing respite from the complexities of modern city spaces that frequently engage in an elaborate masquerade. Lotte World hides little — it is exactly what it appears to be. To be sure, there are "back spaces" and invisible workers — a large workforce of poorly paid cleaners and an elaborate security apparatus, to name but two examples — that deserve critical attention

(Brody 2006; Kang N. 1995; MacCannell 1999). But even these are not particularly concealed. There is no hidden agenda for the consumer at Lotte World — the entire place is designed for people to spend money and to enjoy amusement rides and unusual vistas. While there is something unsettling about this, Stacy Warren reminds us that "cultural activities form an integral component of the socially constructed landscape by acting as channels of discourse, sometimes symbolic and sometimes concrete, that mediate people's relationship with their surroundings and allow opportunities to consider, contest and come to terms with economic, political, and social aspects of place" (1996, 549).

The visitor to Lotte World cares little about the "authenticity" of the place. As Erik Cohen mentions, "the cultural sanction of the postmodern tourist is that of a 'playful search for enjoyment,' or an 'aesthetic enjoyment of surfaces'" (1995, 21), the latter being a particularly apt characterization of the Lotte World experience (Wang 1999, 357). Lotte World embraces the idea of the shopping mall and the theme park in a grand (or perhaps miniature) postmodern gesture of this sort. Linda Hutcheon, writing about the poetics of postmodernism, proposes that the postmodern "is a contradictory phenomenon, one that uses and abuses, installs and then subverts, the very concepts it challenges" (1988). Of course, it has in recent years become de rigueur to characterize both the shopping mall and the theme park as the logical conclusion of postmodern architectonics (Chaplin and Holding 1998; Jameson 1991; Warren 1996). Try as I might, I cannot get away from the conclusion that the contradictory nature of Lotte World validates this stance. What sets Lotte World apart from many other themed spaces is that one has to do very little to arrive at this postmodern critique.

At Lotte World there is a strong embrace of the inauthentic and the unoriginal. Its theme parks borrow, perhaps even steal, design features from other parks, and its shopping mall draws frequent attention to the supporting role it had in a television drama. The "photo spots" that pop up throughout Lotte World insist on the built nature of the environment and seem to comment on its glaring inauthenticity. Citing Eco, Wang notes that "it is irrelevant whether [Disneyland or Disney World] is either real or false, since there is no original that can be used as a reference" (Wang 1999, 356). While Eco emphasizes the concept of the "hyperreal" and Baudrillard mentions the "simulacra," both concepts imply that the consumers of these spaces are critically unaware of this seduction (Baudrillard 1983; Eco 2002). At Lotte World the consumer is not only aware of but cares little about the purely manufactured nature of the world. Interviews with visitors confirm this. Lotte World is not interpreted by its visitors as anything other than what it is. Because of their diminutive size, the gestures toward the natural world, toward historical experience, and toward other built environments are both seen and consumed as miniature models of something else that might well not exist. It does not matter to the visitor.

Notes

This essay is based on fieldwork carried out in 1989, 1994, 2004, 2005, and 2006. It includes interviews in Seoul and Los Angeles. My student Eun Jung Choi has been an incredible assistant, conducting interviews both in Los Angeles and Seoul and giving me her own perspective on Lotte World. Her assistance has made this project far stronger than I would have been able to accomplish on my own. My thanks go to Lee In-sik (director), Lee Choon-ho (chief curator), and Kim Sang-sook (assistant manager), all of the Lotte World Folklore Museum, and Lee Doo-jae (senior executive managing director) of Hotel Lotte, Lotte World, for their hospitality and assistance; without them, this project would have been impossible to complete. I am grateful to Stephen Epstein for his helpful comments on earlier drafts of this chapter and to Scott Snyder for sharing his ideas about Lotte World during a winter visit to the complex. I would also like to thank UCLA's Department of Asian Languages and Cultures, Office of the Dean of Humanities, and Committee on Research for their support, and the organizers of this conference, Ned Schultz and Laurel Kendall, for including me in this exciting project. Finally, I thank the members of the Wildcat Canyon Advanced Seminars in Cultural Studies for their helpful comments on earlier drafts.

1. Lotte World opened in July 1989. It was built by the large Lotte conglomerate, best known for its dominant role in the Korean food industry.

2. The notion that Lotte World is "adventurous yet safe" — a general idea that applies to all amusement parks — was shown to be false when an employee of the park fell from a roller coaster to his death on March 6, 2006. Although operator and rider error were determined to be the cause of his death (as well as a seemingly inept response from the rescue squad), safety at Lotte World became an issue splashed across the front pages of Korea's newspapers. To counteract this negative publicity, Lotte World announced a series of free admission days but did not plan properly for the massive crowds that showed up to take advantage of the offer. As a result, thirty-five visitors were injured in a stampede to get through the amusement park gates on the first of the planned free admission days on

March 25. Consequently, Lotte World shuttered the parks through March 31. By late summer 2006, the controversy had died down, and visitor tallies had rebounded.

3. *Amusement Business Magazine,* December 23, 2002. In 2008, the most recent year for which attendance records were available at this writing, Lotte World registered a steep decline in attendance after a six-month closure for renovations. In 2008, Lotte World had 4.2 million visitors, and Disneyland 14.7 million (TEA/ ERA 2009).

Part II

Korea as Itinerary

The more I examined my data, the more inescapable became my conclusion that tourist attractions are an unplanned typology of structure that provides direct access to the modern consciousness of "world view." — Dean MacCannell, *The Tourist*

While organized travel has venerable roots in European and Asian pilgrimages, mass tourism is a specifically modern and broadly recognizable form that organizes visual experiences into an itinerary (Bennet 1988, 74; Mitchell 1989, 227–236). Encountered in commodity forms such as guidebooks and organized tours, tourism becomes a privileged act of gazing and passing through (MacCannell 1999; Urry 1990). In this section, Hyung Il Pai describes the privileged colonial era gazing of Western and Japanese tourists to Korea and the development of a recognizably modern tourist industry in the colony. Chapters by Okpyo Moon and Robert Oppenheim depict some different forms of alternative tourism in which South Koreans today engage. In common with alternative travelers elsewhere, they claim their own distinction in doing something different from the package tour, but at the same time their "modern consciousness of 'world view'" contains concerns, anxieties, and desires that are distinctive to the contemporary South Korean moment.

Travel Guides to the Empire

The Production of Tourist Images in Colonial Korea

G lobal tourism is often cited as the new colonizing vanguard of modernity, characterized by the search for mythical places, colorful natives, and authentic cultural experiences (Lofgren 1999; MacCannell 1999). Beginning in the mid-nineteenth century, the invention of mechanized vehicles such as steamships and trains capable of transporting hundreds of passengers, and the expansion of trading networks by European imperial powers, were the two main driving forces for the launching of transcontinental and ocean voyages.[1] The opening of the two main transoceanic routes, the Suez (1867) and Panama (1914) canals, as well as the development of communications technologies such as telegrams and telephones also facilitated world circumnavigation. About the same time, the introduction of the portable camera for the amateur transformed photography into the most important tool for recording and cataloguing newly discovered peoples, strange new worlds, and objects as "empirical evidence" in the classification of the "Ethnographic Other" (E. Edwards 1992; Maxwell 1999; Ryan 1997). Ethnic tableaux and dioramas displaying "local color" or the manners and customs in far-off lands also became widely adopted by enterprising trading companies and merchants from Australia to India to show off new products so as to lure visitors to their pavilions at world's fairs staged in London, Paris, and Vienna.[2] By the turn of the century, millions of consumers were already familiar with the dancing geishas, tea gardens, fabricated temple gates, and pagodas, which were designed to enhance the exotic appeal of consumer items from tea, coffee, and spices to curios, silks, and china (Hoffenberger 2001; Lockyer 2000). The popularity of Japanese pavilion displays among European judges, connoisseurs, and the general public was one of the main reasons commercial presses operating from London to the British colonial enclaves in Hong Kong, Shanghai, and the newly opened port cities of Yokohama and Kobe began commissioning travel writers, former diplomats, and academics to publish travel guidebooks targeting customers and potential tourists residing in the capitals of Europe and America (Chamberlain and Mason 1907, 1913; Murray 1894).

Tourism and Japan's empire building in East Asia

In the late nineteenth century, the modernization of Japan's economy, military, and society was engineered by a new generation of former samurai, diplomats, businessmen, and bureaucrats who had been sent on diplomatic fact-finding missions beginning in the 1860s. According to the travel diaries written by prominent returnees such as Fukuzawa Yukichi (1835–1901), they had been most impressed by the spectacles of wonderful things, sights, and bustling crowds witnessed at world's fairs, museums, tourist destinations, terminals, and grand hotels in London, Paris, and New York (Fukuzawa 1934). Japan itself became an emerging imperial power following the military victories in the Sino-Japanese War (1894–1895) and the Russo-Japanese War (1904–1905). Soon, colonial administrators and businesses eager to expand the market for Japanese goods, as well as to search for new resources and customers, spearheaded the industrial development of Taiwan, Manchuria, and Korea. Of all the new territories from Siberia to the South Pacific drawn into the sphere of Japanese military and commercial interests, Chōsen, or the Korean peninsula, has occupied a special place in the imagination of Japan's citizens and rulers for more than a century, for several reasons.

First, its geographic proximity and its strategic location between the Japanese archipelago and Manchuria made Chōsen the prime target of intensive and extensive infrastructure and industrial investment. As early as the 1890s, colonial administrators, *zaibatsu* (conglomerates), and the military were involved in laying down transportation and communication links and military facilities, building harbors, bridges, railways, roads, and a tram system. Major banks and companies such as the Bank of Chōsen, Mitsui Heavy Industries, Ogura Mining Company, the Japan Mail Steamship Company (Nippon Yūsen Kaisha, or NYK), and the South Manchuria Railway Company (hereafter SMR), to name some of the most prominent, calculated that the export of Korea's agricultural products (rice and cotton), the import of military supplies and weapons, and the mobilization of troops to the Manchurian frontier would be profitable enterprises for investors, local contractors, and merchants (Bank of Chōsen 1919). By the 1905 signing of the Portsmouth Treaty, the Korea branch of the Imperial Railways (Chōsen tetsudo, also known as the Colonial Government Railways Company; hereafter CGR) had opened the main north-south artery, the Keifu railway (Kyŏngbu-sŏn) and Jinsen (Inch'ŏn) line, connecting all major cities directly to the ports of Fusan (Pusan), Keijō (Seoul), and Inch'ŏn (Chŏng C. 1999).[3] These efficient transportation links not only facilitated the transfer of freight and mail from the port of Shimonoseki on a daily basis but also drove hundreds and thousands of Japanese settlers to seek their fortunes and jobs on the new frontier (Uchida 2005).

Second, Korea's strategic location made it the transportation and commercial hub of the expanding Japanese Empire (Figure 3.1). Major corporations and empire-building politicians invested heavily in developing tourist and cultural destinations from historical parks, museums, zoos, botanical gardens, hot springs, hotels, and mountain resorts.

Third, the Korean peninsula was the only colony where the Colonial Government-General of Korea Office (1910–1945, CGK hereafter) sponsored more than four decades of continuous archaeological and historical surveys in order to collect documents, register artifacts, and excavate buried objects, which were later exhibited in CGK museums at major historical destinations throughout the peninsula (Pai 1994, 2000, 2001). Imperial University–trained archaeologists were eager to conduct field research abroad because they were prevented by the Imperial Household Agency from excavating imperial tombs in Japan proper (W. Edwards 2003; Pai 2006).

This chapter takes an interdisciplinary approach to tracing the historical and cultural transformation of the Korean peninsula into the favorite heritage destination for Japanese travelers. It is organized into three parts, documenting the international setting and regional dynamics in the coevolution of Japan's empire-building project and the development of a vibrant tourist industry in colonial Korea (Table 3.1). First, I discuss the Meiji background regarding the establishment of a state-coordinated tourist industry by focusing on the oldest and largest travel agency, the Japan Tourist Bureau (JTB), founded by the board of directors of the Japan Imperial Railways (hereafter JIR) in 1912. The JTB was instrumental in coordinating major corporations ranging from the JIR to hotel chains and department stores in order to invest together in the building and promotion of tourist destinations to the masses at home, and in the colonies. Second, I analyze the state production and distribution of tour-

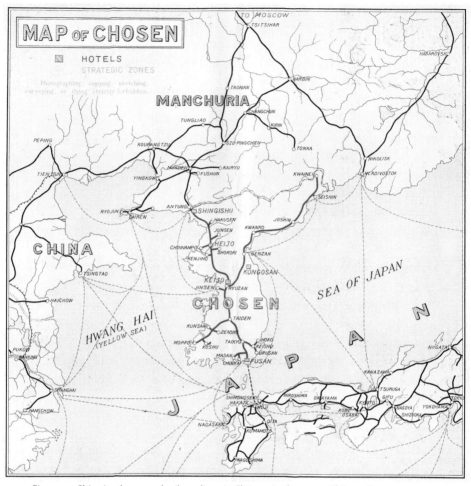

Figure 3.1. Shipping lanes and railway lines in Chōsen. In the 1930s, Chōsen Government Railways (CGR) managed a chain of six railway hotels and one grill restaurant: the Pusan Station Hotel, the Chōsen Hotel in Keijō, the Keijō train station grill, two resort/hot springs hotels in Kŭmgangsan at Onjongni and Changansa, the P'yŏngyang Station Hotel, and the Shinŭiju Station Hotel. *Source:* "Hotels in Chōsen" (CGR, n.d.); courtesy of the International Research Center for Japanese Studies Library Archives.

ist information by analyzing some of the more popular editions of guidebooks to Chōsen (*Chōsen annaisho*) published jointly by the JTB, SMR, and CGR. These colonial corporations owned print media targeting the tastes, hobbies, and expectations of wealthy foreigners and were responsible for remapping the itinerary of "must-see" historical destinations in Korea.[4] Third, I look at some of the most widely circulated tourist images

Table 3.1. Chronology of the Tourist Industry in Japan and Korea,
1874–1943 (Institutions, Transportation, and Heritage Management)

Year	Month(s)	Event
1874	5	Banning of excavations of legendary "burial mounds" and sacred sites by Meiji government
1888		Imperial Office (Kunaishō) sets up office in charge of Preliminary Survey of Treasures
1893		Tokyo Imperial University Anthropological Society Specimens Laboratory established, under Tōrii Ryūzō
1895		Sino-Japanese War; Tōrii's first survey of Taiwan and Manchuria; promulgation of Preservation Laws Governing Temples and Shrines; government takes over the management and preservation of nationally registered art, artifacts, and documents belonging to temples and shrines (beginnings of national treasures system)
1902		Sekino Tadashi sent by Tokyo University to survey art and architecture in Korea
1904		Completion of Fusan-Keijō (Keifusen) Railways Line
1906		Imanishi Ryū surveys Keishū (Kyŏngju, the Silla capital in southeast Korea)
1907		Excavations of Kimhae Shell Mound, Fusan, by Imanishi Ryū
1908		Yi Royal Museum, Zoo and Botanical Garden built in Ch'anggyŏng-wŏn, Keijō (Seoul)
1910		**Annexation of Korea**
1911		Colonial Governor-General commissions Tōrii Ryūzō, who conducts first systematic survey of prehistoric archaeological remains and ethnographic surveys; establishment of the Shiseki Meishō Tennenkinnenbutsu Hozonkai (Historic Sites, Famous Places, and Natural Monuments Protection Committee) in Japan
1911		Temples Protection Act promulgated in Korean peninsula
1912	3, 12	JTB established at Tokyo Railway Station; first printing of bureau-issued pamphlet in English (2,000 copies) and French (3,000 copies)

Table 3.1. (*Continued*)

Year	Month(s)	Event
1912	11, 12	JTB sets up branches in Dalian (SMR Office), Keijō (CGR Office), and Taipei (Taiwan Railways)
1912		Reconstruction of Sŏkkuram funded by Colonial Governor-General begins
1913	6, 10	*Tourist* magazine published as a bimonthly with bilingual (English/Japanese) articles
1914	1	Maps of Keijō, Dalian, and Formosa printed in English (3,000 copies)
1914	2	JTB agents/branches set up in 30 locations around the world
1914	10	Establishment of the Keijō Chōsen Hotel managed by CGR
1915	2	JIR "through" passes linking ship and rail services to Manchuria/Chōsen sold at Tokyo Railway Station Branch (up to 30 percent discounted tickets valid for 6 months)
1915	8	Kŭmgangsan Station Hotel opens in Onjŏngni in what is now North Korea
1915	12	Establishment of the Colonial Governor-General Fine Arts Museum in Kyŏngbokkung
1916		Colonial Governor-General Committee for the Investigations of Ancient Remains and Relics (Chōsen Koseki Chosa ininkai); promulgation of Regulations on the Preservation of Ancient Sites and Relics, the first comprehensive preservation laws governing art and archaeological remains, predating Japan by three years; measurement of Kyŏngju Hwangyongsa temple remains, Sach'ŏnwangsa temple, and Chŏlla-namdo Songgwangsa temple; Koguryŏ tombs in Jian, China, investigated by Sekino Tadashi
1918		Major reconstruction of Pulguksa begins; Colonial Governor-General Construction Department oversees a total of eight years
1918		Kyŏngju Silla tombs excavations (Kuroita Katsumi and Harada Yoshito)
1921		Kyŏngju Museum established
1926		Chōsen Manchuria Office set up in Tokyo, Shimonoseki, and Shinjuku stations

Table 3.1. (*Continued*)

Year	Month(s)	Event
1926		Kyŏngju Branch Museum established; Keijō tram service begins
		Formation of Chōsen Hotel Company to run former CGR hotels: Keijō Chōsen, Fusan Station, Shingishū Station, Kŭmkangsan Onjŏngni, Changanri, Keijō Station restaurant,
1932		and CGR train restaurants
1943		JTB shuts down branches due to expansion of Pacific War

Note: Chronology compiled from JTB (1982). CGR, Chōsen Government Railways; JIR, Japan's Imperial Railways; JTB, Japan Tourist Bureau; SMR, South Manchuria Railway Company.

of so-called manners and customs (*fūzoku shashin*) of the Korean people (Chōsenjin), which were disseminated in postcards and print advertising distributed throughout the empire. I conclude by assessing the contemporary legacies of these Prewar guidebooks, for they were the first to showcase entirely new heritage categories such as Meishō (famous places) and Gyūseki (ancient sites), packaged for a world audience.

Despite the millions of train schedules, pamphlets, and guidebooks estimated to have been distributed at major piers, train stations, and department stores throughout the empire, only a minute fraction survive today. Tourist literature, by its nature, is a disposable consumer item, and therefore in most cases such items were thrown out after the trip. Consequently, the ones most likely to be preserved in research libraries, personal collections, and museum archives in Japan and Korea tend to be sturdy pocket-size guidebooks and attractive postcards that were collected as souvenirs of trips.

State-coordinated tourism policy and the Japan Tourism Bureau (1912–present)

The Welcome Society of Japan, or the Kihinkai (Society of VIPs), was Japan's first tourist board, founded in 1893. Sanctioned by the Imperial Household, its board members included high-ranking foreign ambassadors, dignitaries, aristocrats, and leading entrepreneurs of the Meiji era who operated the society from the Tokyo Chamber of Commerce inside the landmark Marunouchi Building. The preface of the society's 1908 edition of the *Guide-book for Tourists* stated the society's aims: "bringing within reach of tourists the means of accurately observing the features of the country, and the characteristics of the people; aiding them to visit places of scenic beauty; enabling them to view objects of art and enter into social or commercial relations with the people; in short, affording them all facilities and conveniences toward the accomplishment of their several aims, their indirectly promoting, in however small a degree, the cause of international intercourse and trade" (Welcome Society of Japan 1908). Thus, from the beginning, Japan's tourism policy was directed at promoting international trade and commerce. A much larger corporate entity, the Japan Tourist Bureau, was established in 1912 at the Japan Imperial Railways Corporate Head Office (JTB 1982, 8–13).[5] The JIR board soon convinced shipping magnates, department store chains (Mitsukoshi, Takashimaya), and the Tokyo Imperial Hotel management, to mention just a few of the high-ranking *zaibatsu* who were asked to join in the venture aimed at transforming Japan into "the Paradise of the Orient" (ibid., 16; JTB 1926). The immediate financial objective of this Imperial Railways–steered tourist project was to bring in new foreign revenue to help alleviate the severe financial drain caused by the expensive military campaigns in Korea and Manchuria during the Russo-Japanese War. The other mission was more diplomatic in nature; the JTB was charged with devising ways to promote a more "civilized and modern" national image. Japan's image had been much tarnished in the foreign press by numerous demeaning caricatures of the Japanese as a barbaric, war-mongering people and in postcards circulating in the aftermath of the Russo-Japanese War (JTB 1982, 13–14).

The JIR's other important joint venture, in cooperation with the Japan Hotel Association, was the construction of a chain of Imperial Railways–run station hotels emulating customer service standards offered at the grand hotels of Europe and America. The Japan Hot Springs Association also initiated the development of seaside hotels, hot springs, and mountain resorts for escaping the hot summers. Once the JIR began a regular train schedule departing for the ports of Yokohama, Nagasaki, and Kobe, the JTB offices started selling all-inclusive tours to Korea and Manchuria with discounted steamship passage tickets, railway pass coupons, and hotels with a choice of either American or European meal plans for their colonial destinations.

The JTB opened colonial outposts in Taiwan, Manchuria, and Korea in 1912, the same year it was founded in Tokyo. The business goal of the CGR and JTB Chōsen branches was the same as that of their parent company: to attract as many passengers as possible so they could recoup the enormous financial investments spent on building infrastructure to facilitate transportation and communications as well as public works like ports, dams, and waterworks throughout the peninsula. By 1914, branches of the JTB were distributing 3,000 maps printed in English and covering not only Japan but also the colonies, including Keijō, Dairen (Dalian), and Taihoku (Taipei).[6] After World War I ended, Europe was plagued with runaway inflation, and the JTB experienced some tough financial times when foreign travelers were not purchasing travel coupons. As an alternate business plan in 1918, the JTB started selling packaged tours to the colonies for the domestic consumer and launched a Japanese-language advertising business that involved printing and distributing travel brochures, detailed maps, and postcards of seasonal attractions, as well as travel magazines.[7] The rise in domestic ticket sales to the colonies persuaded the JTB to open offices inside the major department store chains such as Mitsukoshi, Daimaru, and Takashimaya. The peak decade for Prewar outbound Japanese was 1925–1935. By then they represented a wide swath of classes and occupations, including teachers, student groups, soldiers, and businessmen. Educated mass consumers who were hungry for news of the latest tourist destinations and leisure trends, near and far, spawned the publication of travel magazines such as the bilingual *Tourist* (1913–1942), in English and Japanese, and *Tabi* (1924–present), a magazine designed for the first time with the Japanese reader in mind.[8] The success of the JTB's world advertising efforts could be felt not only in a wide range of services but also in the national financial coffers. Tourism by the mid-Showa era had become Japan's fourth most important source of foreign revenue, behind cotton, raw silk, and silk products.

The organization of tourist information in "Guides to Chōsen"

The first documented tour group of private citizens to visit the new frontier in Korea and Manchuria set sail in 1906, the year following Japan's much celebrated victory over Russia (Ariyama 2002). The tour was organized by Japan's leading daily; the enterprising Asahi Newspaper Company developed its own plan to capitalize on the consumer craze for Russo-Japanese War memorabilia.[9] With an eye to selling more newspaper subscriptions, the Asahi ran advertisements for a cruise to the frontier, revisiting the great battle sites in Korea and Manchuria that had been featured in best-selling postcards, silk prints *(nishikie),* and photographs (Kōgo 2003). The first announcement recruiting passengers for the "Cruise Touring Manchuria and Korea" (Man-Gan junyū sen) appeared in Asahi's June 22, 1906, edition, and just three days later, all three classes of cabin tickets were sold out, with eighty passengers booked for the trip. This was indeed an auspicious start for a first-time commercial pitch to market Manchuria and Korea as "the new world *[shintenchi]* where one can see for oneself the farthest edge of the Emperor's authority and domain" (Ariyama 2002, 33). Following the media success of the 1906 tour as a contemporary cultural happening, subsequent discounted tours sold out in large numbers, thus giving birth to the packaged educational tour *(shūgaku ryokō)* as we know it today in Japan and Korea. By the late 1910s, there was a growing demand for information about Korea from millions of passengers and potential passengers, including Japanese, Koreans, Chinese, foreign missionaries, soldiers, administrators, educators, and tourists, who were eager to purchase tickets on steamers and railways heading for the continent.[10] Transportation companies from the NYK, CGR, and SMR also joined forces with the JTB to distribute large numbers of detailed guidebooks, maps, and train schedules, as well as picture postcards capturing scenic destinations, peoples, and portrayals of Korean customs *(fūzoku).* These were sold at ticket offices at major piers, railway stations, and department store branches from Tokyo to Keijō to Keelung (Jilong), Formosa.

Despite the wide variety of businesses and publishers engaged in dispensing tourist information in the colonies, the overall organization, content, and layout of photos, maps, and advertisements were remarkably uniform from Japan to Korea to Manchuria. The guidebooks for the colonies were all modeled after an earlier generation of Victorian-era handbooks for Japan penned by foreign advisers and educators hired by the Meiji government *(yatoi gaijin),* such as Ernest Satow, A. G. S. Hawkes, David Murray, and Basil Chamberlain (Satow and Hawkes 1881; Murray 1894; Chamberlain and Mason 1907, 1913). The first chapter of any guidebook covered what was deemed "essential travel information," such as the locations of JTB offices, hotels, transportation links and fares, banking, customs, passports, and post offices for sending telegrams. The introduction also included an "overview of the land," such as topography, population, history, and climate — the latter was always promoted as the "most pleasant and agreeable in the empire," making it an ideal location for summer retreats.[11] A foldout map insert was accompanied by schedules for ships, trains, and transfer information. For the "through" traffic passengers who rode the Fusan-Keijō line (Keifusen), the terminus was Shingishū (Shinŭiju) Station, where they could transfer to the SMR lines departing Antung Station and heading northeast toward Manchuria's new cities. Since most of the passengers arrived by ship docking at Fusan from either Osaka, Kobe, or Shimonoseki, the first place in the recommended itinerary was Fusan, followed by Taikyū (Taegu) along the Keifusen.

The main section of the guides covered the major scenic, cultural, and business destinations found at major cities along the main arteries of the CGR lines, as well as side trips to the seaside, hot springs, and resorts linked by private trams, buses, or shuttle service.[12] The Keijō city tours also recommended excursions to the beach resort of Wŏlmido in Jinsen and to the walls and gates of Suigen (Suwŏnsŏng), after which they could head northwest to the cities of the Heijō region (P'yŏngyang, Kaesŏng, and Chinnampo). These city tours were planned as half-day itineraries, beginning with the Chōsen Jingū (the Main Shintō Shrine on the slope of Namsan) and including Namdaemun (South Gate), the Botanical Garden and Zoo (Ch'anggyŏng-wŏn), Chōsen Sōtokufu (CGK) headquarters building, and the CGK Museum located at Kyŏngbok Palace, and the Fine Arts Museum at Tŏksu Palace (CGR 1938). Transportation fees, admission to museums and zoos, and the costs of food at recommended restaurants, hotels, and inns with a choice of Western, Chinese, Korean, or Japanese were also listed with room prices for the budget-conscious consumer. Last but not least, in the appendix of many guidebooks of the empire, Japanese-operated businesses such as tram and taxi companies, inns and hotels, tailors, pharmacies, and department stores were the major advertisers. Local merchants were represented by geisha restaurants, curio dealers, ginseng shops, and photographic studios.

By the late 1930s the JTB had established operations out of Minakai, the largest department store chain in Korea, with seven outlets in the cities of Keijō, Fusan, Taegu, Taejŏn, Heijō, Hamhŭng, and Wŏnsan. The bureau had two extra offices at Hwashin department store (formerly situated at

Chongno First Street) and Mitsukoshi (now Shinsegye), located at the entrance to Myŏngdong across from the Bank of Chōsen. The major department stores such as Mitsukoshi and Minakai were centrally positioned at main traffic junctions leading to the major thoroughfares (Hon-machi, Kogane-machi) close to the financial centers and the administrative offices of the CGK headquarters (Chōsen Sōtokufu), as well as to Namdaemun Station. Placing ticketing operations in the department store was a strategic move since this was where the upper-class urbanites, both Korean and Japanese, congregated to shop and socialize at cafés in the 1930s (see Cwiertka in this volume). The other JTB branches were at Fusan Pier, Shinŭiju Chōsen Unsō Company, and Ch'ŏngjin and Najin stations.

For nightlife in the cities, the most often recommended choice of entertainment was hiring either Korean or Japanese geishas "to dance and sing for you." Describing "Geisha dances" as a "popular and universal form of entertainment at banquets and other functions in Japan," JIR's 1926 *Guidebook to Japan* added, "Geisha may be hired at any time, anywhere, the charge of the dance depending upon the reputation and number of dances" (JIR 1926, 16). The high demand for young, attractive, and accomplished female entertainers who would accompany male customers to staged performances after the men were through partying at high-class Korean restaurants led to the establishment of a School for Kisaeng (Kisaeng Hakkyo) in P'yŏngyang. The school offered a curriculum of intensive training in musical accompaniment, dance, and popular songs of the day, sung in both Japanese and Korean languages (JTB Chōsen Branch 1939). "Chōsen beauties" in full costume is still the most iconic image of "local color" *(Chōsen fūzoku)* and can be seen in a wide range of colonial print media such as postcards, advertisements for CGR hotels, magazines covers, and front covers of many guidebooks (Figure 3.2).

The southeast corridor of the Korean peninsula, including the cities of Keishū (Kyŏngju), Taegu, and Fusan, was also featured in many guidebooks (Keishū Koseki Hozonkai zaidan 1922, 1935; Figure 3.3) and pamphlets (JTB n.d., ca. 1930s; CGR 1936). When the Gold Crown Tomb, dating to the Old Silla kingdom (ca. fifth century), was excavated in 1921, it was widely hailed as the greatest archaeological discovery of the century.[13] Among other recommended famous places *(meishō)* were tombs of later Silla kings, including Kwennŭng, Hwangnamni, and Kim Yushin myo (eighth century), and freestanding pagodas such as the one at Punhwang-sa.

Figure 3.2. The images of "Korean beauties" in full costume to this day remain the most widely circulated stereotypical image of "Korean manners and customs." *Source:* JTB Chōsen Branch (1939); courtesy of the International Research Center for Japanese Studies Library Archives.

Sŏkkuram and Pulguksa temples (eighth century) were the two largest multiyear architectural reconstruction projects supervised by Sekino Tadashi, a professor in the Tokyo University Architecture Department who supervised the Chōsen government construction engineers between 1912 and 1930 (CGK 1938; Yoshii 2007). By the 1930s the restored ruins of Keishū, and the Keishū museum built in the center of Silla royal burial mounds (ca. third–ninth centuries), became the favorite setting for photo ops by visiting royalty as well as foreign VIPs, including the Crown Prince of Sweden, an amateur archaeologist and collector who founded the Museum of Far Eastern Antiquities in Stockholm (Hamada and Andersson 1932a). The popularity of Keishū as Korea's most spectacular famous place (*meishō*) thus originated with the Keishū tourist boom in the 1930s (CGR 1936; Keishū Koseki Hozonkai zaidan 1922, 1929, 1935).

P'yŏngyang and Kaesŏng on the northeast corridor were also popular destinations whose combined itineraries included Kija's Tomb, Man-

Figure 3.3. Members of the Japanese Imperial Family *(Kaninwaka miya tenka)* and entourage posing in front of a restored eighth-century Sokkuram grotto during their tour, October 1, 1935. *Source:* Keishū Koseki Hozonkai zaidan (1937).

wŏldae (Koryŏ dynastic palace remains), Rakurō (Nangnang Tombs), and Kangsŏ Koguryŏ painted tombs (ca. AD fifth century). The restored tombs of the Han dynasty commandery of Rakurō (ca. second century BC–AD second century), situated south of the Taedong River, were featured in many guidebooks and tourist maps (JTB Chōsen Branch 1939) touting their archaeological significance as the earliest "scientifically" excavated tombs in Asia, since at that time no intact tombs dating from the Han dynasty (ca. second century BC–second century AD) had been identified in China (Kin 1928; *Nippon* 1939; Pai 2000, 127–236). The southwest corridor, where the ancient Paekche (Kudara) capitals of Puyŏ and Kongju (ca. fourth–seventh centuries) were located, became the focus of excavations with the discovery of Paekche tombs, pagodas, and temples in the 1930s.

The only tourist region far from these commercial and historical cities was Kongōsan (Kŭmgang-san, the Diamond Mountains). The mountains' majestic vistas were praised as "the most spectacular natural beauty under the heavens." Photos of the two thousand spiky peaks of Outer Kŭmgang (CGR 1932) were featured in many CGR posters and magazines from the *Tourist* (JTB 1917) to *Nippon*, a heavily illustrated glossy magazine written in German and English targeting Europeans (*Nippon* 1939; Weisenfeld 2000). The CGR built two mountain resorts, one at Onjŏngni Station (1915) and the other at Changan-sa Temple (1924) deep in the mountains, as a hunting lodge–cum–hot springs resort. The hotels could be reached from two directions, either riding on the Keigen line (Keijō-Wŏnsan) or driving north up the east coast by car from Onjŏngi station. The CGR advertised extensively in newspapers and magazines to recruit hikers interested in joining its backpackers group during the summer months. The most widely advertised sports and leisure activity in the 1930s was mountain climbing. It was enthusiastically promoted as a way of training the minds and bodies of the Japanese, who were taught from school age that mountains symbolized the quintessential Japanese national landscape of Fūto (Schwartz and Ryan 2003).[14] Other scenic high mountains in Korea recommended for climbers included Paektusan and Chirisan (CGR 1923). Mountainous regions were also favored by the rugged naturalist types for hunting large game (unavailable in Japan) such as tigers, bears, and wild boar (Bergman 1938).

Sketching an ancient land for the tourist: The narrative of return to the mythical homelands

A typical layout of tourist photos and illustrations featured in guidebooks, postcards, and photo albums juxtaposed images of "old Korea" (*mukashi*) with "now" (*ima*). The former category, identified as "the old country and its customs," usually depicted "rustic Korea" in grainy black-and-white photos dominated by images of peasant women engaged in everyday chores and subsistence activities such as washing clothes by the river, ironing at home, or carrying jars on their heads or children on their backs. Korean men were rarely portrayed in tourist images, unless they were street vendors plying their wares, rickshaw drivers, or old *yangban* noblemen relaxing or smoking in their distinctive black hats. In contrast to the nonthreatening image of the weak Korean male and the quaint rural landscape, *ima* images feature towering edifices to portray Japan's colonial modernity in the form of monumental public works and imposing architectural structures such as the CGK headquarters, banks, post offices, museums, shiny steel bridges, train stations, dams, schools, and hospitals (Gwon 2005). The visual technique of contrasting the "old" versus the "new" was a tried-and-true propaganda strategy widely deployed not only in guidebooks but also in the

CGK-controlled media, from daily newspapers to school textbooks and corporate reports, in order to advertise the successes of Japan's "civilizing mission" to a world audience (Bank of Chōsen 1919; CGK 1929). In many colonial publications these contrasting images of "modern Japan" versus "old Korea" were supplemented by a historical overview explaining the inseparable ties between Korea and Japan since time immemorial *(mukashi kara)*. The following narrative from a guide to the customs of Korea called *Chōsen no hanashi,* printed by the CGR in the 1930s, is a typical example:

> From the time of Empress Jingū's conquest [ca. AD third century?] of the Three Han (Sankan), Chōsen is the country that has had the closest relationship with our nation, a tie that can never be severed. On a clear day, one can see the mountains of Fusan in the country of Chōsen across the sea. It is now only an eight-hour trip across the ocean from Shimonoseki on a boat that leaves morning and night. From there, one can transfer onto a train. In olden times, Kangoku [Korea] was formerly an independent nation, but in August 1910 it was incorporated into the empire. Since then the Chōsenjin have become our brethren for all time to come. Since our races have merged again just as in ancient times, the future prosperity and happiness of our respective countries depends on forging very close ties, just as in olden times [*mukashi*] when Mimana [the ancient Kaya Kingdom] was our colony.... Now anyone can travel in Korea and experience the same beauty and level of efficient and convenient service as we do in Naichi [Japan proper], since there is now no difference between Korea and Japan. This is the way it should be, since we are now one with many of our citizens.
>
> For students joining group tours, we wanted them to see in one glance what a warm and peaceful nation the land and people of Chōsen are. Though there has been some misunderstanding in the past, in fact we are now one and the same people, as proven by the many research investigations that have been carried out by our scholars. Our nation is very concerned about the future destiny of the Chōsen people, and we believe that the development of Chōsen is also our happiness. So our great mission is to bring future happiness to Chōsen as well as the eternal prosperity of the whole empire. (CGR n.d.; my translation)

Thus the archaeological "rediscovery" of Japan's antiquity in the form of excavated prehistoric remains and beautifully restored and photographed Silla temples and tombs (CGK 1915–1935, 1938) was touted as the most tangible body of evidence for a common racial ancestry and, consequently, a shared cultural patrimony between the Koreans and Japanese, or Nissen Dōsoron (Kita 1921; Pai 2006, forthcoming). The colonial travel industry played a pivotal role in promoting this "nostalgic" image of the Chōsenjin, as their long lost poor country cousins who had been salvaged from the dark ages by the timely arrival of the superior Japanese and their "enlightened" government (Pai 2000, 35–43). Furthermore, as we can see in the final paragraph, the CGR and JTB specifically targeted students and tour groups for imperialist propaganda, by emphasizing that the act of visiting Korea was equivalent to affirming their racial and spiritual descent, traced back to the fictitious third-century conquest expedition led by Empress Jingū.

Reclaiming imagined ancestral terrains and imperialists' nostalgia

In sum, the meanings of Korea's archaeological and historical discoveries were manipulated by powerful colonial policy makers and colonial enterprises to justify the annexation of Korea as a predestined "return" and reunion of the two races of Japanese and Koreans (Pai 2006). To convince rich businessmen that the peninsula offered attractive investment opportunities, the JTB and CGK advertised Korea's tourist destinations as the most picturesque and historically "authentic" in the empire, full of decaying ruins, old customs, desirable women, and luxury accommodations.[15] From the perspective of the millions of ordinary Japanese tourists, their visiting, absorbing, and experiencing firsthand Korea's customs and ancient destinations became part of their search for their own national identity as citizens of the growing multiethnic and multicultural empire at the turn of the century (Weisenfeld 2000). This recurring theme of imagined "imperialists' nostalgia" that romanticized the conquered "Other" in time and space, though not unique to the Japanese Empire, reveals the roots of the imagery that is still used in government-initiated tourist campaigns in South Korea today, a century later (Schwartz and Ryan 2003; Selwyn 1996; Pai 2006, 2009).

An epilogue by way of a conclusion

Japanese citizens still constitute the largest package tour groups visiting South Korea. Geographic proximity by air and bargain prices offered by competing tour operators entice them to visit their former colony. In 2007 the Japanese Ministry of Tourism and Culture's official website recorded around fifteen million outbound tourists and eight million inbound tourists.[16] The huge discrepancy between the numbers of outbound and inbound visitors has caused much consternation in the Japanese government since the 1970s, when the purchasing power of the yen began to rise. From the perspective of South Korea, despite the postwar rhetoric denouncing Japanese wartime atrocities, its national tourist policies have always accommodated changing tourist demographics (Korea Ministry of Tourism and Culture 1999b) — American GIs seeking "R & R" in the 1960s; middle-class Japanese salarymen's indulgence in *"kisaeng kwan'gwang,"* a common euphemism for sex tourism in the 1970s; status-conscious young women seeking a shopping haven for counterfeit luxury brands in the 1980s (*Korea Travel Newspaper* 1999). South Korea's tourism board has also kept detailed statistics for four decades, covering Japanese preferences and spending behavior at restaurants, spas, golf resorts, duty-free shops, and souvenir outlets (Korea Ministry of Tourism and Culture 1999a). The main strategy for South Korea is to keep prices competitive, not only to undercut their rival Asian neighbors, but also to compete with Japanese domestic tourist businesses such as golf and spa resorts. Their close monitoring of Japanese tourist preferences has clearly been an impressive success, since Japanese make up the largest proportion of tourists of all nationalities arriving at Korean airports.

In the last five years, the so-called Korean wave — an unprecedented popularity of Korean soap operas, K-pop music, and other popular cultural forms — has deluged China, Taiwan, and Southeast Asia. The total number of foreign visitors to South Korea has increased to about five million annually, largely consisting of middle-aged female fans addicted to Korean soaps, pop singers, and film stars. Currently, the latest best-sellers are three- to four-day itineraries highlighting "fictional" locations, such as recreated historical drama production sets and behind-the-scenes movie sets designed to evoke a sense of history, romance, and nostalgia — the main themes of the most popular Korean soaps such as *Taejangŭm* (Jewel in the Palace) and *Winter Sonata*. However, this time it is South Korea's National Tourism Organization (KNTO), the Korean Film Council, local tourism boards, and major media conglomerates who have recruited TV actors and actresses as both official and unofficial ambassadors of desire, display, and consumption.

Notes

This research has been made possible by two fellowships: Japan Foundation Fellowship (2004–2005) and a visiting research professorship at the International Research Center for Japanese Studies (2007–2008). I want to thank the following professors and staff for their assistance in tracking down original sources for this work: Yoshii Hideo (Kyoto University), Inaga Shigemi and Yamada Shōji (International Research Center for Japanese Studies), and Emiko Yamanashi (Tokyo National Research Institute for Cultural Properties, Ueno). Last but not least, I extend my gratitude to the International Research Center for Japanese Studies Library for giving me permission to reproduce their archives digitally for the figures featured in this chapter.

A Japanese-language version of this paper appears in *The Culture of the Commons: Who Owns Culture*, ed. Yamada Shoji (Tokyo: Tokyodo Press, 2010).

1. Thomas Mason Cook (1808–1892) pioneered this business model by inventing the "guided package tour," in which well-informed and well-connected local guides would personally escort tourists as well as provide translators, tickets, hotels, and porter service. He was also the marketing brains behind the "grand circular tours" in the 1870s when his company started issuing "around the world" tickets, visiting famous places from Switzerland, Italy, Greece, Egypt, India, Japan, and China to North America (Cook and Son 1998).

2. Archaeologists, anthropologists, art historians, and commercial photographers exerted the most impact on who and what the camera's eye selected (E. Edwards 1992). Victorian-era field researchers assumed that the more "authentic" and more "antiquated" remains of humankind's past were to be found in the newly discovered lands where "native" peoples incapable of progress lived a "time-less" existence (Stocking 1991). Such variants of colonial racism also fueled the desire to experience the "Mysterious Orient," by visiting the lands inspired by the Bible, *Arabian Nights,* Rudyard Kipling's novels, and French paintings of half-dressed beauties bathing, lounging in the harem, or dancing for tourists from Turkey to Japan (Beaulieu and Roberts 2002).

3. Some famous place-names and publication titles have been left in their original colonial-era spellings and usage for historical accuracy such as Keelung, Formosa (Taiwan), Keijō (Seoul), Keishū, etc. When first appearing, their current identification will be included in the brackets. Lesser-known tourist destinations and place-names are written in their current Korean renditions.

4. The tourist media I have tracked down so far were all printed in either Japanese or Western languages, indicating that the colonial tourist industry was mainly interested in attracting customers from outside Korea.

5. Over ninety-seven years, the Japan Tourist Bureau has evolved into the

world's largest travel agency. The 150 company affiliates listed on the JTB corporation's official website include some of the same founding *zaibatsu* investors of the Taishō era (1911–1925), such as Mitsui OSK Lines, the Japan Hotel Association, Sumitomo Mitsui Banking Corporation, and the various JIR lines (Hokkaido, Kyūshū, West, Central, etc). See www.jtbcorp.jp/en/company/profile.asp.

6. The appendix of the seventy-year official volume chronicling the history of JTB records that in 1914 the JTB boasted a total of thirty agencies. They were in London, Antwerp, Paris, Port Said, Marseilles, Rotterdam, Manila, Sydney, Singapore, Penang, Colombo, Seattle, San Francisco, Honolulu, and other cities (JTB 1982). "Through" steam/railway tickets good for six months to tour Japan and its colonies could also be purchased at the branches of the Thomas Cook and Son Company, American Express Company, and other affiliates by 1926 (JTB 1926).

7. The JTB started selling "through" tickets to the domestic consumer in 1919. They remain the company's main source of revenue today (JTB 1982, 32).

8. By 1936 the number of inbound tourists reached 42,586, annually spending a total of 107,688,000 yen (JTB 1982, 50). Though it represented only a small fraction (4 percent) of Japan's overall trade (including exports and imports), the amount exceeded the nation's persistent annual trade deficit of 94,000,000 yen (Leheny 1998, 125).

9. Between 1904 and 1906, the Ministry of Communications issued five different sets of picture postcards depicting the progress of the war and the victory celebrations (Morse, Rimer, and Brown 2004, 18). When these postcard sets were issued on the signing of the Portsmouth Treaty, which officially made Korea a protectorate, thousands of people lined up to buy them, causing a near riot. This famous incident was captured in one of the many memorable postcards in the exhibition on Japanese postcards organized by the Boston Museum of Fine Arts in 2005 (ibid., 111).

10. According to CGK-published statistics, the state railways' business records indicated that the number of passengers increased by a factor of 10 — from 2,024,000 to 20,058,000 — in a span of sixteen years (1911–1927). For the same years, the length of railway lines increased from 674 miles to 1,455 miles, while freight increased from 888,000 tons to 5,570,000. Revenue from receipts also grew ninefold, from 4,095,000 to 36,364,000 yen (CGK 1929, 43).

11. This narrative of an overview of the land was a long-established formula for empire guidebooks designed so that the would-be colonialist arriving on the shores would be able to read in one glance the living conditions and judge the level of civilization.

12. For example, all tour buses and trams left from the main junction at South Gate Road (Namdaemun), where the "through" ticket passengers disembarked

for rest or for sightseeing on the way to China or Manchuria. By 1929 there were three private electric tram companies operating thirty miles of rail in Keijō (CGK 1929, 43).

13. The excavations were conducted by Kyoto University professor Hamada Kōsaku and his student Umehara Sueji and published in the Colonial Governor-General Committee on Korean Antiquities special excavation report series (Hamada and Andersson 1932b; Pai, forthcoming).

14. After the founding of Japan's National Parks Association in 1927, two of the largest national parks in the empire were established in Taiwan in the 1930s: Niitaka-Arisan and Tsugitaka-Taroko (Kanda 2003).

15. I have not been able to track down year by year statistics for the number of Japanese tourists who traveled to Korea in the 1920s and 1930s. I suspect that records are lacking because, by the late colonial period, all citizens who were part of the official empire (Naichi-jin), including Japan, Korea, Taiwan, and Manchuria could travel throughout the empire without having to pass through customs. I did locate one published source, compiled by the JTB office in Manchuria, that provided the following group tourist statistics for the year 1940: 9,109 JTB-led tour groups to Manchuria and Korea; 398,299 tour group members, including Manchurians, Japanese, and foreigners; 320,000 train schedules distributed; and 548,905 tourist pamphlets distributed. These figures do give us a glimpse into the vibrant tourist industry in the late 1930s and early 1940s, before its total collapse after the outbreak of the Pacific War in 1943 (Namigata et al. 2004).

16. According to statistics provided by the Japan National Tourist Organization (JNTO), the 2,235,963 Japanese travelers to South Korea in 2007 made up roughly a quarter of the total number of outbound Japanese. Taiwan came in a distant second as a destination, attracting 1,385,255 Japanese visitors. For the latest tourism statistics by country and region, visit the JNTO website at www.jnto.go.jp/eng/ttp/sta/index.html. Due to the world economic downturn in 2008, the total number of Japanese outbound tourists (15,987,250) reflected a 7.6 percent decline from the previous year's. From January to November 2009, due to further deterioration of the Japanese economy, the number of outbound tourists (14,153,000) represented a 3.8 percent decrease from the number in 2008.

Guests of Lineage Houses
Tourist Commoditization of Confucian Cultural Heritage in Korea

One early summer day in 2004, Kim Won Kil, the primogenital descendant of a well-known Andong *yangban* (noble) lineage, demonstrated a simulated Confucian ancestral rite at the persistent request of a tour group, the local branch of a national women professionals' organization. With subsidies from the Korean Ministry of Culture and Tourism, the members of this group regularly organize events that usually involve experiences of Korean traditional culture such as the tea ceremony, how to properly wear Korean traditional dress *(hanbok)*, or traditional knot tying *(maedŭp)*. On this occasion they would view a Confucian ancestral rite in a *yangban* household in the Andong region, a place with strong associations to the elite *yangban* culture of Korea's late traditional Chosŏn period (1392–1910), as another, more novel way of understanding Korean tradition.

The demonstration took place at Kim Won Kil's residence, a lineage house *(chongtaek)* built in the seventeenth century and handed down to him as the primogenital heir *(chongson)* of a branch of Ŭisŏng Kim lineage (Moon et al. 2004; see Figure 4.1). Mr. Kim first led the visiting women to the house shrine where the tablets of his paternal ancestors were stored in four separate compartments, one for each generation from his parents up to his great-great-grandparents. As he performed the rite, Mr. Kim gave the women detailed explanations of each stage, including the meaning of the offering, the proper layout of different dishes on the table, the correct procedures, and the propriety associated with each act. When he performed "the rite of taking out the tablet" *(ch'uljurye),* the first stage of the Confucian ancestral rite, instead of removing one of his ancestral tablets from the shrine, he used a specially prepared wooden tablet with white paper pasted on its face *(paekju).* An ancestor tablet usually contains all the official titles the particular ancestor held during his or her lifetime as

Figure 4.1. The Ŭisŏng Kim lineage house in Chirye Artist Village.

well as those posthumously given.[1] A "white tablet" is a literal blank slate, a receptacle of nobody's spirit. Mr. Kim offered the first sacrificial cup of wine himself, but in another variation on custom, he let the women offer the second and third cups. After the rite, all the participants shared the ancestral offering food, just as descendants usually do after ancestor rites. The group then made a small payment to Mr. Kim and his family to cover both the cost of the offerings and an honorarium for their lessons and services.

This incident offers a fine example of a work of cultural heritage being transformed into a piece of performance, something to be taught and learned, appreciated and consumed. In this process of transformation, however, Mr. Kim's demonstration necessarily breached several of the basic rules of a Confucian ancestor rite. First, it took place in the middle of the day, around noon, although it is most properly held at midnight, to mark the beginning of the ancestor's death anniversary.[2] In the demonstration, time was irrelevant, since the rite itself did not venerate any specific ancestral spirit. Second, the major participants were women, whereas Confucian ancestor rites are celebrated exclusively by male lineage members.[3] In normal procedures a woman enters the shrine only in the form of a wooden tablet after her death and if she has borne or adopted a son who will perform the ancestor rite for her, but Mr. Kim had invited unrelated women into his ancestral shrine. Perhaps the greatest violation of Confucian propriety was that Kim Won Kil, the primogenital descendant of Chich'on Kim Pang Köl (1623–1695), a well-known *yangban* lineage, had performed a mimicry of an ancestor rite and was remunerated for the service.

In Andong such incidents provoke concern, anxiety, or even fear that a valued Confucian heritage, an essential feature of Korean culture at least since the Chosŏn period, is under threat (Deuchler 1992; Janelli and Janelli 1982; Kim Kwang-ok 1992, 1996). Others, including Mr. Kim himself, might argue with equal concern that precisely because the Confucian heritage is at risk of being lost and forgotten, such compromises as evidenced in the demonstration ancestor rite are essential to its perpetuation. The paradox sits at the nexus of three related circumstances: a broad-based Confucian revival in 1990s South Korea, the development of "experience" tourism, and the particular circumstances of Andong lineage houses and households in the final decades of the twentieth century.

Confucianism revisited in 1990s Korea

From the colonial period (1910–1945) until the 1980s, the Confucian tradition of the preceding Chosŏn period was negatively regarded as the main cause for the fall of the dynasty and as an impediment of modernization. In the 1960s and 1970s the Park Chung-hee regime promoted Confucian ideas in the contexts of education and the state-society relationship (Moon 2005). This contributed in the 1980s to the disdain among those in the pro-democracy Popular Culture Movement (*minjung munhwa undong*) for Confucianism as both reactionary and authoritarian, faulting neo-Confucian philosophy, with its temperance and emphasis upon reason, for having historically suppressed the spontaneous will of the people. The protest culture celebrated the cultural expression of peasants and other oppressed people over the high culture of the rulers and the *yangban* (Abelmann 1996; Kwang-ok Kim 1994). Movement activism gradually waned after the successful reinstallation of a civilian government in 1993, but the issue of Korean national-cultural identity that had been central to the movement's thinking remained.

With the successful hosting of the Seoul Olympics, Korea's new economic prominence, and the successful reestablishment of civilian government, South Koreans were ready to look more positively on their own heritage, anxious to win recognition for Korean distinctiveness in a globalizing environment. As significant numbers of Koreans began to travel abroad, they also had reason to rethink their own traditions and identity, to consider what it was that distinguished them from other cultures and peoples.[4] Social commentators described a sense of loss or an identity crisis, which they attributed to Korean experiences of colonization, war, economic development, modernization, and above all the pervasiveness of Western cultural influences, which were believed to have fundamentally changed Korean ways of thinking, lifestyles, and patterns of social relationships. In the search for Korean national-cultural identity, many came to appreciate that Confucianism had once helped define what it meant to be Korean. In the 1990s an elite group of foreign-trained young social scientists, known within Korean academic circles as the School of Tradition and Modernity, evangelized the compatibility of Asian philosophy — and Confucianism in particular — with modernity, capitalism, and democracy.[5]

The revival of interest in Confucianism in the 1990s can thus be characterized as a postmodern search for roots in an increasingly globalizing world and as part of a collective nostalgia for things past as a counterweight to Westernization. Developments in domestic tourism in the 1990s were fueled in part by similar concerns. In 1998, when the Kim Dae Jung government renamed the Ministry of Culture and Sports as the Ministry of Culture and Tourism, and the renamed ministry made the development of a Confucian Cultural Zone a part of its master plan, it explicitly linked Confucian revival to the development of tourist sites as part of a larger national identity quest.

Development of alternative tourism

From the 1990s, domestic tourism was one area where popular interests in culture and history could be effectively consumed. If a family vacation of three to four days at a seaside or mountain resort indicated an emerging urban middle-class lifestyle in the 1960s and 1970s, subsequent periods have seen an increasing diversification of travel patterns, including more thematically oriented trips, solitary or small peer group travels for all ages, and various kinds of experience tours. These new travel interests are reflected in such programs as *Kŭgose kagosipta* (I want to go there), first broadcast by KBS in 1994, or in the explosive popularity of Yu Hong-jun's *Na ŭi munhwa yusan tapsagi* (The chronicles of my field study of cultural remains), whose first volume was published in 1993 (see Oppenheim in this volume). The former emphasized "getting away" from industrialized cities, escaping from concrete apartment blocks, air pollution, hectic lives, and traffic congestion — a return to nature or to an imaginary premodern simplicity.[6] Yu, on the other hand, stressed that travelers should seek after not just natural beauty or historical remains per se but also a rediscovery of and nostalgia for Korean things, for "our things" *(uri kŏt)* that are being lost and forgotten in the flood of Westernization (Cho Hae-joang 1994a).[7] As a reflection on Korean history and culture, his work critiqued the supposed modern Korean tendency to desire things foreign or Western while neglecting one's own heritage.

The "old house culture experience," or *kot'aek munhwa ch'ehŏm,* is one form of the many experience tours that have become popular in Korea since the 1990s, from Buddhist temple stays to nature experiences. A promotional description of an old house experience in Andong is revealing:

> In traditional times, our ancestors yielded the warmest part *[ttattŭthan araetmok]* of the room to the guests. They did their best to provide their guests with good food and comfortable bedding to make them at home. At Andong, you may stay at an old lineage house where such traditions are still alive and can be felt. Even without modern conveniences, the Andong old lineage house experience will greet you with the warmth of a mother's bosom. . . . You are invited to a place that will give you real rest and recovery from the exhaustion of everyday life [in the busy city].

The key words in this advertisement are warmth, hospitality, and mother's bosom as the antitheses of a hectic, impersonal modern life in congested, polluted cities. People, it is said, come back to these places because they feel as comfortable and relaxed amid clean air and quiet surroundings as if they were in their old hometown *(kohyang).* The Andong recipe so far does not differ much from other *hanok ch'ehŏm* (Korean-style house experiences) that have become popular in many other places in South Korea where these houses, at risk of disappearing under the flood of shapeless apartment blocks, have been either rescued or reconstructed through the efforts of culture movement activists and opened for tourism. In Chŏnju, an old city in the southeastern part of Korea, for instance, a special zone called *hanok maŭl* (village of Korean-style houses) was constructed in the 1990s where traditional Korean-style houses *(hanok)* are either relocated or rebuilt. *Hanok* can also be visited in Pukch'on and Namsan in Seoul and in Sokch'o, Taejŏn, and Kyŏngju. Although some of these houses offer only daytime cultural experiences, others offer lodging. Together with the Buddhist temple stay program introduced around the time of the Seoul Olympics in 1988, *hanok* visits are rapidly gaining popularity among both domestic and foreign tourists seeking to "experience tradition."

For many urbanized Koreans who live in modern but characterless apartment blocks, an overnight stay in these places can be truly an exotic and refreshing experience. Such houses have a traditional *ondol* floor, covered with oiled paper and heated from underneath. Sleeping on such a floor has become a rare and nostalgic experience for most Koreans. In the morning, one wakes up and slides open the paper-and-lattice door to see the garden just outside, and if one is lucky, birds may sing in the fresh air, a house dog may bark, or some garden chickens may be busy pecking at grain. Meals are served in brassware or at least in earthenware on a communal table with dozens of dishes, including grilled fish and proper Korean-style soup. So few urban Koreans have such a breakfast these days that the smell of grilling fish or bean paste soup in the morning itself evokes a poignant hometown image and the taste of a mother's cooking.

Tradition does not mean an exact return to the past, since some of these houses have flush toilets and washbasins inside the house, and the floors are heated with oil or gas, not wood or charcoal. Also, meals are usually followed by coffee even after traditional rice tea *(sungnyung)*. The *hanok* experience provides only a partial and selectively reconstructed past, but for most tourist consumers this does not really matter, since "tradition" for them evokes synthesized images and feelings rather than a specific temporal past with all of its historical details intact.[8]

The lineage house experience:
Reconstructing the *yangban* culture

Since the introduction of the local government system in the mid-1990s, South Korean municipalities have endeavored to build a distinct local character, partly for tourist purposes and partly to increase financial viability by drawing more subsidies from the central government. The lineage house experience is compatible with Andong's self-presentation as the "hometown of Confucius and Mencius" *(ch'urojihyang)*, where one may find Confucian culture in its original form.[9] To the degree that "authenticity" carries value, the lineage house experience *(chongtaek ch'ehŏm)* in the Andong area stands out from other types of *hanok ch'ehŏm*. As places where the primogenital descendants of prominent *yangban* lineages have lived generation after generation, *hanok* in Andong have usually been carefully preserved, some for hundreds of years. Because they are officially designated cultural properties, it is difficult to change the form of an Andong lineage house. Many lineage houses have, in addition to the main house buildings, shrines *(sadang)*, ritual halls *(chaech'ŏng)*, lineage halls *(chaesil)*, study rooms *(sŏdang* or *kangdang)*, and private museums *(yumulgwan)*. Each house has its own historical tales and often much-glorified stories about the great deeds, eminent scholarship, loyalty to the country, and self-sacrifice of the ancestors of the specific lineage concerned. Those that also have private museums exhibit the evidence of these claims in material form.

Visits to these places combine pleasure with education in what Creighton calls "edutainment" (1997). As we have seen, Kim Won Kil gives instruction in the ancestral ceremonies of his house. At Yŏlhwadang, the Chinsŏng Yi lineage house, introductory classes on the writings of the Korean Confucian philosopher Yi Toegye are offered, and at other lineage houses a dialogue with the master of the house is included in the visit.

For many modern Koreans who choose to visit these places, an old house culture experience in Andong offers not simply an opportunity to stay overnight in a quiet and peaceful environment or to satisfy innocent nostalgia for things past. It also appeals to a specific kind of collective nostalgia borne by modern Koreans whose own past and history are lost to them. Although they do not have much concrete knowledge of their own ancestors, through the old lineage house experience they can temporarily become *yangban* themselves, consuming *yangban*-ness. One young mother who stayed at one of the lineage houses with her family wrote that she felt like a *manim* (lady of the house) when she woke up in one of the *ondol* rooms in the house and thought that a real *yangban* gentleman might walk out from the next room.

When a middle-aged woman stayed at one of the lineage houses with her daughter who was studying in the United States, the daughter confessed to her mother that the visit had made her reevaluate her feelings about Korean family values.[10] From her experience in the States, she used to think that although Americans consider love and affection among family members to be of primary importance, Korean family relations were very businesslike. In Andong she found a tradition that really does value family relations and that had theretofore been unknown to her. Similarly, a high school graduate wrote a comment on the website of one lineage house, thanking the landlord couple for providing him with a family-like atmosphere and for giving him heartwarming advice when he was depressed after failing his college entrance examination. The visitor went on to say that after returning from his stay at the lineage house, he found new energy to go on and to try again.[11]

Heritage legislation and struggles for survival in Andong

Kim Won Kil, who was a pioneer in opening the lineage houses to tourism in the 1980s, faced many obstacles. The very factors that enhance the authenticity of an Andong lineage house experience — their monumental status and their identity as homes of prominent *yangban* families — have also made it difficult to develop them as tourist sites. The most formidable resistance came from the *yangban* descendants themselves, many of whom considered it unthinkable to let anyone "whose roots are not known" (*kŭnbon ŭl morŭnŭn*) stay at the sacred place where their ancestors had lived. It is even more difficult for *yangban* descendants to imagine serving strangers by providing meals and bedding like servants. They would rather leave their ancestral houses standing empty than turn them into tourist facilities, and many such houses have been vacated as the primogenital descendants pursued jobs elsewhere with no intention of moving back into the empty house. Owners of houses that had been designated as cultural treasures were not allowed to modify the structure of the building without a complicated series of negotiations with the authorities, a factor that also discouraged the descendants from returning.

Kim Won Kil managed to persuade the relevant officials to allow him to install several flush toilets and shower facilities in his compound and started to receive guests amid much opposition and criticism. Some blamed him for attempting to earn a living by "selling the ancestors." Others could not accept the idea of degrading the status of *yangban* descendants by engaging in a kind of service industry. For his part, Kim firmly believed that it was more shameful to leave the house empty and let it decay. In 1989 he started Chirye Ch'angjak Yesulch'on (Chirye Artist Vil-

Figure 4.2. Imch'ŏnggak, the Kosŏng Yi lineage house.

lage) and appointed himself mayor of the village.[12] He then began to invite well-known novelists, poets, scholars, and musicians to stay in his house while engaging in their artistic endeavors. For him, Chirye Artist Village was not an ordinary lodging place but a kind of cultural facility, although he also opened some of the rooms to ordinary tourists.[13]

Later, some of the descendants of other *yangban* lineages with ancestral houses followed his lead and opened their houses to public lodging. In the Andong area, these include Yŏlhwadang (Chinsŏng Yi lineage house),[14] Imch'ŏnggak (Kosŏng Yi lineage house; see Figure 4.2), Tapdong Chongtaek (Kosŏng Yi's main lineage house), Suaedang (Chŏnju Ryu lineage house), Nong'am Chongtaek (Yŏngch'on Yi lineage house), and Kunjari (Kwangsan Kim lineage houses).

The perpetuation of lineage houses by lineage heirs faces many obstacles, one of the most significant being that few women are willing to marry into these families and take on the burden of preparing dozens of ancestral ceremonies and receiving countless guests according to the *yangban* family tradition, often without modern household conveniences. In some cases, the wives of primogenital lineage heirs have become embattled with the officials from the Bureau of Cultural Properties Preservation over the installation of gas pipes that are routinely prohibited in cultural property zones out of fear that a fire could occur.

The primogenital descendants of eminent *yangban* lineages in the Andong area, no matter how glorious the family history, have encountered serious marital problems. In one case, the young mistress of the house (*chongbu*), who had faithfully served her aging mother-in-law for ten years, simply disappeared one day, taking the children with her. After several years, the lineage elders were finally able to trace her and the children to the United States and persuaded her to consent to a divorce so that the primogenital heir could remarry. The heir needed a wife at home to prepare the ancestral rites and look after his mother, but to the dismay of the lineage elders, he chose a divorcée with a child of her own as his second wife. The elders justified the marriage to a divorced woman, a violation of *yangban* propriety, as preferable to having no *chongbu* at all. In another case, to the shock of Andong *yangban* society, the elders of one lineage are said to be seriously considering looking for a wife for its primogenital heir from among Korean Chinese (Chosŏnjok).[15] Because many lineage houses in the Andong area are faced with such difficulties or are places where only the old *chongbu* resides, there is no easy solution to the problem of maintaining the house and continuing its living culture.

According to Kim Won Kil, it is only by letting people live in them that old houses can be preserved and maintained; the buildings themselves need to be heated and aired regularly. This idea is not easily accepted by those in the Bureau of Cultural Properties Preservation, a body whose sole purpose is the preservation of material remains. In fact, the bureau's preservation policy has actually caused people to give up living in the old houses. To address these issues, Kim Won Kil set up a corporation, Kot'aek Munhwa Pojonhoe (Old House Culture Preservation Society), in 2004. With fifty-eight owners of old lineage houses throughout the country as members, the corporation was intended to bring consensus among the owners of old houses in their struggle against the preservation authorities. Mr. Kim had already made a huge personal effort, sending endless letters and petitions to the Ministry of Culture and Tourism and to the Bureau of Cultural Properties Preservation regarding his ideas for the most appropriate and productive ways of preserving and maintaining Korean traditional-style old houses. He also toured the country, giving lectures and instructions to the owners of other such houses in order to gain their support. In Andong some lineage organizations have been won over to the idea of joining the Old House Culture Preservation Society and reconceptualizing the lineage house as a "place for experiencing traditional culture" (*chŏntong munhwa ch'ehŏm jang*) by opening it up to the public.

As a result of these efforts, the preservation authorities finally agreed to let the house owners install basic modern amenities, including updated kitchens fueled with gas, shower facilities, and flush toilets. A budget of one billion won (approximately US$1 million in 2006) was assigned to this end, and the corporation was asked to select and prioritize houses for renovation. Although the Andong area has the largest number of, and arguably the most magnificently scaled, old houses in the country, regional parity had to be considered. In the end, ten houses from a total of fifty were chosen from the Andong area as the first beneficiaries of the renovation subsidy under the new measure. Each selected house constructed the needed facilities in locations that would least affect the outer appearance of the house. Thus, in the case of Imch'ŏnggak — the house of Yi Sang Ryong, who served as the state head of the Korean Government in Exile in Shanghai during the Japanese colonial period — shower and toilet facilities were installed in the former horse sheds, while in Chirye a few more shower stalls and toilets were added to an existing building behind the main house.

Some old house experiences are run by the lineage descendants themselves, but, partly out of consideration for *yangban* propriety and partly as a consequence of practical difficulties faced by aging lineage descendants, the running of others is entrusted to nonlineage managers. For example, the Imch'ŏnggak is run by a young couple who have a keen interest in the traditional culture movement. While all the old lineage houses emphasize their claims to being not ordinary inns but sites of cultural experience, certain discrepancies can be noted in the concept of "cultural experiences" as provided by lineage people and by outside guest managers. Where the *yangban* descendants themselves are in charge, they offer instruction about their vanishing Confucian elite culture with its family values, ancestral rites, and respect for elders, or instruction on the literary works of particular lineage ancestors. The hosts' claim of authenticity is backed by their being the descendants of *yangban* and thus the legitimate heirs of the heritage they represent. This claimed authenticity eludes outside managers who are acting as temporary employees and do not have the necessary knowledge of *yangban* culture. Perhaps as compensation for this deficiency, these managers often introduce more "folkloric" cultural experiences, inviting the guests to participate in pounding the rice cake *(ttokch'igi)* or flying old-fashioned kites *(yŏn naligi)*. What is experienced and consumed during this latter kind of lineage house stay is inevitably very different from what is experienced in a stay at a lineage house run by house owners who see themselves as evangelists for *yangban* culture, as Kim Won Kil does.

Tradition vanishing and being commoditized

Chirye Artist Village now receives more than three thousand visitors every year, about 40 percent of whom are foreigners (Kim Won Kil's statistics). Most of them are short-term guests who stay just one or two nights, but occasionally there are those who spend one to several months engaging in artistic pursuits as writers, painters, or poets. The largest group of visitors may be termed experience tourists; they include college students, families with school-aged children, scholars and artists, culture movement groups, history study groups, diplomats, and foreign tourists seeking a uniquely Korean experience. Thanks to an Internet booking service, student groups from as far away as England, Canada, and Australia are among the visitors to these lineage houses. In recent times it has also become popular to use these places for overnight seminars, workshops, or small conferences, and they are thought to be particularly appropriate venues if the theme of the event is anything related to Confucianism or Korean culture.

The experience of the ancestral ceremony *(chesa ch'ehŏm)* is another attraction of Chirye Artist Village, as it is still the only place in the Andong area that offers it. After his success with the local professional women's group, Kim Won Kil decided to open up all of his family's ancestor rites to tourists visiting his residence. The dates of the ten annual death day rites of Mr. Kim's paternal ancestors are now advertised as "days for experiencing Confucian culture" *(yugyo munhwa ch'ehŏm ŭi nal),* and some Koreans who have immigrated to other countries book a few months ahead via the Internet to come for the event. The father of an immigrant family that had made this trip said that Mr. Kim's demonstration of the ancestor rite showed "our proud tradition" *(charangsŭrŏun uri chŏntong),* which immigrant parents wish to show to their children who are at risk of losing their own cultural identity by being brought up in a foreign country. The rare opportunity of observing a *yangban* ancestor rite also attracts the attention of education-conscious mothers, folklore enthusiasts, and college students who regard the tradition as either lost or vanishing.

The story of the demonstration of ancestral rites and its commodification also indicates that the tradition is being fundamentally transformed from a private family event into a public performance. When, in the spring of 2006, I visited Chirye with a group of graduate students to see one of these rites, I noticed that Mr. Kim paused for the camera when he took out the tablet from the shrine for the ceremony. All those who came for the event, especially the students, were asked to come into the kitchen and help prepare the ritual food and set up the table. They were asked to carry plates of offering food in the dark from the kitchen across the garden and up several stairs to where the rite would be held. All the guests — the graduate students, a Norwegian couple, and a few other tourists who booked specifically for the event — were allowed to take photographs freely throughout the ritual even right up at the table. Before the ritual table was dismantled, the meanings of the offerings were kindly explained to us in every bit of detail, and we were encouraged to take pictures.

After the rite, when we all shared the offerings at a communal table, we were lectured about the importance of keeping our tradition in this world where our things are disappearing and being distorted. Mr. Kim's retired father, in his late eighties, opined, "Every woman who's been to the States comes back with children of three different surnames. Now it has even come to pass that people can take their mother's name."[16] He was arguing that only with accurate knowledge of our traditions and by making an effort to keep them can we restore order and sense in this world turned upside down. Kim Won Kil has made it a mission to give people the opportunity to observe and experience "our tradition" by letting them participate in "properly practiced" ancestral rites. According to him and the other lineage elders present on that occasion, Confucian ancestral rites are becoming like an Intangible Cultural Heritage asset to be protected in contemporary Korea, because so few people understand their meanings these days.[17] By opening their family rites for members of the public to see, lineage descendants can teach them how to respect the elders and the ancestors and the basic importance of family, the essence of the Confucian tradition. The lineage elders hold that these values are still important in this age of globalization. They believe that the reason Korean TV dramas are popular among other Asian peoples today (the phenomenon often referred to as the Korean wave, or *hallyu*) is not that they show good-looking actors and actresses but that they have Confucian family values embedded in them. In this regard, the old house culture experience could be considered the very starting point of *hallyu*.

Consuming history and tradition

Despite the earnestness of those promoting the old house culture experience for educational purposes, how many tourists actually go back to their homes with more respect for their elders or a renewed sense of the importance of the family? I doubt that the members of the professional women's club, with their own busy lives, had any intention of reinstalling elaborate ancestral rites as Mr. Kim performed them. Confucian rites belong to the male realm, and these traditions are understood to differ from house to house *(kagarye)*; women are not in a position to introduce any new elements even if they wish to.

Apart from the descendants of a few prominent *yangban* lineages, most people in contemporary Korea do not know who their own extended ancestors are, let alone their lineage background. Specific ancestry does not constitute any meaningful source of identity in the everyday lives of most urban Koreans. If they were directly involved and if they fully understood the meaning of what they were doing, they would know that participating in other people's ancestral ceremonies itself is a most inappropriate thing to do, let alone bowing to a stranger's ancestor *(nam ŭi chosang)* unless one is a special guest, such as an eminent son-in-law. It may be exactly because the tradition has been lost for most of them that they can appropriate the *yangban* rites as part of "our collective tradition" and see it as something to be honored.

To the eye of a professional anthropologist who has observed many elaborate ancestral rites as they are practiced in contemporary Korea, the rite shown at Chirye can be described only as a very simple one with abbreviated offerings.[18] However, few spectators noticed these details, as they lack the knowledge required to appreciate these differences. Although their families practice ancestral rites at home, many young people simply follow in the footsteps of their fathers or grandfathers without knowing or bothering to learn the meanings involved. At Chirye one can at least observe the proper ritual paraphernalia, including wooden tablets kept at the ancestral shrine, the proper ritual table and tablet chair, the specially made ritual utensils, and the proper ritual robes with matching hats worn by the descendants officiating at the rite. Most of these things, if not all, can be seen only at the *yangban* lineage houses these days. When people come and observe all these as part of "our tradition," it does not really matter whether the forefathers of the individual spectators ever practiced their own ancestral rites according to this *yangban* formula. It does not matter whether they are Buddhists or even Protestant Christians (who in ordinary contexts are prohibited by their faith from Confucian rites of ancestor veneration), the ancestral rites in this context are presented as "Korean" rites above and beyond religious distinctions. In short, it may be precisely because these things do not have any immediate relevance to the spectators' real lives that they can be consumed and appreciated as "our good old tradition."

Conclusion

Old lineage houses can be considered as material embodiments of *yangban* cultural heritage of the Chosŏn period and of the Confucian tradition that *yangban* culture is believed to have enacted. It is perhaps because so many of these structures remain in Andong that the region has been equated with the Chosŏn period. Most of the lineage houses in Andong were actually built during the Chosŏn period, and much of the history related to them is from the period. Recently these houses have been opened to the public partly as a result of the municipal policy to promote tourism and partly as a result of the house owners' initiatives to find a more realistic way of preserving and maintaining them. With the emergence of alternative tourism in the 1990s, the old house cultural experience was promoted and marketed in the Andong area as an opportunity for learning about the Confucian cultural tradition of the Chosŏn period as it is enacted in the everyday lives of the descendants of prominent *yangban* lineages. In this context, *yangban* are newly constructed as every Korean's common ancestors *(uriŭi sŏnjo)*, and, in the process, the private family realm temporarily transforms into public performance.

Notes

1. Although women did not hold official positions during the Chosŏn period, a married woman received a title that corresponded to her husband's rank. When a man did not hold any official position during his lifetime, the inscription on the

tablet would simply read *haksaeng,* meaning "student" and that of his wife would be *yuin,* meaning "a person to be worshipped."

2. This midnight norm has long been broken, as most households now perform the rite in the early evening or even before the dinner hour so that it will be easier for the descendants, who may now live at a distance from each other, to share the ritual meal after the ceremony. While this change is largely for the sake of convenience, it is also popularly believed that the institution of midnight curfew (abolished in 1983) provided a handy excuse for this adjustment, especially in urban areas.

3. Women prepare the offerings prior to the ritual, and in some regional customs, the wife of the primogenital heir makes the second cup offering, *ahŏn* (Moon 1998).

4. The ban on overseas travel, imposed as a means of foreign currency control, was eliminated in December 1989.

5. In the 1980s, a discourse of "Asian values" had been popular throughout the region and undoubtedly influenced this effort. The School of Tradition and Modernity included political scientists, economists, sociologists, philosophers, and historians. Since 1997 the group has published a quarterly journal called *Tradition and Modernity (Chŏntong kwa Hyŏndae).*

6. This of course reflects the more general trend of alternative tourism. Arguing for the association of the developmental stages of capitalism with forms of tourism, Urry suggests that rejection of certain forms of mass tourism, proliferation of alternative sights and attractions, the growth of "green tourism," and aestheticized consumption of a place are travel forms associated with late capitalist societies (1995, 141–151).

7. For a similar phenomenon in Japan, see Creighton (1997); Ivy (1995); Graburn (1995); and Robertson (1998).

8. On the proliferation of discourses on native place *(furusato)* in Japan and various civic efforts to capitalize on them, Ivy wrote, "Through the loss of urban Japan's rural roots . . . the ideal of native place has expanded to become a more capacious metaphor, one both multiple and generic" (1995, 104).

9. *Ch'urojihyang* literally means "home of Confucius and Mencius." A place was called *ch'urojihyang* when it was known for high propriety and eminent scholarship. King Chŏngjo is said to have first conferred the title of *ch'urojihyang* on the region in 1792 in honor of Yi Toegye (1501–1570), a famous Korean Confucian philosopher from Andong who is enshrined at the Tosan Confucian Academy. In 1981, when Kong De Cheng, who is regarded as the seventy-seventh primogenital descendant of Confucius, visited the academy and was elected as its honorable guest director, he honored the town by invoking this title once again.

10. *Monyŏgan* (Between mother and daughter), "*Kajok iran?* (What is fam-

ily?)," June 12, 2007, Dongi Saramdŭl (People of Dongi, a company specializing in Andong tours), www.dongi.net.

11. Suaedang (Chŏnju Ryu lineage house), www.suaedang.com.

12. Chirye Artist Village, www.jirye.com.

13. The original Chirye village was submerged under water when the Imha Dam was constructed in the 1980s. Most of the villagers left the place around this time, but one house was reconstructed above the dam.

14. Although the Andong city homepage (www.andong.kr) lists it as one of the old lineage house experience places, Yŏlhwadang is not in fact the Chinsŏng Yi lineage house, the home of Yi Toegye, but a separate lodging specially constructed in the vicinity to accommodate those who wish to visit this famous lineage.

15. The practice of marrying a Korean Chinese woman or a woman from a Southeast Asian country such as Vietnam, Thailand, or the Philippines is widespread among the eldest sons of Korean rural households faced with a similar difficulty. One person I interviewed whispered that the marriage had already been contracted, but this being a delicate matter, no one else was willing to confirm the claim or identify the household.

16. He was referring to the recent change in the Korean Family Registry Law that is considered the most triumphant and long-awaited victory of Korean feminists.

17. In other words, they are as valuable and endangered as the performing art forms and handicraft techniques that receive official protection and support from the government as part of the national intangible heritage.

18. Family members gave different reasons for the variation of abbreviation in their rites. While cooked meat offerings are more common practices at death-day rites at home, some said that, by offering meat and fish raw, they were following an ancestral decree. Mr. Kim's wife offered the practical observation that when the now-vanished village had some sixty households in it, the preparation of the rites at the main house used to be assisted by many female relatives from the village. When all of the Chirye village — with the exception of the main lineage house — disappeared with the construction of Imha Dam, it became impossible to prepare the rites as in the past.

Crafting the Consumability of Place

Tapsa and *Paenang Yŏhaeng* as Travel Goods

onsumption is about objects and about transactions. What is perhaps most unusual about travel as a consumptive activity is the way that it irreducibly blends the two. It is not simply a scene where objects are transacted; transactions with the world are themselves the ultimate "objects" consumed in traveling. This makes travel a limit case for consumption studies, but such cases can at times reveal otherwise unseen dynamics.

This chapter focuses on two South Korean "off the beaten track" travel genres. *Tapsa*, or *tapsa yŏhaeng* — field study travel — has long been a term associated with the academic practice of taking field trips to the actual sites of history, and before that still with literary travel (Delissen 2004, 23–24), but has come to refer more recently to a sort of heritage tourism that revolves around visiting historic sites and monuments in the Korean landscape, alone or with a group, and getting to know them better through both study and direct experience.[1] *Paenang yŏhaeng*, meanwhile, means "backpack travel" and refers mostly to backpacking abroad — the sort of self-arranged solo or small-group, often "budget" travel to other countries that is epitomized internationally by the Lonely Planet guidebooks. Both of these practices grew to relative popularity during the 1990s amidst rising economic prosperity and the decline of legal restrictions associated with South Korea's pre-1987 authoritarian past, conditioned more specifically by such factors as increasing individual automobile ownership and the loosening of exit visa regulations that formerly had greatly constrained leisure travel abroad. Both practices have been pursued most characteristically by the central beneficiaries of this new prosperity, members of South Korea's expanding middle class, with college students and educational professionals (such as middle and high school teachers) often especially numerous. Yet beyond the economic, occupational, and educational status of the bulk of their participants, *tapsa* and *paenang yŏhaeng* have been "middle-class" consumption activities in a more important sense, as sites for the *performance* of class *distinction* from both the authoritarian structure of older forms of mass tourism and the perceived immoral excess of elite consumption, as well as of class and status *commonality* with those projectively held to be "people like us," both inside and outside Korea (Abelmann 2003; Bourdieu 1984; Eckert 1993; Lett 1998; Nelson 2000).

It is with both this general concept of consumption as an arena for making deeply ethical and political claims about who one is in the world and the specific character of travel in mind that this chapter also experiments with a second, methodological axis of comparison. Light is sometimes best grasped as a particle and sometimes as a wave — so it was said in high school physics — and in the service of illuminating these two Korean travel genres, I describe first their "object-like" and then their "transaction-like" characters. I begin with a treatment of *tapsa* and *paenang yŏhaeng* as defined entities implicitly analogous to other objects within a politics of meaningful consumption. I then turn in the latter half of this essay to an approach that problematizes precisely those processes of definition and closure that make travel encounters appealingly available, detachable, and transportable for travelers — the methods through which their degree and kind of involvement with other places is regulated and limited by themselves and by others. Rather than assuming that human beings newly meeting are naturally either connected or disconnected, I take both to be equally crafted effects. I thus play upon a double entendre expressed in the title of one of John Urry's books on tourism, *Consuming Places* (1995). My goal in the second half of the essay is to show the interrelation of the collective work by travelers and "the traveled" that makes places consumable and the management of both the promise and the threat of being consumed. Marx (1977, 163) famously disclosed within the apparent dumb thingness of the commodity a variety of "subtleties" and "niceties." Here, likewise, "to go and come back" *(kattaoda),* as one says in Korean, will be found to conceal some interesting metaphysics relevant to the performance of ethical self-positioning that travel as consumption entails.

Elementary structures of contemporary Korean travel

Daniel Miller (2002a, 261), probably the leading representative of present-day British anthropological interest in the topic of consumption, remarks at one juncture that "semiotics without structuralism was never much use." His point, at least in part, is a familiar one from studies of the meaningful character of consumption connected to anthropologies on both sides of the Atlantic. Even such global commodities as Coca-Cola and McDonald's carry a specific significance in Trinidad or Korea or (indeed) the United States only in (structural) relation to other commodities and possibilities for consumption, relations that are eminently local, contextual, and historical (ibid., 246; Watson 1997; for Korea, see Bak 1997).

As meaningful consumption options, *tapsa* and *paenang yŏhaeng* would at first glance appear to be directly opposed. *Tapsa* is about Korean things and, in some representations, about Koreanness. *Paenang yŏhaeng,* on the other hand, is not merely in some way "symbolic" of the global — it is itself a globalism, literally a way of going out and seeing (smelling, tasting, . . .) the globe, or at least some non-Korean places on it. Yet the two have also been mutually conjoined in their common positioning against still other travel possibilities, a positioning that helps ameliorate contradictions in the ethical claims they otherwise make (see Lévi-Strauss 1966; D. Miller 2002a, 257).

Tapsa rose to national popularity in the early and mid-1990s largely on the strength of a best-selling series of books written by art historian and critic Yu Hong-jun (1993, 1994, 1997).[2] In stylized, literary prose, Yu described his own *tapsa* visits to historic sites throughout South Korea — new volumes added around the turn of the millennium would recount Yu's subsequent travels in North Korea (1998, 2001) — interspersing his account with a good deal of cultural, social, and political critique. There were many pleasures to Yu's texts, and the ensuing popularity of the practice of *tapsa* clearly had complex causes. Yet this call to see the beauty and wonder of Korean things was timed rather perfectly to catch a rise in public sentiment, moral discourse, and attendant social campaigns that promoted the consumption of Korean over imported goods in the wake of Uruguay Round pressure to open the Korean rice market — the occasion, if not the cause (such campaigns have a longer history), of what Cho Hae-joang somewhat sardonically termed a "boom in finding Us" (1998, 73; see also Han Kyŏng-gu 1994; Nelson 2000, 107–136). Ostensibly, at least, Yu's text invited a cultural or consumer nationalist appropriation from its very first line. Yu recalled an exchange with an official of New York's Metropolitan Museum of Art who, presumably after glorifying the holdings of his own institution, had asked him about the status of museums in

South Korea, thus displaying a blithe obtuseness to the cumulative effects of colonialism, war, and poverty on the international disposition of cultural properties. The reader was invited to cheer Yu's plucky reply, which began the book: "In our country, the whole of the national territory is a museum" (1993, 5).

The popularization of *tapsa* largely engendered by Yu also intersected, however, with complex regional histories of the practice. In the late 1990s, I was doing ethnography in the historic city of Kyŏngju, site of the capital city of the Silla kingdom (traditionally 57 BCE–935 CE) and one of the areas on the Korean Peninsula densest with historic monuments and remains. For much of Kyŏngju's modern existence, these ancient things have defined its relation to a succession of national states (Pai, this volume). They have been the pride of Kyŏngju citizens yet, at times, have also been perceived as the bane of their prosperity, largely because of the preservationist restrictions on economic development established in their name. In this milieu, *tapsa* had for decades been among the constituent practices of amateur historical organizations created by Kyŏngju residents and run on a club basis with a central, long-term membership (Figure 5.1). For them, it had been a technique of the body for knowing history and a technology of place, a practice of orientation within Kyŏngju's historical terrain (Mauss 1973; Oppenheim 2008a). These groups, which included many local teachers and other educators, had also sometimes sought to use *tapsa* as a means to enlighten[3] their fellow residents as to the true value of their historical surroundings — some members, for example, were central in the establishment of an extracurricular "museum school" (loosely affiliated with the Kyŏngju National Museum) for the edification of local children (Kungnip Kyŏngju Pangmulgwan 1994). In the 1990s, however, in conjunction with the end of authoritarian rule and the resumption of elections for local officials for the first time in decades,[4] newer Kyŏngju organizations such as the Silla Cultural Institute sought to build on the national popularity of *tapsa* after Yu's books to offer a more open — and, to some detractors, touristic — form of *tapsa*, often led by semiprofessional guides. Beyond their core membership, these newer groups tried to engage an even wider array of persons, including not only Kyŏngju residents but also visitors to the city. *Tapsa* came to be seen to bear another order of sociopolitical significance as a site for the mediation of resident and nonresident perspectives, a potential forum for a more constructive dialogue that might create mutual understandings toward the resolution

Figure 5.1 A *tapsa* group and leader on Kyŏngju's South Mountain, 1998. Author's photograph.

of controversies over historical preservation and development that continued to wrack Kyŏngju, and sometimes national, debate — controversies that in practice seemed too often to run on a multisided incomprehension of other points of view. Kyŏngju residents tended to leave Silla Cultural Institute *tapsa* speaking of a dislocation from valuable historical things now overcome — "We had never really noticed the things around us" was a common formula — while outsiders were reciprocally encouraged to understand the ambivalence with which many residents have seen the very same objects.

This new Kyŏngju *tapsa* often seemed to exist in harmony with other foci of the consumption of Korean tradition that likewise gained popularity in the 1990s. The Silla Cultural Institute, indeed, traced its origins to the activities of a Buddhist tea shop formerly run by its director, and green tea was both sold on the institute's premises and offered before or after many *tapsa*. This same director often appeared on *tapsa* days wearing the neotraditional Korean clothing *(saenghwal hanbok)* that became fashionable (if not widely worn) during the latter half of the decade; the wife of another Kyŏngju *tapsa* organizer opened a shop selling "our clothing" *(uri ot)* next to her husband's group's office (cf. Ruhlen 2003). I do not mean to give the impression that there was a great deal of consistency in the consumptive selections or practices of those who participated in *tapsa*. But whereas, for example, one *tapsa* leader's taste for McDonald's (albeit the *pulgogi* burger, which features Korean barbecue) drew little remark in internal group discussions, the common practice of seeking out Korean rice beer *(makkŏlli)* at the end of a long day of hiking to view cultural objects was highlighted as congruent with the conduct and meaning of the event. Although I likewise received diverse answers when I asked coparticipants in institute *tapsa* the reasons for their interest, one man made an explicit connection to the four-character phrase that came, in 1990s consumer nationalist discourse, to suggest the consubstantiality of Korean bodies and Korean foodstuffs and other goods (cf. Han Kyŏng-gu 1994, 62–63). "Do you know *sint'oburi* [literally, 'body and earth are not two']?" he asked. "It's important to know your own country."[5]

Paenang yŏhaeng, meanwhile, was also becoming increasingly prominent in the South Korea of the same decade. This travel genre had no singular dominant representation or charter text on the order of Yu's series of *tapsa* books. But as positioned in newspapers, in new dedicated magazines like the eponymous *Paenang yŏhaeng* (first published in November 1996), in books devoted to youth culture, and in the name of a video café *(pidio pang)* in provincial Kimhae selected with exquisite attention to the au courant, backpacking abroad at first glance seemed to stand opposite *tapsa* as against a turn inward to Korean tradition. An inaugural editorial in the first *Paenang yŏhaeng,* entitled "Let's Become Jonathan [Livingston] Seagull," was devoted to the need to learn to fly amidst internationalization *(kukjehwa)* and globalization *(segyehwa)* (Kim Sŏng-yŏl 1996).[6] At least rhetorically, some writings of the era were meanwhile rendering the "new generation" *(sinsedae)* as provocatively postmodern, as imbued with the "death of history," or as possessing an individualism rooted in the self-generative spirit of remix culture (cf. Cho Hae-joang 1994b, 179–203; Mimesisŭ 1993, 5–6). A book on South Korea's Generation X, during the relatively short Korean career of that particular concept, bore the antipious and *tapsa*-unfriendly subtitle *New Bad Things Are Better Than Old Good Things* and situated its chapter on *paenang yŏhaeng* amidst others on other native customs and objects: coffee, dance, fashion, computers, and sex, not necessarily in that order (Kim Chin-man 1995).

Notwithstanding these easy contrasts, and the mutual capacity for *tapsa* to be pushed to stand for a nativist journey to the center of the Korean soul or for *paenang yŏhaeng* to appear as a shockingly free embrace of the foreign, other signs of the times posited a more complex relationship of similarity and difference. Titles could also do other work. Yu Hongjun had called his best-selling books *Na ŭi munhwa yusan tapsagi* (The chronicle of my field study of cultural remains); the cover of the first volume showed a figure in the landscape in solitary contemplation of one of the pagodas at Kyŏngju's Kamŭnsa. In 1997 an author named Chŏn Yu-sŏng published the first volume of his account of a 103-day *paenang yŏhaeng* trip to Europe, calling it *Nam ŭi munhwa yusan tapsagi* (The chronicle of [my] field study of *other people's cultural remains*) (emphasis added). Its humorous cover showed Chŏn in the characteristic hat of the *yangban* literati of Chosŏn-dynasty Korea (1392–1910), popping up from a manhole amidst a group of overweight, shorts- and sneakers-wearing, camera-toting, Hawaiian shirt–bedecked, stereotypically unglamorous white tourists; he thus appeared not only as a Korean busting in but as an aristocrat among the crowd yet as apart from it, via ironic distance, as the figure on Yu's book had been. Indeed, it was also the case that many of the participants in Kyŏngju *tapsa*, of various ages, had already been on foreign *paenang yŏhaeng* or hoped to go one day; the strict polarities of some cultural critique held little interest for them. Especially in the depths of the Asian financial crisis in 1998, usually known in Korea as simply "the IMF," *tapsa* sometimes appeared as a cheaper and perhaps patriotic but not fundamentally dissimilar alternative to *paenang yŏhaeng.* Under the heading "Backpack Trips for Inspiration in Overcoming the IMF," *Paenang yŏhaeng* magazine offered a selection of itineraries centering on domestic cultural objects (*Paenang yŏhaeng* 1998). The man who mentioned *sint'oburi* in connection with *tapsa* himself ran a Pusan travel agency and was thinking of offering domestic services in an effort to overcome his own decline in foreign travel business.

This blending of meanings and practices points further to a common antithesis that both *tapsa* and *paenang yŏhaeng,* as "off the beaten track" forms of travel, posited in the "package tour" as metonym for highly directed and scripted travel experience and cultural encounter. A writer on the Korean *paenang yŏhaeng* website Backpacker.net, for example, in early 2006 described her recent trip to Japan. She had signed on to a group tour because of its cheap flight and hotel combination and, in an effort to fit in, she had "thrown [her] backpack far from [herself]," but despite such good intentions on arrival she "could not endure the suffocating power of the package *[p'aek'iji]*" and thus took off on her own.[7] Even though Kyŏngju *tapsa* with the Silla Cultural Institute was a guided group activity, with many cameras in evidence, jokes were not infrequently made at the expense of the flag-following cultural tour group, whose members snap photographs without actually seeing or understanding. What is familiar in the West as the stereotype of the "Asian tourist" could also be encountered in *tapsa* circles, but it was displaced onto the Japanese tour group as often seen in Kyŏngju.

Opposition to the package tour furthermore allowed both *tapsa* and *paenang yŏhaeng* to be positioned against ethical hazards that populated 1990s South Korean discourses on culture and consumption, resulting in a mediation of the most obvious vulnerabilities of their own respective ideological locations. Writ large, "the package" could, in effect, be opposed to both antiauthoritarian and anti-overconsumptive *(kwasobi)* ends (see Nelson 2000). After valorizing the Korean nation-museum in comparison with foreign alternatives, Yu Hong-jun (1993, 6, 132) went on to attack the sterility of the conventional museum itself, along with the informational signboard, the textbook, and (more indirectly) the school class trip — classical locations of scripted and prescriptive state nationalist cultural discourse (cf. Grinker 1998, 135). In contrast with these figurations of stifling authority, he presented *tapsa* not simply as another opportunity to learn about cultural things but also as a process of learning to see and understand independently (Oppenheim 2008b, 91–92). On Kyŏngju *tapsa,* meanwhile, a sort of conspicuous frugality was the norm; when I once mentioned that I was paying the (hardly princely) sum of 15,000 won to stay overnight in a *yŏinsuk* (rooming house), I was told that I could do better and spend less. Frugality, of course, was also built into the notion of "budget travel" in which *paenang yŏhaeng* participated, but took on a special resonance in a setting where the supposed free-spending habits of conventional Korean tourists abroad were central to the moral panic surrounding excessive consumption and national crisis (Nelson 2000, 124, 165–166). Texts about *paenang yŏhaeng* at times emphasized its instrumental role as a form of "open education" useful for cultivating Korean strength amidst global competition (Kim Sŏng-yŏl 1996). Notwithstanding its own hype of the new, the aforementioned Gen X book described young people who, after saving money through part-time jobs *(arŭbait'ŭ),* traveled on "theme" *paenang yŏhaeng* to learn the marketing practices of foreign bookstores or the techniques of Japanese anime for future use at home, or who, without such blatantly economic goals, took their mothers along as an act of devotion (Kim Chin-man 1995, 141–146). On foreign vacation, the filial developmentalist subject was not dead — indeed, he or she was hardly resting. Securely virtuous, amidst consumer nationalist discourse, in its focus on Korean culture, *tapsa* thus displaced the shadow of authoritarian culturalism by adopting a concern for individualized self-cultivation otherwise associated with "new generation" pursuits, while *paenang yŏhaeng*, securely connected to the realization of personal ambitions, domesticated itself within an older heroism of the productive national citizen.

From social contexts to transactional framings

At a very basic level, Daniel Miller and many other anthropological scholars of consumption are writing against the individualistic and universalizing assumptions of classical and neoclassical economics, which posit and valorize a model of exchange based upon rationally calculating individuals who attempt to maximize utility in order to fulfill individual needs most effectively. According to such assumptions, market exchange is a transhistorical aspect of human behavior that a priori may be disaggregated from other human activities — not for nothing did Adam Smith (1976, 19) trace a course to the "wealth of nations" from hunter-gatherers trading tools and meat. Miller and other critics respond to this sort of abstract universalism by asserting instead the embeddedness of consumption activities, whether capitalist or noncapitalist, in specific historical and sociocultural contexts; it is impossible, they say, to separate calculative individual "utility maximization" from complex social worlds of meaning and taste or, indeed, from the generation of needs by such social forces as advertising. Miller joins a long line of theorists who have contested the sovereignty of the economic and read it back into the social (Miller 1995b, 1998, 2002b; Polanyi 1944; Slater 2002, 236–237). In suggesting, as I have so far, that *tapsa* and *paenang yŏhaeng* as consumption options must be understood in relation to the location of middle-class South Korean subjectivities with respect to revaluations of tradition and cosmopolitanism, moral discourses on "overconsumption," and legacies of authoritarian rule, I have effectively embraced this sort of perspective.

Yet there is a second perspective in recent economic anthropology and sociology that I adopt toward an exploration of other dimensions of these

Korean travel practices in the remainder of this essay, one championed centrally by Michel Callon and (with modifications) Don Slater in debate with none other than Miller himself.[8] This approach also rejects "the market" as a global aspect of human behavior, but contra Miller it likewise rejects common anthropological notions of "society" as a uniform context for meaningful action within which exchange is embedded or as a sui generis entity into which the illusion of market rationality may simply be dissolved (Callon 1998b, 50–51; Duranti and Goodwin 1992; cf. Durkheim 1915; Latour 1986, 2005; Riles 2000; Slater 2002, 242). Callon believes in markets in the plural, in concrete, emergent, actively organized settings — made local *transactional* contexts — in which the self-interested "calculativeness" presumed to exist naturally in economists' rational actors is in fact circumscribed and formed into existence. However socially meaningful objects of consumption may be, however otherwise connected to the participants in an exchange in webs of relatedness, there is nonetheless a carefully arranged setting in which parties to a transaction "enter and leave . . . like strangers," negotiating price and passing money and goods between them, and then are "quits." The transaction is closed, and they may never see each other again (Callon 1998b, 3, 19; Slater 2002, 235, 239).

For Callon, market exchange and its subjectivities are thus neither natural nor illusory, but rather a highly contingent localized achievement. His central problem is how such market settings, zones of calculativeness, are made or "formatted" through mechanisms that may be procedural, institutional, technical, informational, legal, or metrological. He uses the example (citing Garcia 1986) of a regional French strawberry market that came into being in an area where, formerly, strawberry growers had had long-standing relationships with their wholesale distributors (with, we may imagine, prices set by custom with some sense of mutual obligation for each party to go easy on the other in times of difficulty). Calculativeness came partially to displace such ties through a set of technical intercessions: the rental of a warehouse where strawberries could be compared side by side, the severing of berry lots from producer identities through numerically coded data sheets, the establishment of an auction procedure, and so on (Callon 1998b, 19–23).[9] Together, these interventions amount to a multidimensional process of *framing,* a concept Callon develops in dialogue with Pierre Bourdieu (2000), Erving Goffman (1974), Arjun Appadurai (1986a), and particularly Nicholas Thomas (1991). Framing, with all of its constructive aspects, has simultaneously the character of a limited, circumstantial *dis*entanglement of persons and objects that may otherwise be entangled in relations.[10] Disentangled persons may relate calculatively within a transaction because they owe each other no future obligation. Disentangled objects become alienable, able to be fully ethically detached from one party and attached to another.[11] Crucially, however, Callon also emphasizes that framing is never total. Because the persons and objects in a transaction may remain otherwise entangled, because they are in a sense simultaneously present inside and outside the frame, there is always the possibility of *overflowing,* which might unravel constituted relations of calculability and alienability. Callon's perspective thus licenses attention both to the formatting mechanisms that constitute framing and to the crafted and contestable "edges" of frames (Callon 1998a, 1998b, 16–19; Callon, Méadel, and Rabeharisoa 2002; Slater 2002).

The relationship between Korean travel practices and Callon's focus on the architecture of transactional (market) exchange may seem a bit tenuous. Yet if, beyond seeing travel genre choices simply as objects of consumption akin to others, we foreground their internal transactional character and thus come to understand leisure travel as, in fact, a fairly miraculous metaphysical achievement of being able to "go and come back," living for a time in other places and "consuming" them while incurring strictly limited obligations beyond the financial, then perhaps the link to disentanglement through framing may not be so obscure. Through what techniques are the entanglements and disentanglements of travel regulated, and by whom? In prepackaged tourism, framing may be highly routinized and solidified, like the tinted windows of a bus or the steel fence around a five-star hotel campus that separates guests from the embracing poverty. The overall landscape of obligation in prescriptively antithetical modes like *tapsa* or *paenang yŏhaeng* is more contingent and emergent, but it is nonetheless the framing of disentanglements that permits the simultaneous promise of desirable and chosen entanglement in other places to be realized. It is what allows them to be crafted as travel goods and as good travel.

The rest of this essay returns to how *tapsa* has been locally staged in Kyŏngju for outsiders, as well as the self-constituting practices of Korean backpackers abroad. I pay attention to the formatting and negotiated edges of frames that in turn mold and contest the *calculability* of travel for travelers and the double *alienability* that both makes places available and makes travelers able to get to and from places "and be quits," as well as relations of *overflow* that define both dangerous and desirable interactions that are thus structured to exist beyond the circumscribed interchange itself. Overflow is not simply the unpredictable but also the predictable figured to lie outside an act of framing. Thus I argue that, beyond the contextual location of Korean travel genres as consumption options, their internal transactional architecture is a relevant aspect of their articulation with ethical landscapes of place and cultural commitment.

Formatting Kyŏngju *tapsa:* Getting to know us

Above, I noted the 1990s creation of a "new" Kyŏngju *tapsa* by the Silla Cultural Institute and other groups that was, by design, more available to city outsiders and to nonmember locals, while outlining as well their stated political project of fostering improved dialogue between the two about, and at the scene of, Kyŏngju historical things. These aims were crafted in tandem by the sort of pragmatic framing that Callon and his allies highlight: the program of bringing about a new ethical entanglement of residents and visitors and historic terrain proceeded through a disentanglement of *tapsa* from extant webs of local obligation and reciprocity that made it available for wider consumption. This remaking gave *tapsa* a different transactional character, making it more calculable in its costs and alienable in the sense that visitors could, if they wished, come and go as strangers with only the most circumscribed short-term commitments. And this change, in turn, inscribed the shape of other ethical possibilities.

Most basic among these crafting mechanisms was the manner in which *tapsa* was repriced. The Silla Cultural Institute in the 1990s was probably the most visible of Kyŏngju cultural groups, with an office above a major intersection and a glossy magazine with fairly wide circulation. Its invitation to newcomers and outsiders, moreover, extended to demands it did not make. Older Kyŏngju historical organizations such as the Friends of Silla Culture had been conducting monthly *tapsa* for years, but one gained access to these *tapsa* activities only by becoming a member of the group, which entailed relatively high annual membership dues (over 100,000 won in 1998) paid on a lump sum basis, a degree of acceptance by other group members, and a reciprocal responsibility for the ongoing cultural activity of the organization. In contrast, one could join the Silla Cultural Institute's regular monthly Sunday *tapsa* and gain the services of its semiprofessional guide simply by appearing at its office and paying a single-event fee of 15,000–17,000 won on the day of the trip, without regard to status or prior connection to the group.[12] While membership in the institute was possible, it was also relatively inconsequential, costing only 20,000 won annually and bestowing only a 2,000-won discount on monthly *tapsa* and a presence on institute mailing lists. In short, institute costs were structured to emphasize event fees over membership and thus to permit one-time or trial participation with only a relatively small financial outlay. With this low barrier to entry, if some participants in institute *tapsa* professed a desire to achieve a deeper appreciation of culture or history of the sort presumed among both the Friends and the ideal readership of Yu Hong-jun's books, many others, including some regulars, admitted to consuming *tapsa* in a state of distraction — it was "something to do" or a nice alternative to conventional mountain hiking.

This delimitation of financial costs and reciprocal obligation had an analog in the organization of the normal institute *tapsa* itself. Relative to Kyŏngju predecessors and other touchstones, both the experience and the knowledge that *tapsa* promised were repackaged, with the latter made alienable in a newly tangible form. The usual *tapsa* Sunday began shortly before 9:00 a.m., with participants' arrival at the institute office. At a desk by the door, each paid the event fee and received in return a photocopied, illustrated booklet that on its cover noted the date of the *tapsa* and its iteration number in the complete series of institute events (ranging in the 60s–70s in 1997–1998) and inside provided a page or two of explanation, with references, of each major cultural site or object to be visited in the course of the day. Although some of the most self-consciously "advanced" participants kept running *tapsa* notebooks, as Yu Hong-jun and the very genre conventions of the *tapsa* account invited one to do (cf. Delissen 2004, 24), for most the premade booklet, perhaps supplemented with marginal notes, constituted the transportable record of knowledge and impression, the alienable take-home trace of *tapsa*.

Just after 9:00, after remarks from the institute director and the guide for the day, the latter would give a few minutes of preview of the day's sights, and then the actual *tapsa* would begin. A day would pass in movement from site to site, with the guide offering explanation at each and taking questions, sometimes with knowledgeable participants adding their own perspectives. Even if movement during the day was on foot (as it was on many courses), the event as a whole was usually bounded by the use of a chartered bus in the morning and a return to the institute offices on the same bus in the afternoon. Disembarking, thanked and bade farewell by the guide and institute staff, participants were "quits," and many of them indeed immediately left for the bus station or their cars.

So far in this section, I have called attention to the small procedures — the parceling of financial obligation, the objectification of portable knowledge, and the staging of an official beginning and end to the event — through which took place the crafting of the edges of the frame of a more singularly transactional Kyŏngju *tapsa,* one in which persons might indeed "enter and leave as strangers" to other participants and to the cultural terrain without ongoing entanglement but one that, on the very same basis, was also more available to "strangers" in the sense of geographical, ethical, and knowledge outsiders to extant Kyŏngju networks. This shift might simply be taken as the "commodification" or "touristification" of *tapsa,* and certainly some in Kyŏngju who were critical of institute practices expressed thoughts along these lines, but my hesitation to offer such a concept as an analytical endpoint is underlain by my sense, noted above, that institute *tapsa* at the same time sought to engineer the ethical encounter of Kyŏngju and outside perspectives at the scene of culture. Institute *tapsa* discourse interspersed information about cultural objects with discussions of the problems of development and burdens of preservation in the historic city, the politics of regional self-governance *(chibang chach'i),* and other issues that outsiders presumptively "failed to understand." Even as the institute disentangled *tapsa* from a web of local practice and obligation, it also sought to produce new entanglements of precisely such mutual understanding, but these took on their ethical quality from the way in which they were figured in relief *as overflow* — that is, as outside the primary transactional framing of obligation. It was, in short, precisely the fact that one *might* leave as a stranger that co-constituted the ethical possibility of *choosing* not to.

The way such possibilities came into being in the course of institute *tapsa* was in the formatting of routine moments that may best be thought of as invitations or "gates" — openings through which one might elect to pass. The interspersion of Kyŏngju issues with cultural knowledge was itself one, but most prominent was the institute habit, toward the end of each *tapsa,* of stopping in a convenient clearing so that participants could offer self-introductions and sing for the amusement of the assembled. Public speech genre conventions and the precedents of institute staff and *tapsa* regulars pushed each person, couple, or set of friends to relatively formal self-presentations and the performance of sincerity and mutuality; outsiders often spoke of their gratitude in getting to know Kyŏngju better, and residents of their new appreciation of Kyŏngju's historic terrain, while both tended to express their pleasure at meeting and their promise to continue to participate. The end of the day usually provided the chance to begin to make good on these sentiments, for the same disembarkation from the bus that marked the official boundary of the *tapsa* usually opened onto an informal opportunity to join others in a meal or drinking. Within the larger institute structure, long-term participants might "graduate" from the normal guided *tapsa* to a more informal and advanced "youth" *tapsa* organized by mutual effort.[13] In both cases, the edge of the frame figured also the potential to step beyond in ways already limned and scripted.[14]

Formatting *paenang yŏhaeng:* Being there

As I was writing this chapter, Backpacker.net, now defunct but then perhaps the most prominent (mostly) Korean-language website devoted to *paenang yŏhaeng,* featured on its homepage a photograph that encapsulated its obvious connection to backpacking as a global practice of wealthy nations, something of its sociological distinctiveness, and its self-presentation as antithetical to package tourism. The image showed a Backpacker.net member as the only Korean seated amidst a group of Western backpackers on the steps of a European-looking building, in evident conversation with one of them. The Westerners all looked to be in their twenties, but the Korean, one learned by linking to his member profile, was a male teacher from Seoul in his sixties who listed Spain and Nepal among his seven trips abroad. Indeed, while younger members are certainly numerically predominant on the website, the man in question was not alone among others of his age, and my sense from a variety of encounters is that *paenang yŏhaeng* is less exclusively generational than may be suggested by either the Lonely Planet analogy or the common location of the practice within Korean youth culture — many likely travel now because they could not earlier. On his own page the Seoul teacher offered an ode to the freedom, insouciance, and "romance" of travel headed simply *"kŭnyang,"* a word at once suggestive of the elemental simplicity of backpacking ("just") and one's noninstrumental reasons for going ("just because"). *"Kŭnyang"* donning a backpack and setting off is good, "in search of the romantic" *(nangman ch'aja).* Simply do it; do it for its own sake.[15]

Such rhetoric of authenticity pervades the discourse and practice of *paenang yŏhaeng*, as it does international backpacking more generally.[16] In Callon's terms, backpacking is apparently premised upon and ostentatiously seeks overflow, some sort of entanglement with distant places or the people occupying these places that goes beyond that experienced by the "typical tourist," an entanglement that at the extreme approaches the existential — Being there by being there. The magazine *Paenang yŏhaeng* has associated its eponymous practice with contemporary examples of foreign travel literature, such as author Pak Wan-sŏ's account of Nepal and Tibet (1997; Pak Ŭn-gyŏng 1997). Some other writers on Backpacker. net adopted a different literary persona in emphasizing not the carefree quality but the rigors of travel and of life lived closer to the edge — one blogger gave a sparse, present-tense, first-person account of waiting at the bus stop in Tulum, Mexico, in the dark early hours of the morning, sipping coffee alone with little money in his pocket.[17] Another uploaded a photo of an Indian funeral pyre encountered on his own travels to accompany a meditation on death.[18] Meanwhile, *paenang yŏhaeng* seems to participate in a broader shift in Korean travel photography directed at the traveling subject, from a predominance of static frontal poses framed to include a foreign sight in the background, demonstrating presence, to stagings that emphasize some sort of active participation in place or in transnational backpacking culture — such as drinking with Australians in one's Prague hostel.[19] This last example underscores *paenang yŏhaeng* as also a practice of cosmopolitan entanglement, a claim upon commonality with those who move rather than those who only reside.[20] English, the lingua franca of many travel settings, was used in revealing ways on the otherwise Korean-language Backpacker.net. One blogger wrote in excellent but also clearly Korean English, as if toward a broader readership, while the traveler to Tulum mentioned above wrote in Korean but included at the end of each post an English-language poetic meditation on travel drawn from a popular source, such as a song by Annie Lennox or one sung by Pippin in *The Lord of the Rings*.[21]

Yet if this desirable overflow and these inalienable experiential entanglements are the most loudly proclaimed aspect of *paenang yŏhaeng*, they come into being against the background of a crafting of disentanglement from more undesirable commitments and connections. The bidirectional alienability of travelers themselves, their ability not only to go but also to come back, unencumbered, and thus to consume foreign places "off the beaten track," depends on the careful technical management of the potential for other overflows that may include the physical (challenges to the safety of travelers), the financial (being cheated), and the ethical (the accrual of obligations to a destination). Metaphorically, the problem of backpack travel is the engineering of a situation in which one may not just see, as stereotypical "specular" mass tourism does, but also touch and "be touched" to some extent, *while simultaneously* remaining sufficiently untouchable.

Although *Paenang yŏhaeng* shares aspects with conventional travel magazines, and Backpacker.net in its public overlays and multiple tunnels to spaces for individual expression ("My Backpack") resembled other social networking websites, amidst the growth of *paenang yŏhaeng* such media have had significant tutelary roles within a larger collective process of learning to consume foreign places differently (Hindman 2009).[22] One early reader letter published by *Paenang yŏhaeng* pleaded for more advice beyond destinations, "not on the 'what' but on the 'how'" of travel — more practical information toward self-organized travel on a budget (Hwang Wŏn-uk 1997). To the extent they have delivered, *paenang yŏhaeng* media have not only represented the practice but have been among its formatting elements, its "separative technologies" (Slater 2002). Very concrete suggestions as to zones of danger to avoid and how not to be trapped into overspending have been interspersed among suggestions for more authentic encounters abroad; "being there" has had as its constitutive infrastructure a procedural scripting of how to get away — the calculative groundwork of alienability, of how not to leave too much of oneself or one's wallet behind.

The fine crafting of the edges of entanglement and disentanglement in uncertain situations, of transactional frames carved out against the potential attachment of other obligations, has also taken place through *paenang yŏhaeng* narratives. One traveler described for the Backpacker.net audience his negative and at moments frightening experience with local guides on a trip to the Egyptian pyramids. After he asked how to get to them and declined to pay for an unmetered taxi from Cairo, a young man approached him and volunteered to help, presenting his student and military identification cards to overcome the backpacker's initial distrust and thus differentiating himself from the other "hateful" touts in the street. The young man brought the Korean to a stable, from which another guide led him on horseback into the desert. Soon enough, however, this second guide began to mention, casually at first, his family's need for money and then began intermittently to drive the pair's horses at a gallop, throwing the author, an inexperienced rider, into a panic. After the requests became more direct, the Korean eventually refused to give him money during the journey — because the guide had broken his promise and "treated [him] wrong" — but offered to give him some upon their mutual safe return to the stable. When the trip was over, and the promised money angrily and reluctantly paid but paid nonetheless, the Korean went back to accost the young man who had arranged the whole desert trip. The young man apologized and offered to take the backpacker to his home for dinner, but the latter refused; the Korean spent the rest of the day deflecting other offers, entreaties, and invitations in an effort to get back to his guest house alone, with the young Egyptian man importuning him all the while to "please accept my brotherliness."[23]

This was, of course, a common enough kind of backpacking encounter, replete with power dynamics, unfamiliar and ambiguous situations, perceptions and realities of relative wealth and poverty, and initial good cheer giving way to threat and recrimination. A reader taking this as an exemplary lesson might well revise his or her own mental checklist of safe travel dos and don'ts. Yet it finally also both illustrates and participates in travelers' attempts to establish the ethical boundaries of encounters with other places and peoples when those boundaries are being contested. It may have been transparent, tactical, and cynical, but by using kinship metaphors, the young Egyptian was trying to entangle the Korean in a nonmarket economy of obligations — did not this (relatively) rich foreigner owe him something as a function of hospitality and status generosity beyond the transactional frame? For *paenang yŏhaeng* participants, as perhaps for many backpackers more generally, "brotherliness" may be appealing only so long as it is on their own terms, and deeper involvement in a local setting may be viable only so long as the path of clean return and detachment from unwanted moral claims, back to their room and to mobility, remains clear.

Conclusion: Two travel genres, two ways

In this chapter, I have considered *tapsa* and *paenang yŏhaeng* as linked travel practices and ways of consuming places in and beyond contemporary South Korea. Following authors such as Daniel Miller, I began by treating these two genres of travel as objects of consumption that articulate projects of meaning-making, emergent cultural logics of a post-authoritarian, postdevelopmentalist, globalizing setting. Conceptually, I thus opened by treating types of travel in the same way one might treat other unitary consumption goods. Yet however fruitful this may be, in the consumption of place, perhaps especially "off the beaten track," experiential object and setting are unusually difficult to distinguish and define a priori. I thus turned in the latter half of the chapter to a perspective that focuses on the framing mechanisms of transactional (market) exchange, using it to discuss the contested crafting of the edges of experience and entanglement with places — the architecture of calculability, alienability, and overflow that secures both the encounter and return moments of "going and coming back" and thus actively circumscribes travel as a good available for transaction. Read methodologically, this has been an essay about the difference various economic anthropologies make.

Miller's emphasis on local, contextual meanings is attuned to the usual focus of American cultural anthropology. Callon, in contrast, is more clearly interested in effects, what made frames do. Yet framing itself also constructs the meaningful and ethical contours of the consumptive encounter. In this formatting and the conjoined making of overflow as overflow, entanglement and disentanglement as well as human connection and disconnection are co-constituted and given qualitative shape. Making travel into goods makes versions of good travel. Kyŏngju *tapsa* made available for outside consumption also made available at its edges an ethical posture for outsiders of willful understanding of Kyŏngju concerns; in such small pathways lay an invitation to a specific moral economy of nation and locality amidst the political transformations of 1990s South Korea. The framing of *paenang yŏhaeng* traces zones of spiritual versus practical encounter — the former made free to occur only by grace of a control over the latter — and in doing so locates Korean sympathies and commonalities in the world much differently from, say, the way widely read anti-imperialist dependency theories of the 1980s did (see G. Shin 1995). Thus it is that the cultural logics of consumption of place are shaped not only by external context but also by the internal architecture of consumability itself, the logic of its transactions.

Notes

1. In considering *tapsa* elsewhere, I focus more centrally on its academic antecedents and its politics of knowledge and materiality (Oppenheim 2008b, 83–112).

2. Made widely famous through these books, and a public figure since their publication, during the No Mu-hyŏn government Yu was appointed to an important public office dealing with cultural affairs, the Cultural Properties Administration.

3. "Enlightenment" (or "civilization"), as a project directed toward others, has been a recurrent emphasis of Korean nationalist reformers and colonial and post-colonial states since the nineteenth century (cf. Schmid 2002). While I do see echoes of these projects in Kyŏngju, I hasten to add that their local proponents have rarely been as contemptuous of the "unenlightened" or as forceful in the pursuit of their goals as many national authors of such campaigns have been.

4. Elections for city council members resumed in 1992, and those for municipal executives (e.g., mayors) in 1995.

5. Of course, my presence at such events was not irrelevant. One woman who had brought her young daughter on *tapsa*, only to have the child's interest flag, pointed me out for the sake of a guilt trip, saying, "Look, there's a foreigner who is interested in our things." Laura Nelson (2000, 130) comments on the projective dialogicity of the theme of "the watching world."

6. In the 1990s, Richard Bach's tale could carry something of the individualist flavor with which it was imbued, as a "do your own thing" narrative, in 1970 when it first appeared in the United States. In South Korea it had been a quintessential adolescent *(ch'ŏngsonyŏn)* story, read by middle school students outside and against the tightly structured (and government-controlled) academic curriculum and sometimes informally extolled by their teachers as well. (I am grateful to Hyunjung Lee for this information.)

7. An Mi-yŏng, "Ilbon ŭl tanyŏwasŏ . . . ," Mai paekp'aek (My backpack), January 24, 2006, www.backpacker.net.

8. The debate took place in a 2002 issue of *Economy and Society* devoted to a consideration of Callon's 1998 edited volume *The Laws of the Markets,* and it included several other participants beyond those I name here. I owe my attention to this exchange to the much-recommended work of Amy Levine (2004, 103–105), who herself works through the debate toward a consideration of the "virtual."

9. That many of these changes were orchestrated by a local government economist, trained in neoclassical theory, points to a dynamic crucial for Callon that is less important to the present paper — that is, the formatting effect that economics itself exerts upon economic activities (Callon 1998b, 22–32). It may have been the case that, because the world had markets, it gave birth to Adam Smith, but for Callon the more important point is that because it had Adam Smith (and Friedrich Hayek, and Milton Friedman, and economics textbooks that quote them all), it now has markets in abundance.

10. Slater (2002, 242) cogently distinguishes between "embeddedness" as a global claim of the social character of economic activity and Thomas and Callon's notion of the variable "entanglement" of entities.

11. Relative to Callon, Slater especially highlights this question of alienability. Gifts, which carry the obligation of a future gift in return and, as objects, thus in a sense retain and extend the moral presence of the original giver, are the classic anthropological example of exchanges not based on the (full) alienation characteristic of market transactions (Mauss 1967).

12. It is, of course, emblematic of this relative openness to outsiders that the Silla Cultural Institute was my first point of contact with Kyŏngju cultural organizations. I saw its sign while walking down the street, went up to the office, and began asking questions. I came to find or to know about other organizations only after a matter of months, through the expansion of my network of contacts.

13. "Youth" (ch'ŏngnyŏn), here, was used in its broad Korean sense inclusive of persons in their thirties or forties.

14. My analysis here bears echoes of Martin Heidegger's treatment of circumspective relationships with everyday objects that demand one's attention (1962, 102–104). The ethical possibilities of Kyŏngju tapsa become more deeply such through a made obtrusiveness that takes place through the action of framing.

15. www.backpacker.net, homepage, and Sŏng Tae-hyŏn, member page. Nancy Abelmann and Jung-ah Choi (2005, 134–135), writing of the film Attack the Gas Station, argue that kŭnyang, as the reason given for the film's signature act, inscribes a filmic posture against the "grand narratives" of previous South Korean political and subjective meaning-making and toward a "celebration of 'difference' and the 'individual.'"

16. The earliest Western sociologies of tourism to treat backpacking, not insignificantly written in the early 1970s, took this self-presentation at face value perhaps to a fault and treated the ideal-typical backpacker as a countercultural questing figure (E. Cohen 1973, 2003).

17. Cho Hŭi-ch'ang, "Iyagi yŏhaeng — Chungnammi 4. Sinŭi kwihwan (T'ullum)," Mai paekp'aek, February 10, 2006, www.backpacker.net.

18. Yi Su-ho, member page, www.backpacker.net.

19. Moreover, frontal "presence" photos, when taken, have tended toward less static and more informal poses. These observations on photography are admittedly impressionistic, gleaned from the sources I discuss here as well as photos I have seen since 1991 in both public settings and private albums.

20. Among the best perspectives on this gap is Jamaica Kincaid's A Small Place (1988).

21. Cho Hŭi-ch'ang, "Iyagi yŏhaeng — Chungnammi 4. Sinŭi kwihwan (T'ullum)," Mai paekp'aek, February 10, 2006, www.backpacker.net; "Iyagi yŏhaeng —

Chungnammi 9. Manch'ŏnŭi ch'ŏnyŏ haehyŏp (P'unt'a Arenasŭ)," Mai paek-p'aek, March 6, 2006, www.backpacker.net.

22. There were also "*paenang yŏhaeng* information sessions," often sponsored by travel agencies, which proliferated in the late 1990s.

23. Chang Chŏng-dae, "39 Yŏksaŭi tosi K'airo esŏ mannan saram tŭl," Mai paekp'aek, March 3, 2006, www.backpacker.net; "40 Yŏlsaŭi Sak'ara p'iramit — Mal t'ago tallinda," Mai paekp'aek, March 8, 2006, www.backpacker.net.

Part III

Korean Things

The conditions of transnationalism under which most people in the world now live have created new and often contradictory cultural and economic values and meanings in objects — that is, in material culture — as those objects travel in an accelerated fashion through local, national, and international markets and other regimes of value production. These emerging conditions . . . offer a critical moment in which to reexamine the ways objects come to convey and condense value and, in doing so, are used to construct social identities and communicate cultural differences between individuals and groups.
— Fred R. Myers, *The Empire of Things*

A long tradition in anthropological writing, from Marcel Mauss (1969) to Arjun Appadurai (1986a), regards things as more than things, sees objects as embedded in and sometimes as significant markers of social relationships, and finds that even the most ordinary objects can be encoded with moral and emotional significance. Fred Myers gives particular credit to the work of Annette Weiner (1992) and Arjun Appadurai in moving material cultural studies away from the quid pro quo economics of classical exchange theory to a new emphasis on how "objects come to convey and condense value and, in doing so, are used to construct social identities and communicate cultural differences between individuals and groups" (Myers 2001b, 3). Appadurai's influential *The Social Life of Things* moved the commodity into the domain of anthropologically significant goods and focused attention on an object's shifting signification as it moves from one domain of experience to another (Appadurai 1986b; Kopytoff 1986; D. Miller 1995b). As noted in Robert Oppenheim's chapter, Daniel Miller has solidly claimed the world of mass consumption as ethnographic terrain (1994, 1998, 2002a).

For students of material culture, "object" is construed in the broadest sense, from things such as postcards, CD covers, and souvenirs to sites in the material landscape such as department stores, theme parks, and preserved *yangban* houses. While the social life of things has relevance throughout this volume, the two chapters in this section focus on smaller, tractable objects whose significations have altered over the course of Korean modernity. The *changsŭng* poles that Laurel Kendall describes and kimchi as the subject of Kyung-Koo Han's chapter both bear strong, sometimes emotional, traditionalist associations that sit uncomfortably with their current availability as commodities.

The *Changsŭng* Defanged

The Curious Recent History of a Korean Cultural Symbol

Devil posts — road idols whose primary function is to protect a village from evil spirits — Korea — Case label in the Hall of Asian Peoples, American Museum of Natural History

They stand in the American Museum of Natural History's Hall of Asian Peoples, a pair of Korean "devil posts" *(chang-sŭng)*, imposing, with bulging eyes, deeply contoured faces, and Dracula mouths full of pointed teeth.[1] Bearing their ideographic inscriptions — "Male General under Heaven," "Female General under the Earth" — they loom over a case filled with diverse charms, masks, and statues from different corners of Asia, a case anachronistically devoted to "animism" and intended to illustrate "some of the good and bad animistic spirits which Asian peoples acknowledge." (The viewer can only imagine whether these leering "devil posts" are benevolent or malign.)[2] As a large and commanding presence, *changsŭng* had come to symbolize "Korea," as tiki gods stand for the South Pacific and totem poles evoke the Pacific Northwest. A century ago, Westerners encountered this same demonic *changsŭng* in early missionary and traveler accounts of Korea, a material marker of pagan exoticism that would later be purchased in miniaturized form by American GIs souvenir hunting in the PX and by tourists in the Bando-Chosun Arcade. You can find similarly ferocious little *changsŭng* in Seoul/Inchon airport souvenir shops today, competing with masked dancers and dolls dressed like brides, grooms, and antique Korean royalty. The *changsŭng* in the AMNH exhibit case did indeed remind me of Korea, of Seoul in the early 1970s, where I had seen similarly garish *changsŭng* outside restaurants featuring Korean cuisine. As I remember, Hanilgwan and most certainly Korea House each had a pair, too freshly made and brightly painted to have ever inhabited a village. By the late 1970s, enormous *changsŭng* posts loomed over the Korean Folk Village near Suwŏn and decorated tourist promotion brochures. They aren't pretty, but they fit the basic requirement of a souvenir or a collected curiosity, something really different, exotic even to the eyes of urban South Koreans. But by the turn of the millennium, the *changsŭng* had taken on a different cast, less Other than "us."

In this chapter, I chart the *changsŭng*'s journey from a village guardian and road marker to a museum artifact and consumable souvenir to a saturated symbol of a multiplex Korean experience, from an image photographically reproduced by outsiders to signify a strange and distant Korea to its multiple contemporary reproductions as expressions of innate Koreanness. In Susan Stewart's terms, I look at the *changsŭng* as an object generated by means of multiple and changing narratives (S. Stewart 1984, xii). I am concerned, particularly, with how the *changsŭng*'s transformation from demon visage to face of the Korean folk has been and continues to be negotiated, paying particular attention to the manner in which those who produce *changsŭng* in the borderland between handicraft and art navigate the material production of meaning (Babcock 1986).

The *changsŭng*'s contemporary face

In the neighborhood of galleries and elegant traditional restaurants that is Seoul's Insadong, *changsŭng* are everywhere, outside restaurants, inside drinking establishments, glistening with varnish to protect their gold-toned wood from the elements. In the handicraft and souvenir shops they range from small mass-produced souvenirs, now mostly all made to mold in Chinese factories, to rare antique stone *changsŭng* and distinctive artistic sculptures in wood four to six feet high. One innovative gallery briefly featured ceramic *changsŭng*. Two old stone *changsŭng* mark a convenient meeting place and photo opportunity at the northern entrance to Insadong's main street. An archival photograph of young men in white clothes and bachelors' pigtails bowing reverently before a row of *changsŭng* hangs on the wall of my favorite café.

On the street, the new *changsŭng* seem playful. Some carvers have shaped the *changsŭng*'s body with artful attention to the twists and knots in the wood and the roots that spring out as hair. These *changsŭng* have faces more friendly than frightening, the demonic fangs less in evidence or more like the canines on some friendly cartoon tiger or Korean *tokkaebi* goblin. Some carry the faces of much-reproduced wooden masks from the cultural heritage site Hahoe Village near Andong, an icon meeting an icon. Could these whimsical creations ever have commanded the reverence shown to the fierce *changsŭng* in the old photograph? These playful new creations wear equally playful new messages. The central *changsŭng* in the pocket park just off the southern entrance to Insadong echoes the rallying cry of Korea's World Cup efforts: "Go for the dream" *(kkumŭn iruŏyajinda)*. Up the road, a *changsŭng* at a restaurant doorway proclaims this venue as the Insadong hangout of Guus Hiddink, the Dutch soccer coach who led the South Korean team to a surprising string of successes in the 2002 World Cup. Another pair, exotic-looking with atypical necks and dangling earrings, represent "Great General Chanho," after Korean American baseball pitcher Park Chan-ho, a totemic baseball stuck in his chest, and "Woman General Se Ri" for Se Ri Pak, the "magic princess" of golf, appropriately adorned with a golf ball. *Changsŭng* and sports, *changsŭng* and restaurants, *changsŭng* as souvenirs, *changsŭng* as pricy interior decoration, but what is a *changsŭng*? "What do you tell your customers?" my field assistant and I ask a sales clerk in one of the shops selling miniature *changsŭng,* mostly now produced in Chinese handicraft factories. "I tell them, 'It's traditional,'" she says.

On a warm spring night in 2006 Ch'oe Hyŏng-bŏm's exhibition, "Iron Dreams Are *Sottae* Dreams, Wooden Dreams Are *Changsŭng* Dreams" (Ch'ŏlŭiggum sottaeŭiggum, namuŭiggum changsŭngŭiggum) opens at the Mogin Gallery up a quiet Insadong ally, drawing the expected artistic, literary, and quasi-bohemian crowd. One room contains fanciful riffs on the *sottae* poles that elevate wooden ducks into the sky as heavenly messengers. Bird forms on spikes sprout from such quotidian objects as an antique iron, an old Underwood typewriter, and the poster image of a helmet with barbed wire; old iron scissors morph into birds. The *changsŭng,* in warmer wood, have multiple forms. Picasso-like abstractions have misplaced eyes, noses, and genitals, all suggested by the form of the wood used to embody them. A *changsŭng*'s hollow belly makes a cavern for a little Buddha statue against the painted backdrop of a mountain. Another *changsŭng,* sprouting green grass hair, has the body of a cylindrical "bee house" whose aperture suggests a gaping mouth. Another breaks with type; instead of a *changsŭng*'s rough and basic eyes, nose, and mouth, this one has the finely drawn facial features of a general in a Korean classic comic book. In an alcove room, lit with candles, a female *changsŭng* sprawls on a traditional Korean meal tray, her legs of bowed wood spread wide, her pubes drawn in black ink, an allusion to the earthy custom of joining the *changsŭng* posts in marriage, male on top of female, before setting them up at the entrance to the village (Yi P. 1997, 271). A set of miniatures make an even more explicit comment, the male general sporting an enormous penis, the woman general with a gaping hole in the appropriate place, both endowments accommodated by the original shape of the wood. Portraits of old wood and stone *changsŭng* in stark rural landscapes hang sedately on the gallery walls, as if silently contemplating this riot of new *changsŭng*. These photographs are also the work of Ch'oe Hyŏng-bŏm, who wandered the Korean countryside with his camera until he became so captivated by the *changsŭng*'s mutable faces that he had to try to make them himself.[3]

In an exhibition of *changsŭng* and *sottae* held in the plaza of the Sejong Cultural Center to commemorate the reopening of the Ch'ŏngye Stream in the fall of 2005, sculptor Lee Garag (Yi Ka-rak) presented his own witty riffs on the *changsŭng* with this opening statement: "The *changsŭng*'s traditional form is carved with a modern sensibility. The carver's thoughts are given poetic form." The sculptor's own interpretations were appended to the sculptures. A *changsŭng* with a gaping mouth, missing teeth, and no fangs bears cosmological ideographs for "heaven, earth, and man." According to the artist, "the meaning of all things is explained in the *changsŭng*." A large family of *changsŭng* are marked with an array of folksy kinship terms that might be used in a large rural extended family. A *changsŭng* made from a twisted trunk and wearing a particularly foolish expression bears the ideograph for "nothingness" *(mu)* followed by a question mark. In my favorite rendering, a woman general stands grinning beside a male general's pole, his potential face marked only with horizontal lines. In an appended label, the artist explains, "I have shown what the Female General Underground would look like as she waits anxiously to see what the Great General under Heaven will look like."

Changsŭng as artistic expressions, as "tradition," in stark images of a rural past, *changsŭng* meant to provoke a smile — how distant they all seem from the demonic *changsŭng* in the museum case and whatever its bared fangs conjured for the Western missionaries who dubbed it a "devil post." In these new *changsŭng*, the vanishing village meets the World Cup and earthy rural humor stokes the wit of transgressive gallery art. Students of material culture have charted the multiple trajectories of material objects as they move between different regimes of value, their meanings negotiated and renegotiated through acts of consumption (Appadurai

1986a; Kopytoff 1986; Myers 2001b), sacred and quotidian objects become "commodities," sometimes as "art" and "artifacts" in museums and galleries (Morphy 1995; Steiner 1994), and particular handicraft productions become sites for the imagining of an Other (Jonaitis 1999; Phillips and Steiner 1999a; Spooner 1986) or for the celebration of an ethnic or national "us" (Myers 2001a, 2001c). Even my brief tour of Insadong suggests that all of this is at play in the production of (different kinds of) *changsŭng* as multi-sited distillations of meaning and value, different ways of thinking "Korea" and "Korean." But where the trajectory of an object biography commonly ends in a Western art gallery or museum or with a first world appetite for "folk" or "primitive" art stoking local production (Causey 2003; Forshee 2001; Graburn 1976; Phillips and Steiner 1999b), in the story I have to tell, the once-appropriated *changsŭng* image comes home to a relatively affluent Korea where sophisticated consumers and art-savvy producers invest it in new ways, both spiritual and commercial.

What is/was a *changsŭng*?

Folklorists describe the *changsŭng* as a guardian post of wood or carved stone in human form, commonly set up at the village entrance to protect it from malevolent sprits, epidemics, and other misfortunes but also found at temple gateways, where *changsŭng* dispatch demons, and used in dynastic times as road markers.[4] As village guardians, *changsŭng* received periodic veneration with wine, food offerings, and supplication as part of a sequence of rites enacted by ritually "clean" officiants, usually at the New Year, to honor the village gods and secure good fortune for the community.[5] Wooden *changsŭng* crumbled after a few years of exposure, and villagers periodically replaced them during the annual celebration. Ritually clean elders selected the tree. Villagers cut it down in an auspicious hour and brought logs of a suitable size down the mountain to where several villagers carved *changsŭng* faces with crude village tools. They painted on features and inscriptions with black ink and sometimes smeared the *changsŭng* with red earth to repel malevolent forces before setting them up with appropriate ceremony and celebration.

As enforcers of village morality, the *changsŭng* demanded respect and sometimes commanded fear. Like the ritual elders, those who carved *changsŭng* purified themselves by abstaining from meat, liquor, and sex and had no recent births or deaths in their families. Ritual lapses could re-

Figure 6.1. *Changsŭng* that used to frighten children on their way to school. Keystone View Company half stereograph. LC-USZ62-72671.

sult in misfortune both for those who performed the ritual and for the village as a whole. In 1989, newspapers carried the story of a stolen *changsŭng* and the subsequent death of the village chief, interpreted as divine punishment for his failure to protect it (Pak I. 1999, 193). A few people who had grown up in villages with active *changsŭng* traditions told me that they could still recall their feelings of dread when they passed the *changsŭng* on their way to school (Figure 6.1).

The face of an Other

Protestant Christian missionaries understood this veneration of spirits in material form as "idolatry," in Europe as a papist deviation, bowing down to the golden calf, and outside the West as one of "the marks of heathenism" (Gale 1898, 243; cf. Freeberg 1989; Gell 1998, 96–99). In missionaries' eyes, Koreans "made offerings to pictures,"[6] kept "fetishes" in their homes, and indulged in a "widespread materialistic idolatry" of which the *changsŭng* was a part (Poleax 1895, 144; Gale 1898, chap. 13; Gifford 1898, 106–117; Oak n.d.). In an age before the Western elevation of non-Western "primitive art," missionaries and other Western travelers to Korea reported that the *changsŭng* left a "painful" impression (Oppert 1880, 117), had a "ludicrous or absurd appearance" (Griffis 1911, 280), or were "hideous" (Cavendish 1894, 176; Moose 1911, 194). James Gale describes the *changsŭng* as grotesque, "cut roughly with grinning teeth, horrible face, the most ferocious eyes and ears" (1911, 86), while others see the *changsŭng* as "rudely carved" (Clark 1961, 198; Jones 1902, 42; Poleax 1895, 143). Even so, the awful form fascinates. They document it with photographs and use it to illustrate their accounts of life in Korea, committing their own fetishization in taking the *changsŭng* as visual evidence of "heathenism" and "idolatry," causing it to stand out, in Peter Pels' definition of the fetish, as something "'curious' and 'rare' from the everyday world of commodities" (Pels 1998, 103). Today many Korean Protestant Christians continue to regard the *changsŭng* as idols. Shopkeepers and sculptors all claimed that Christians do not purchase even the small decorative *changsŭng* that are sold as Korean handicrafts and souvenirs.[7]

From the late nineteenth century the *changsŭng* also entered the Japanese inventory of things Korean and the work of Japanese and Korean folklorists. Japanese folklore scholars, without the same religious ax to grind, saw the *changsŭng* as a curious feature of Korean material culture, speculated as to its origins, documented is distribution, and, like Western missionaries and travelers, sketched and photographed it. As early as 1890, Suzuki Kentaro offered a description of the functions and putative origins of the *changsŭng,* and in 1902, Yagi Shozaburo published a detailed study, based on fieldwork and illustrated with sketches and photographs (Knez and Swanson 1968, 72 #207, 76 #220). *Changsŭng* appeared in ethnographic and folkloric accounts throughout the colonial period.[8] First-generation Korean folklorist Son Ch'in-t'ae, writing in Japanese in 1933, produced a work on *changsŭng* that would be much-cited and to some degree modeled by subsequent generations of Korean folklorists, with its typology of *changsŭng,* list of variant terms for *changsŭng,* compendium of historical references to *changsŭng,* and speculations on their ultimate origins (Knez and Swanson 1968, 66 #186).

Through the dissemination of these different accounts by missionary, traveler, and colonial ethnographer — and especially the reproducibility of photographs — the *changsŭng* became "quotable" in Thomas Hine's sense of a widely disseminated iconic image that "works" because it resonates with consumer expectations that "might or might not be at odds with the meaning of the original upon which the icon was based" (cited in Jonaitis 1999, 121).[9] In 1919 a popular audience first encountered the image that now graces my favorite Insadong café when the Keystone View Company circulated it as a stereograph with the caption, "Natives praying to wooden devils, Chosen" (see Figure 6.1). In 1933, *National Geographic* used a pair of toothy "devil posts" as the lead image for a feature on Korea (Deering 1933, 111). Early twentieth-century photographs of *changsŭng* circulated freely between Japanese-language ethnography, popular consumption, and Western reportage on Korea (Gwon 2005, chap. 3). Although Sten Bergman's travelogue *In Korean Wilds and Villages* (1938) does not mention them, his illustrations include one of Murayama Chijun's ethnographic photographs of *changsŭng*,[10] originally published in a photographic album of Korean customs (Kim Tu-ha 1990, 538) and also circulated as a tinted postcard (Huang and Yi 1988, facing title page; Gwon 2005, 61).

In this same period, *changsŭng* were being produced, exhibited, and marketed, in effect "commoditized," independent of village, temple, or roadside settings. As early as 1889 a *changsŭng* was part of the exposition of Korean products at the Trocadero Palace in Paris, and later it appeared in local expositions inside Korea itself (Kim Tu-ha 1990, 503; Gwon 2005, 128, 142). The Peabody Essex Museum (then Peabody Museum) in Salem, Massachusetts, acquired pairs of *changsŭng* in 1927 and 1930.[11] After the Pacific War, the distinguished, if controversial, Japanese folklorist Akiba Takashi kept a *changsŭng* in front of his office at Aichi University, interpreted as a salvaging of "his experiences in colonial Korea . . . to recreate them in his office and at home" (Chun 2002, 165–166), in effect having the *changsŭng* stand for his own ties with Korea.[12]

In the manner of totem poles and tiki gods, *changsŭng* were also being miniaturized for souvenir consumption. The Museum of Anthropology at the University of British Columbia has a tiny Korean tableau, purchased sometime between 1898 and 1935 (Elizabeth Lominska Johnson, pers. comm., September 28, 2005). Five small wooden figures in Korean dress, including a grandfather in a long, white overcoat wearing a high-crowned black *kat,* a woman carrying a bundle on her head, and a bearded laborer with a burden on his back stand flanked by male and female *changsŭng,*

Figure 6.2. This Japanese woodblock print, probably from the 1930s, uses familiar postcard imagery, including *changsŭng*. Private collection.

a tiny three-dimensional inventory of much-photographed Korean curiosities. Gwon Hyeok Hui's research on the material culture of the colonial period describes how miniatures of this type were produced in Japan and transported to Korea to be purchased by returning Japanese tourists, and he has traced the familiar forms to widely circulated postcard images (Gwon 2007). This same Korean typology appears on a Japanese woodblock print of a Korean village scene, the grandfather now riding a small Korean pony, a woman carrying a clay jar on her head, and a row of *changsŭng* as background, composed with children leaning against them (Figure 6.2), as in that well-circulated photograph attributed to Murayama. The woodblock print and the souvenir miniature are fortuitous single fragments, but of genres usually produced in multiple. After liberation, Korean carvers would reproduce miniature *changsŭng,* alone or as part of little genre tableaux, for a new foreign audience that shopped at the US Army PX (Gwon 2007).

Rescued from the jaws of oblivion

If, in the first half of the twentieth century, the *changsŭng* had become icons of "Korea," by the time of the Korean War they were beginning to disappear from the countryside. Earlier reports had caused Cornelius Osgood to look for *changsŭng* when he conducted fieldwork in a village on Kanghwa Island in the late 1940s. A pair had disappeared from the neighborhood in the recent past, and the local fishermen told him how they had once supplicated the *changsŭng*, tossing scraps of food and wine libations with prayers for a good catch. "People bowed in passing and children were afraid of them, especially at night" (Osgood 1951, 126–127).

With the revival of Korean folklore studies in the 1960s and 1970s, the *changsŭng* became one more aspect of a vanishing rural Korea that called for careful documentation and preservation, not only of the *changsŭng* themselves, but of the "intangible culture" of ritual and belief through which they were constructed and venerated (Kungnimminsokpangmulguan 2003, 16–47; Yi T. 1984).[13] Folklorists worked with a particular urgency in the early 1970s when overenthusiastic participants in the rural-development-oriented New Community Movement (Saemaŭl Undong) sometimes razed religious sites in villages, including *changsŭng*, and discouraged the seasonal village rituals in the name of "anti-superstition" and thrift (Ch'oe K. 1974; Cho Hung-yŏn 1990, 36, 214; Im 1999, 18).[14] In more recent times, Christians have also been accused of late-night arson, setting fire to *changsŭng*, sacred trees *(sŏnang)*, and Mountain God shrines *(sansin'gak;* Ch'ŏn 2001, 228). In a well-publicized and frequently recollected incident in 1991, when the Tongjak Ward Office restored *changsŭng* to a site in Noryangjin where they had stood in dynastic times, the Christian community rose in protest and someone attempted to torch the female *changsŭng* in the dead of night.[15] Folklorists attributed the conflict to the perpetuation of "ignorance and misunderstanding" from the early Western missionaries to the now sizable Korean Christian community, an assumption that gave added urgency to their own work.[16]

That Tongjak Ward had replaced its long-vanished *changsŭng* testifies to a popular enthusiasm for folkloric revivals from the 1980s and a particular new interest in *changsŭng* from at least the end of that decade. Between 1988 and 1996 the National Museum of Folklore conducted a province-by-province survey of *changsŭng* (Kungnimminsokpangmulguan 1988–1997) and established on the museum grounds a park of replicas illustrating variations in regional styles, not garishly painted and demonically carved *changsŭng* but rustic forms that replicated the *changsŭng* of specific villages and weathered in the elements as wooden *changsŭng* were meant to do. As a measure of popular interest in *changsŭng*, the Minhaktongjihoe, a society of amateur folklore buffs, made their own weekend-by-weekend survey *(tapsa)* of regional *changsŭng* under the leadership of Kim Tu-ha, who presented the results in his encyclopedic study of *changsŭng* (1990, i).[17] Both scholarly and popular publications about *changsŭng* proliferated, the later ones lavishly illustrated.[18] In addition to existing souvenir and novelty production, carvers began to take commissions for large *changsŭng* that would stand in public parks, pocket parks, amusement arcades, private homes, in front of old peoples' homes, in front of village halls, in front of rural railway stations (inscribed as "Railway Changsŭng," or "Watch out for oncoming trains"), and as posts for signboards advertising other folkloric activities such as pottery production.[19] At the entrance to Hahoe Village, a carver produces "traditional" *changsŭng* even though the carver comes from another area and throughout its long prior history, Hahoe Village did not have *changsŭng* (Moon 2000, 93–94 n. 3).

The 1980s were a pivotal decade in South Korean thinking about the rural past; rural traditions — shamans, village rituals — once held responsible for Korea's "backward" state, came to be celebrated as part of a unique national essence, celebrations that took place both under official sponsorship and as opposition movement culture.[20] Popular folklore publications, folk performances, and folkloric motifs gained a broad audience even as (and not coincidentally) the hardships of village life faded beyond the lived experience of urban consumer memory. In 1988 a pair of *changsŭng* graced the entrance to the Seoul Olympic Park (Kim Tu-ha 1990, 572–574), and some carvers link the *changsŭng*'s current popularity to the 1988 Seoul Olympics, a genealogy that might also account for the identification of some *changsŭng* with sports (as we saw in Insadong). The new *changsŭng* also owe something to the Popular Culture Movement (Minjungmunhwaundong),which wedded protest theater to folk motifs and created new customs using traditional music, performance, and material cultural forms. From the mid-1980s the student movement raised newly minted *changsŭng* on several university campuses (Im 1999, 19), inscribed to capture the moment as "National Unification Changsŭng" (Tongil Changsŭng), "Great General Democracy" (Minju Taejanggun), or "Great General Who Liberates the Masses" (Minjunghaebang Taejanggun). These protest *changsŭng* went up amid percussive music and dancing, and with ritual offerings of rustic wine and rice cake, all intended to replicate the communal spirit *(kongdongch'e)* of village rites. These events did not include the full sequence of rites to village deities and elided the ritual dangers and taboos associated with setting up a village *changsŭng* (Kim Tu-ha 1990, 576–582; Yi Chong-ch'ŏl 1992, 521). At Yonsei University a particularly poignant pair were named "Male General of Paektu" and "Female General of Halla," capturing the popular reunification movement image of a couple sundered by national division in this evocation of Korea's northernmost and southernmost mountains as husband and wife (Kim Tu-ha 1990, 580–581; cf. Jager 1996). The "new" *changsŭng* moved beyond the campuses and, bearing appropriate slogans, appeared in support of the labor movement, the farmers' movement, and the pro-democracy movement (Kim Tu-ha et al. 1991, 109–113). This tradition continued in the ecological protests of more tranquil times. A pair of *changsŭng* went up at the foot of Pukhan Mountain in 1997 to protect a national park from the construction of an expressway (*Korea Newsreview* illustration, July 18, 1997). By chance, I encountered a group of *changsŭng* protesting a planned highway that would disrupt a quiet road of country weekend residences.

The Popular Culture Movement had brought the *changsŭng* into the domain of traditionalist-modern Korean cultural practices and had reinvented a celebratory ritual evoking village communalism that sometimes included setting up a *changsŭng*. These experiences have recuperated the *changsŭng* from the empty signification of a souvenir image. Contemporary commentators claim the *changsŭng* as a "symbol of Korea" (Im 1999, 5), a "widely regarded symbol of the masses [*minjung*]" (Yi Kwan-ho 2005, 4) or "something uniquely ours . . . something that can only be seen in our country" (Kim Tu-ha 1990, 20–21). The link between *changsŭng*, the rural past, the folk, and nationalist essentialism permits such novel uses as the Kyŏnggi Province Peace Festival 2005's website appeal for funds to build two "wish" *changsŭng*—"Support children in North Korea and show your will for the unification of families of the Korean Peninsula"[21]—or the South Korean performing arts troupe that, as part of their performance at the University of Hawai'i, carved a pair of *changsŭng* out of palm trees (Edward J. Shultz, pers. comm., June 5, 2006).

The face of self?

Scholars have also found new ways to rehabilitate the *changsŭng* in the service of Korean culture, writing against the grain of its prior image as visually demonic and ritually dangerous, as something that inspired fear in children, "especially at night." They note that although the *changsŭng* may wear a fierce expression, it is for a benevolent purpose, to protect the village from illness and misfortune by frightening away any malevolent incursion (Kim Tu-ha et al. 1991, 33). Yi Pilyŏng observes, "Although some *changsŭng* seem to be angry, they are only pretending. Some *changsŭng* have the appearance of grandfathers scolding their grandchildren out of affection for them, and there are *changsŭng* who recall well-intentioned country elders" (1997, 267). Suggesting that the village guardian's face is not so frightening after all, some commentators describe the unambiguously fearsome, fanged *changsŭng* as overdone "artist's creations" (Kungnimmin-sokpangmulguan 2003, 33) or, as one carver explained to me, a subgenre of *changsŭng* used by shamans and their followers for their own spooky purposes. The village *changsŭng*'s crude carving, grotesque to missionary eyes, becomes a virtue, an expression of simple but mysterious beauty or a warm folksy image: "Clumsy but not hateful, they have a friendly feeling" (Kungnimminsokpangmulguan 2003, 33); "Their eyes popped like a brass bell, snaggle-toothed, staring like a fool, mouth a gash from ear to ear, long unkempt whiskers, wearing a battered official's hat, standing vacantly at the entrance to the village or by the side of the road" (ibid., 16); "The *changsŭng*'s rough beauty [*kusuhanmŏt*] and jocularity are the product of our own distinctive aesthetic, wise, sincere, and sorrowful but not without a touch of humor" (Kim Tu-ha 1990, 22); "Like those who live close to the earth, baring soul and temperament with a naive eye and unadorned expression, the *changsŭng* might be said to resemble a simple-minded buffoon" (Huang and Yi 1988, n.p.). In its haphazardly carved and mysteriously abstract expression, the village *changsŭng* becomes the essence of the folk: "Typically smeared with dust and dirt, the *changsŭng*'s misshapen face is the face of our common people" (Kim Tu-ha et al. 1991, 8).

Contemporary postcard images pose the *changsŭng* not as a curiosity or a grotesque but as a sculptural form animated with its own personality. These artistic images, sold in Korean-language bookstores rather than at tourist sites, are produced for Korean consumption. Set in the empty landscapes of a depopulated countryside, the *changsŭng* call upon the viewer to see and embrace dimensions of Koreanness that, once abandoned, might disappear without a trace. In a similar vein, a couple of the carvers I spoke with hold workshops for students and teachers so that young Koreans will "know the *changsŭng*," so that it will be part of their education in national culture.

The sculptor Lee Garag (Yi Ka-rak) inscribed this sentiment on one of

Figure 6.3. Running *changsŭng*, by Lee Garak (Yi Ka-rak).

the contemporary *changsŭng* he exhibited in the Sejong Cultural Center Plaza (Figure 6.3):

> The *changsŭng* is an object that distills the history of the eastern country of Korea
> A face covered with the joys and sorrows of a Korean is the *changsŭng*'s face
> I am not a *changsŭng*
> But insofar as I am a Korean
> The *changsŭng*'s face could not but be my own.
>
> This being so, yesterday
> Today, tomorrow, I intend to be carving *changsŭng*[22]

Those who give form to *changsŭng*

In a country with a literate, educated population where works on national folklore are widely consumed by a popular audience, I was not surprised when the carvers sometimes sounded very much like the scholars I had been reading as they described the *changsŭng*'s traditional functions, regional distribution, and why the scary-seeming faces really weren't meant to be frightening. To fit the image of the *changsŭng* as a benign expression of Koreanness, the carvers I interviewed admitted to carving less severe, more approachable *changsŭng*. Beyond this, three carvers who make changsŭng as gallery art or high- and handicraft — Mr. Tak, Mr. Shim, and Mr. Pak[23] — emphatically and repeatedly insisted to me that their work is "not a commodity" (*sangp'um),* that it is something more spiritual. They were, of course, simultaneously making a case for their work as "art," distinguishing it from *changsŭng* kitsch, but the claims went beyond this. All in their forties or early fifties, they are young enough to have identified with the Popular Culture Movement and its claims for the expression of a collective Korean spirit experienced through direct contact with the music and arts of the common people, including a playful revival of ritual offerings made to *changsŭng*.

As carvers, they vest their work with a spiritual aura, distinguishing the act of carving from any odor of mechanical reproduction. Mr. Tak insists that *changsŭng* carving can be learned not from books but only intuitively: "You learn what a *changsŭng* is by carving them." He spoke of how a *changsŭng*'s face emerges as the carver peels away the bark, each face distinct to the piece of wood itself, not formed by the maker's prior design or his knowledge of regional styles. The play between misshapen wood and sculpturally distorted features and body parts, usually to comic effect, is a prominent feature in the work of all three sculptors. According to Mr. Sim, "It comes from the shape of the wood; you can't just trim the *changsŭng* round. It comes into being through humorous exaggeration *[haehakchŏgŭro ŏmjŏngnan chohuabŏp]*." He described the contemporary artist's insurmountable dilemma, attempting to self-consciously replicate in his workshop a form carved collectively by naive farmers armed with only crude gouging tools to produce a spontaneous effect — "Sometimes the eyes don't even match, because different people have carved them." His words reminded me (almost suspiciously) of Yanagi Soetsu's writing on the indigenous Zen spirit of Korean craftsmen (1978), the crude Korean rice bowls that were so painfully replicated by master ceramicists of

Japanese tea wares, words I had taken, when I first read them, as colonial romanticism. But in conversations with the three *changsŭng* carvers, nostalgic romance has an indigenous inflection (cf. Ivy 1995, 10 nn. 7, 12–13; S. Stewart 1984, xii). This carver idealizes the collective production of village *changsŭng* as a perfect material realization of that otherwise ephemeral concept dearly held by the Popular Culture Movement, "the collective body" *(kongdongch'e)* of village society as realized in village rites and communal feasting. The collective body was evoked by the pro-democracy movement of the 1980s in acts of politicized mimesis — the revitalized rituals, drumming, and dancing that preceded political demonstrations and were taken as a sacramental communion with the *minjung,* the long-suffering Korean masses.

What surprised me most in my conversations with these three carvers was how they have all managed to — in some sense — reenchant the *changsŭng* in their own practice. They perpetuate the legacy of the popular culture revival in making some sort of rice cake offering to the *changsŭng,* as part of their work. Mr. Tak carves many images for restaurant owners and affirms that all of his customers offer rice cake when they set them up, usually turning to the carver for instructions on winding a white cord between the male and female pair, dangling a dried fish from it, and setting up a steamer of rice cake, a pig's head, and rice wine. "If they don't do it they won't have good fortune *[chaesu]* in their business." In this instance, the village guardian has been transported to a modern setting — a restaurant — as an icon of "tradition," a street-side advertisement for the ambience inside, but it has also become, if not the fearsome village guardian of old, at least a tutelary of good business.

The carver Mr. Shim makes an offering when he receives a large shipment of wood or an exceptionally large commission, following the logic of Korean popular religion. He does this, he says, because *changsŭng* "are not commodities." When he went to France to carve *changsŭng* for a park, he organized a *kosa* — a ritual offering — to install them; in the absence of Korean farmers' music, he asked for local musicians and got a French military band.

Mr. Pak assumes that those who buy his art from a gallery generally regard it as art and install it in their homes without a *kosa,* although he speculates that "old people might." His own feelings for the *changsŭng,* however, are more complex. When we asked Mr. Pak if he believed that the *changsŭng* had a spirit *[sin],* he answered with no hesitation, "I believe,

I bow, I pray, and when I do my work, I bathe, I don't drink, and" — he grinned — "I'm someone who likes to drink." Mr. Tak and Mr. Pak described artisans' taboos against sex and other pollutions that they claimed to observe when carving *changsŭng*. Mr. Tak described a slip of the knife as a common punishment for negligence, and Mr. Pak rolled up his trouser leg to show us a gash on his own shin.

Mr. Na considers himself a pioneer of the *changsŭng* revival, but he does not share the younger carvers' claims to *changsŭng* spirituality. A successful designer of antique furniture reproductions and *sottae* poles, Mr. Na, now in his sixties, had a successful business in producing large *changsŭng* for bars, restaurants, and theme parks from the late 1980s until the Asian Financial Crisis of 1997. Mr. Na is a formalist. His approach to *changsŭng* carving is academic, based on careful research of existing *changsŭng* aesthetics, and knowledge of the "classical" *[kojŏn]* principles of Korean design, to which he makes constant reference in conversation. He insists that good *changsŭng* production, the ability to convey the "image" of Korea, emerges from a thorough knowledge of the history and philosophy behind *changsŭng* and the range of regional styles. Although he also asserts that the old *changsŭng* weren't really frightening — they were dignified *(wiŏm)*, exhibiting severe authority *(kwŏnwi)* to frighten inauspicious things away — he feels that contemporary *changsŭng* should convey a "friendly feeling so that people can get to know them." His own *changsŭng* were visually appealing *(pogijohahage)*, inviting to the potential customers of the bars and restaurants that installed them outside. "Really frightening *changsŭng* are for museums," he said. But while Mr. Na has made what he considered to be necessary modifications, he also assumes (as the Ministry of Culture and Tourism assumes when it designates Intangible Cultural Heritage) that there are limits to the degree that "our heritage" *(uri yusan)* can be adapted without its being irrevocably damaged. He is contemptuous of the younger carvers' willingness to work playfully with the shape of the wood and scorns their expressive, individualized styles. "A *changsŭng* does not have a laughing face. If people see them laughing, they get the wrong impression," he says.

Mr. Na regards "Korean tradition" as a thoroughly secular construct; he does not hold that spirits were ever associated with *changsŭng*: "People used to believe that *kwisin* [ghosts, demons] lived inside old trees. Not in the *changsŭng*. They were objects of veneration, like Buddha images, a place where people prayed to have their desires fulfilled."[24] He claims that he never had anything to do with offerings made to the *changsŭng* he carved and was vague about whether his clients might make *kosa* offerings when they installed them, but he affirmed, with a touch of patronization toward the folk, that such actions "have a good intention." Mr. Na's comments resemble the discourse of the early folklore revival, a desire to accurately preserve and perpetuate traditional culture but from a perspective of scholarly detachment. The distance between these sentiments and the gash on Mr. Pak's shin measures the degree of folkloric reenchantment evident in South Korean popular culture since the 1980s.

Conclusion

In his influential *The Social Life of Things,* Arjun Appadurai enjoined anthropologists of material culture to follow the object as it moves from one domain of signification to another. If recent writing on objects, commodities, souvenirs, and works of art causes us to assume a trajectory where things ultimately fall into the reinscribing maw of "the West"—from sacred object to commodity to museum artifact, to invoke a much-cited example—this story of the *changsŭng* suggests a more complicated peregrination to arrive at what one of the carvers described as "our ultimate folk handicraft" *(kajang minsokchŏgin kongyep'um).* What goes out as Other, as heathen idolatry and colonial curiosity subsequently trivialized into a souvenir, comes back recuperated as an artistic expression of self, an image creatively, sometimes playfully, restored in multiple manifestations, from unabashed commodities to art that claims to be anything but a commodity and something more than merely sculptural. This process took place through a close mingling of folklore scholarship, handicraft, and art production. Its realization would be possible only in a place like Korea (or Japan or some European states), where the imagined community is imagined as monoethnic, where national essentialisms are expressed through performance, photographs, and three-dimensional arts and crafts, and where relative prosperity permits self-consumption through such forms as popular folklore texts, illustrated coffee table books, decorative handicraft, and gallery art.

Notes

I am grateful to all those who took the time to talk with me and share their understanding of *changsŭng,* particularly the busy carvers and sculptors. This project would have been impossible without the enthusiasm of Ms. Sung-ja Kim, who worked as my field assistant. I would also like to thank Hong-nam Kim, then director of the National Folk Museum of Korea, and Kwan-ho Lee, senior curator, for sharing valuable information, as well as Susan Bean of the Peabody Essex Museum and Elizabeth Lominska Johnson of the Museum of Anthropology at the University of British Columbia for answering my many queries about *changsŭng* in their collections. Daenim Park of the National Research Institute of Cultural Properties provided me with a useful bibliography of Korean-language sources on *changsŭng*. This project also benefited from the archival work carried out by Kristen Olson and Christina Vuong during their internships in the Department of Anthropology, American Museum of Natural History. My research in Korea was supported by a visiting lectureship at the Academy of Korean Studies and by the Belo-Tanenbaum Fund of the AMNH. I alone am responsible for the shortcomings of this effort.

1. AMNH 70.3/2435 and 70.3/2436.

2. The AMNH *changsŭng* had been commissioned in 1978 from the Yurim Miyewŏn, a shop in Suyu-dong, Seoul, specializing in wooden handicrafts (Anthropology Archive, AMNH, accession envelope 1980–8). I would be most grateful for any further information about this enterprise.

3. His photographs of *changsŭng* have been featured in exhibits, in art books, and on postcards (e.g., Ch'oe H. 1993).

4. This summary follows general descriptions in Huang and Yi (1988), Im (1999), Kim Tu-ha (1990), Kim Tu-ha et al. (1991), Kungnimminsokpangmulguan (2003), Yi Chong-ch'ŏl (1992), Yi Kwan-ho (2005), Yi P. (1997), and Yi T. (1984).

5. As guardians of the village entrance *changsŭng* were lower spirits in lower shrines relative to the village tutelary, who was usually enshrined on elevated mountain space (Yi T. 1984), or in the democratic sentiments of recent decades, *changsŭng* were "closer to the people than other village spirits" (Kim Tu-ha et al. 1991, 12).

6. General Commission on Archives and History, United Methodist Church, Korea scrapbook 2, #25327).

7. The *sottae* poles mounted with wooden ducks or geese pose no such problem because they lack human form, and *sottae* of all sizes are well represented in shops and in wood sculptors' workshops, where the floors are littered with tiny wooden birds and twigs for miniatures.

8. See Yokoyama, cited in Knez and Swanson (1968, 85 #243), and prewar Japanese scholarly publications cited in Kim Tu-ha (1990, 499–514, 533, 538, 540–550). Akiba's discussion of the numerous theories of the *changsŭng* most likely predates the postwar English-language publication available to me (Akiba 1957, 8).

9. Surprisingly, in light of what would become, for a time, the standardized image of a *changsŭng,* the sculptures in many old photographs lack fangs and a few have no teeth at all.

10. www.flet.keio.ac.jp/~shnomura/mura/contents/album_6k.htm, #138.

11. The Peabody Museum purchased them (E20110 and E20111 in 1927 and E2089 and E20810 in 1930) from the Yamanaka Company, vendors of art and curios who had supplied several other Korean objects in the museum's collections (Susan Bean, pers. comm., September 5, 2005).

12. For a discussion of the ambiguities of Akiba's legacy as an enthusiastic student of Korean culture who was also a colonial scholar, see Ch'oe K. (2003).

13. Note also the number of sources from this era in Huang and Yi's comprehensive bibliography (1988, 170–172). Chang Chu-gun's 1959 photograph of a Cheju Island *tol harŭbang* (stone grandfather, a local variant of *changsŭng*) half buried, with discarded tires and an oil drum beside it, was published retrospectively by the National Museum of Folklore as "a measure of how cultural artifacts were disregarded at that time" (Kungnimminsokpangmulguan 2003, 44). This statue subsequently became Cheju folk artifact #2.

14. In April 1972, through the efforts of folklorists, village shrine trees *(sŏnangdang), changsŭng* enshrinements, and similar sites received legal protection as cultural properties (Kim Tu-ha 1990, 22).

15. The Christian community gathered 5,700 signatures on a petition opposing what they saw as an officially sanctioned act of idolatry or, in the words of one minister, "symbols of cheap culture, which shifts men's responsibilities onto pieces of wood" (M. Lee 1991, 29).

16. *Changsŭng* set up by students on the campus of (Christian) Yonsei University were similarly torched.

17. The museum's survey located 543 surviving *changsŭng* in South Korea. Kim Tu-ha's group surveyed 317 (Im 1999, 19).

18. See, for example, the citations in note 4 above.

19. This list is based on carvers' descriptions of their commissions and my own observations. One carver distinguished the signboard-bearing *changsŭng,* which can be made in a day and has no special meaning, from those that are actually intended to protect a house or business.

20. See, for example, C. Choi (1991, 1993), Howard (1989), Kendall (1998), Pai and Tangherlini (1998), and J. Yang (2003).

21. www.english.peacef.org/theme/stone/about.aspx.

22. Transcribed from the exhibited work itself. My translation.

23. Owing to the requirements of the Internal Review Board of the American Museum of Natural History, I am using pseudonyms for my interview subjects.

24. He brushed aside our observation that believers consider Buddha statues to be animated.

The "Kimchi Wars" in Globalizing East Asia

Consuming Class, Gender, Health, and National Identity

Kimchi, Korea's characteristic relish of pickled vegetables, garlic, fermented fish or seafood paste, and red chili pepper, is celebrated today as the central element of Korean cuisine, said to be universally palatable, delectable, nutritionally beneficial, and environmentally correct. Kimchi has been hailed as Korea's original health food and as a possible preventive for SARS and "bird flu." Kimchi has successfully overcome its prior identification as a smelly and combustible food and emerged as a potent symbol of national identity in a rapidly globalizing world (Han 2000). But even as kimchi's virtues are extolled as a source of national pride, South Koreans are actually eating less and less kimchi than in the past, and only rarely is it made at home.[1]

In this chapter, I focus on the consumption of kimchi in modern South Korea, suggesting that a deep sense of national anxiety about globalization undergirds kimchi's prominence as a national symbol in a country traumatized by colonization, war, division, and rapid industrialization and urbanization. I analyze two incidents dubbed the "Kimchi Wars" (*kimchi chŏnjaeng*) by the Korean press: the kimchi/*kimuchi* conflict with Japan in 2004[2] and the uproar over imported Chinese kimchi in the fall of 2005.[3] The experience of these two "wars" brought home to South Koreans the enormously complex and often arbitrary relationship between national identity and authenticity, particularly when the forces of globalized production and distribution are literally and figuratively invested in a recognized cultural tradition.

A brief social history of kimchi

Kimchi, as it is consumed today, was a relatively recent innovation in Korean cuisine. Red chili pepper was introduced to Korea, probably through

Japan, during or immediately after the Korea-Japan (or Imjin) War at the end of the sixteenth century. Even so, pickled vegetables with chili pepper are now regarded as an essential component of Korean cuisine and are consumed almost every day and at almost every meal (Han 2000). Kimchi is eaten not only with cooked rice but also with noodles, stuffed buns, rice cakes, beef, and pork and with drinks. It is so taken for granted that restaurants are expected to provide it gratis. Many Koreans crave kimchi when eating Chinese or Western food, which tastes greasy to a Korean palate, and many Chinese and Japanese restaurants in Korea, and even a few Western restaurants, serve kimchi without being asked. Other restaurants emphasize the authenticity of their cuisine and their classy status by refusing to serve kimchi. Uncouth people are unable to eat a meal without kimchi, while independence from a dietary obsession with kimchi is considered a mark of class and refinement (Han 2000). Even so, many Koreans seek out kimchi when they travel abroad, to avoid being deprived of it even for a brief time. But while kimchi has long been a staple of Korean dining, its status was peripheral, not central to the meal; it was a relish that was always supposed to be eaten with other food. This gave kimchi a somewhat ambivalent place in the meal structure of Korea; as a basic item, something always served, it was not counted as one of the proper side dishes in traditional Korean table d'hôte. Kimchi made the rice palatable, and its relative importance decreased in inverse proportion to the number of side dishes. A meal consisting of steamed rice, soup, and kimchi was regarded as a poor man's diet. Add three side dishes, and then you had a modest *sam-chŏp pansang* (meal with three side dishes); add seven, you had a luxurious *chil-chŏp pansang* (meal with seven side dishes). A Korean host would apologize, saying, "There is no *panch'an* [side dish]. I can serve only *pap* [steamed rice] and kimchi" (Han 2000, 221–236).

As the food habits of Koreans have changed, their consumption of meat, sugar, processed foods, and other items has increased rapidly, and obesity is now a serious problem in Korea. Experts blame misguided eating habits as the main cause of high blood pressure, diabetes, and other nutrition-related diseases. A new interest in healthy cuisine has fostered a new regard for traditional Korean food. Kimchi, soybean paste, and other foods that had been despised during the last few decades of intensive modernization as smelly, labor-intensive, and insufficiently nutritious are now being praised for providing vitamins, valuable inorganic compounds, and fiber and for boosting the metabolism. But in contrast with the recent past, these traditional foodstuffs are only rarely made at home and are commercially mass-produced and marketed.

Kimchi production was not commercialized until the late 1960s, when the first serious attempt at industrial production was undertaken for Korean troops in Vietnam.[4] Whatever the taste and quality of the first canned kimchi, it was very popular with these target consumers because kimchi could now be consumed in places where it could not be produced. After the Vietnam War, kimchi was exported to the Middle East for Korean construction workers during the late 1970s and early 1980s. But in spite of the immediate popularity of industrially produced kimchi abroad, Koreans at home were not yet ready to purchase and consume it, probably because of its comparatively poor quality and taste. Another reason was economic. Unskilled labor was abundant, and it was often cheaper for large organizations to make kimchi in-house. Only slowly did schools, companies, hospitals, and military units begin to purchase kimchi for their dining facilities. With developments in technology and packaging, the quality of commercially produced kimchi kept improving.

After the initially cold reception for industrially produced kimchi (Yi Chin-Haeng 2001), domestic demand accelerated. Changes in living arrangements and an increase in the number of working women resulted in increased consumption of factory-produced kimchi. In addition, more and more people began to eat out.

The decline of the kimchi network

Before kimchi production and consumption were commercialized, Korean women depended on what I call a kimchi network, a group of kinswomen who would gather to prepare a whole winter's supply of kimchi (*kimjang*) and/or participate in the exchange of kimchi. The network provided not only kimchi but also the opportunity to learn how to make "better" kimchi and how to live together. A young daughter would participate in *kimjang* as an apprentice and learn the basics of making kimchi as well as the art of living with female relatives and members of the house, who would exchange labor and information. She might master the basics of the art of making kimchi before marriage. When married, she would become a member of a new kimchi network at her husband's house and would begin to learn different ways of making kimchi from her mother-in-law. As her knowledge and skill matured, she would assume more important roles. Finally, especially if she was married to the eldest son, she would become the key player in the network and eventually take control of *kimjang*.

After the kimchi was made, a housewife might have sent some of it to her parents at her natal home, initially so they could enjoy a different taste, and later, when her mother became too old to make kimchi, to ensure that her parents had a continuous supply. This cycle worked both synchronically and diachronically. Kimchi and labor for kimchi were shared by those who participated in the annual *kimjang* and other kimchi-making events. Women would participate in *kimjang* in several different households.

This kimchi network is now an endangered cultural practice. One of the most obvious reasons is the change in living arrangements. More and more families have moved to *ap'at'ŭ* (apartment housing), where it is extremely difficult to make and preserve kimchi.[5] There is little spatial flexibility in the typical apartment, so it is difficult to pile up, wash, cut, and soak Chinese cabbages in salt water overnight. Some desperate housewives resort to using the bathtub. One joke about a mother-in-law shows both the importance and the transformation of the kimchi network in modern Korea. A young housewife would like to have homemade kimchi, but she is usually unwilling or unable to make it well; she is so busy that she cannot help her mother-in-law make it. Her mother-in-law, who wants her son and grandson to enjoy homemade kimchi, is willing to give her some. An average good mother-in-law, when her kimchi is ready, makes a phone call to her daughter-in-law and tells her to come to pick it up. A better mother-in-law makes kimchi and personally delivers it to her daughter-in-law's home. But the best mother-in-law does not enter her daughter-in-law's apartment but leaves the kimchi with the janitor; back home, she calls her daughter-in-law to tell her where she can pick it up.

Many Korean housewives (like the mothers-in-law in the anecdote) still take pride in being able to provide tasty kimchi for the family, but the number of such housewives seems to be rapidly decreasing while the number of those who do not know how to make kimchi is growing. Making kimchi might become a lost art for housewives in Korea in the near future. One expert predicted that more than half of the total amount of kimchi will be produced by big kimchi companies in five years. Kimchi's peculiar status as a peripheral element of a meal may be one reason why fewer and fewer Korean women now make it at home. For many women, kimchi is so basic that it does not feel appropriate to buy it at the market, but for others, because it does not count as a proper side dish and is difficult to make, preparing it does not seem worth the labor involved.

Another reason many younger housewives no longer make kimchi is the change in the value of women's work. Until the early 1980s, Korean housewives were expected to be thrifty and practical, living for their husband and children and, in those rare traditional households, for their parents-in-law. They were managers of no-frills consumption. Since their own beauty was for their husbands only, an ostentatious interest in cosmetics or bodily appearance was not encouraged and was even frowned upon. However, in the 1990s a new word, *missy-jŏk,* was coined by the media to denote married women who wanted to appear as fresh and stylish as unmarried women; the *missy* epitomized a new feminine consumer in an increasingly affluent society. Today, being a housewife in the traditional sense is increasingly regarded as unrewarding, and women are encouraged to describe themselves as interested in "self-realization" or finding "meaning in life." Modern Korean mothers as well as their daughters think there are more important things to learn than how to make kimchi.

A *missy* wants to feed her family good kimchi, but she is not willing to undergo the burdensome process of making it. Fortuitously for the busy contemporary woman, the kimchi that used to require much time and effort to produce and mature before serving, has now become a food that can be purchased in the market and consumed immediately. In other words, it has become possible to enjoy kimchi as a sort of instant food. This is quite ironic because kimchi is often praised by the Korean press for the "slowness" of its production and its healthiness, in contrast to the characteristics of hamburgers and other fast foods. For kimchi enthusiasts it does not seem to matter whether kimchi is made at home or not. The "slowness" of kimchi seems to refer to the fermentation process itself, regardless of how the kimchi is actually produced, and in the new millennium it is quite common to find kimchi, together with *toenjang* (soybean paste) and other traditional food, celebrated as "slow food" in Korea. In fact, several stores sell their "slow food" kimchi over the Internet.

Making the commodity palatable

As the double-edged media image of the desirable but self-indulgent *missy* suggests, consumption is an ambivalent act with a recent history of illegitimacy. In poorer times, government campaigns denounced extravagance and needless consumption as the enemy of the developing nation; production and thrift were praised as a source of national salvation. It has been difficult for those brought up under such circumstances to feel comfortable purchasing such a basic food item as kimchi. To overcome the moral disapprobation associated with consumption, Korean kimchi makers have developed marketing strategies that emphasize values such as hominess, tradition, authenticity, naturalness, the environment, safety, cleanliness, and nativism. Tellingly, the advertisements do not emphasize the convenience or benefits to women of simply buying kimchi instead of making it. Instead, advertisements for kimchi and other traditionalist goods make a nostalgic appeal to "motherly love" as manifest in the traditional methods and ingredients used to produce this component of a unique, traditional national cuisine (cf. K. Stewart 1988; Boym 2001). For example, a TV commercial for a brand of soybean paste shows a famous actress talking with her son-in-law, who is gratefully enjoying a dish that uses soybean paste. Satisfied with her son-in-law's response, she says that *meju* (soybean cake) should be ripened with the maker's care, sincerity, honesty, devotion, and so on. The son-in-law is deeply moved and asks if she personally made it. The mother-in-law laughs and says he shouldn't ask such a question. Sometimes the commercials tell an outright fabrication. The TV commercial for Haetbahn, a ready-cooked rice for a microwave oven, declares that the product is "rice cooked by Mother" or "rice that Mother cooked with devotion." For young Koreans who have been eating rice cooked in an electric rice cooker since childhood, such an advertisement borders on what Appadurai (1996) called "armchair nostalgia."

The Chonggajip company, which produces the best-selling kimchi in Korea, offers a fine illustration of this kind of marketing strategy. Its 2006 TV advertisement emphasizes motherly love and care only and does not discuss any details of the product. It starts with a housewife's memory of her childhood. She remembers her mother washing the hot kimchi so that she could eat it. That washed kimchi was obviously more than kimchi; it was mother's love. When she was a high school girl, she broke several bowls trying to help her mother with *kimjang,* but her mother did not scold her and simply smiled a quiet smile. When her wedding day came, she saw that her mother, who was saddened by the parting, had tears in her eyes. And then she remembers the kimchi her mother made and sent to her new home. Thus Chonggajip kimchi is more than kimchi. It is a mother's love. As the story is being told, we see watercolor paintings of the child and mother, the schoolgirl and mother, the mother's tears, and so on, with the song "Sealed with a Kiss" as background music. This advertisement for kimchi emphasizes belonging, nurturance, care and love, motherhood, and Koreanness.

Chonggajip kimchi is far more expensive than lesser brands, but it sells well. Chonggajip tries to persuade Korean housewives that its factory-produced kimchi is more than kimchi. It tries to make customers forget that it is fast kimchi, an industrially produced commodity. The brand name "Chonggajip" is another exercise in armchair nostalgia; it means the "Main House" of a prestigious lineage and so connotes tradition, prestige, authenticity, trust, duty, discipline of the house members (especially the daughter-in-law), devotion, and care and love for the ancestors and the elderly (see Moon in this volume).[6] In this context, kimchi provides an excellent example of what has been called the nostalgia business, the search for authenticity (Bendix 1997), or anticapitalist commercialism. Consumption offers new business opportunities to postmodern capitalists whose products promise to restore a sense of the good old days that modern capitalists destroyed in the industrialization process.

The success of this marketing strategy implies that one needs more than McDonaldization claims of efficiency (cf. Ritzer 2004) in order to produce and sell kimchi in Korea, where even the instant food industry seems to be increasingly emphasizing naturalness, traditionalism, hominess, (grand)motherliness, and the family atmosphere of its products. Kimchi producers, interested in creating a domestic market, had to persuade housewives not only that factory-produced kimchi is okay but also that some brands, not produced in the most efficient way, are actually better than others.

Kimchi and class

As a commodity, kimchi has become one of the most important class indicators in South Korea. Because enjoying homemade kimchi is a cultural ideal for Koreans, one can infer a person's class from the kimchi they have access to. Some affluent families manage to maintain the kimchi network, thanks to full-time or part-time helpers. Other families have relatives and friends in the countryside who can send them kimchi, thanks to the development of packaging and home delivery services. Some women are able to rely on a mother figure as a source of kimchi: an aunt, a relative, or a friend of a relative in the ideal rural town. A woman may alleviate her guilt by spending more money on a well-known brand of kimchi or taking the trouble to participate in a kimchi studio run by department stores and top-brand kimchi companies where she "makes" her own kimchi with the salted cabbage and other ingredients available for purchase.[7] She also believes the advertisers' claim that this expensive kimchi will make her husband and children healthy and happy as well as granting them higher social status. Kimchi shopping is, in this sense, a sacrifice vested with love (D. Miller 1998).[8]

The cheapest kimchi is now imported from China and sold in the traditional market and on Internet sites to restaurants and individuals. Because of rising costs, many Korean food companies have stopped making kimchi and instead import it from China, selling it under their own name. What is called OEM (original equipment manufacturing) for industrial products is practiced for kimchi too. Many housewives felt uncomfortable with Chinese kimchi at first, but more and more of them turned to it, finding that it was not really that different from the kimchi produced by small firms in Korea — at least until the second Kimchi War.

Higher-priced kimchi is manufactured by large Korean companies and sold at more prestigious places like department stores and large supermarkets. Some stores sell, under their own brand, kimchi produced by other companies. The most famous brand is Chonggajip, followed by labels such as Cheiljedang and Pulmuwon. In competition with this top-brand kimchi is the kimchi made and delivered to order. Although small-scale kimchi producers such as the Green Truck Uncle of Apkujŏng-dong are small in number, they have loyal customers. Their kimchi is more like homemade, fresh and safe. It is an example of the boutique kimchi favored by middle- and upper-middle-class housewives. The highest-priced kimchi is from the Chosun Hotel and the Shilla Hotel, the most luxurious hotels in Korea. The Chosun Hotel used to sell kimchi in a corner of Shinsegye Department Store in Seoul's expensive Kangnam District. The price was exorbitant, but some housewives would buy it and proudly present this prestigious kimchi to important guests. Although the most prestigious kimchi was still that made at home by experienced women, this hotel kimchi could serve as a nice substitute.

Kimchi goes global

One unexpected result of the industrialization and commercialization of kimchi production is the loss of variation in taste and a resulting standardization. Before production was industrialized, kimchi differed according to household, province, and season, depending upon the availability of ingredients and variation in climate. Although the customers for commercially produced kimchi were from all over South Korea, the kimchi factories were located in Seoul and the surrounding Kyŏnggi area and produced kimchi that imitated Seoul tastes, which were considered the least objectionable and most common. One reason why the flavor of Seoul and Kyŏnggi-area kimchi has become the commercial standard is not that it was the most popular but that it met the least resistance when served in blind tastings to customers from different regions. Kyŏngsang people may not love Seoul kimchi, but they can put up with it, something they find more difficult to do with Chŏlla kimchi. Chŏlla people may similarly favor Seoul kimchi over Kyŏngsang kimchi. Industrialization thus brought about the birth of "Korean" kimchi. This generic kimchi is sold in airports and at tourist spots instead of the distinctive kimchi of certain areas or seasons. Although there are as many as two hundred different kinds of kimchi, this fact is now conveniently ignored; one kind of kimchi comes to mind for Koreans as well as foreigners when they hear the word "kimchi." In an increasingly globalized world, this is only natural. Koreans are not only imagined as a nation that enjoys the same food; commercialization is making Koreans accustomed to the same flavor of kimchi nationwide. The commercialization of kimchi production reinforces the consciousness of Koreans that they constitute a single ethnic group. One tends to compare Korean kimchi with other foods, for example, Japanese *tsukemono* (pickled vegetables), and in doing so, one thinks unquestioningly of a representative type of kimchi, a naturalized component of the Korean nation and the South Korean state.

The Asian Games of 1986 and the Olympic Games of 1988 in Seoul were turning points in the consumption of kimchi, and export-oriented kimchi producers found a new market in Japan and elsewhere (Yi Chin-Haeng 2001). It was during the 1988 Olympics that Koreans began to actively ask foreigners to try kimchi for its taste and nutritional value.[9] Kimchi proved to be so successful that it became synonymous with Korea. Now foreigners, especially the Japanese, began to eat kimchi too (Han 2000).

Many Japanese had heard about or even seen kimchi, but very few had eaten it prior to the mid-1980s. Kimchi was the food of the colonized, and so it was looked down upon. In colonial times and during and after the Korean War, Koreans had been characterized as "kimchi-smelling." Japanese and Westerners seemed to consider kimchi as a marker of the odd and backward status of Koreans, obsessing about it in the manner of those European missionaries who had devoted much attention to African nakedness (Comaroff 1996). The ethnic cuisine boom in the so-called era of internationalization and the Seoul Olympic Games helped overcome the Japanese prejudice against kimchi. The growth of the kimchi market in Japan provided a new chance for Korean businesspeople to invest in kimchi production, and they expected ethnicity — the aura of Korean authenticity — to give them a competitive edge over Japanese firms in the kimchi market.

Kimchi's popularity can be understood as providing Koreans with a kind of compensation for the homogenizing forces of globalization. Following the Kim Young-sam regime's motto, "What is most uniquely Korean is most global [globally popular]," kimchi was a primary example of distinctively Korean things that can be popular on the global stage. In the big transaction called globalization, Koreans no longer had to feel like victims and losers insofar as they had succeeded in "globalizing" something uniquely Korean and making money from it, even as Koreans themselves were eating less kimchi than in the past.

The Kimchi War with Japan:
A question of honor or of business?

The *Korea Times* ran an editorial on July 7, 2001, celebrating the "Triumph of Kimchi": "Kimchi, Korea's undisputed national dish, was finally acknowledged on Thursday with an international standard by the general congress of the Codex Alimentarius Commission (CAC), based in Geneva." The editorial interpreted the CAC decision as meaning that kimchi would be referred to internationally as kimchi, while the term *kimuchi,* indicating the Japanese imitation, would no longer be officially used. According to the editorial, this granting of international status to kimchi meant that Korea's traditional cuisines could be developed into international dishes, depending on "our" efforts. Moreover, the editorial emphasized that this decision recognized Korea as the "suzerain state" of kimchi. Koreans were deeply moved because this decision was interpreted as a failure on the part of Japan, which had "dared to challenge Korea with its imitation, *kimuchi*."

According to the editorial, Korea had to compete with Japan to obtain the international standardization of the CAC, because Japan had mounted an international campaign against this move. Japan did so because export of its *kimuchi* would face restrictions if Korean kimchi was designated the standard. The *Korea Times* ended its editorial by exhorting the related government authorities and kimchi exporters to "double their efforts to further develop the Korean food."

This editorial gives the impression that the Kimchi War with Japan ended with Korea's glorious victory at the CAC. A cursory look at titles of newspaper articles such as "Kimchi Found to Be Authentic," "Kimchi Crushes the Attempt of *Kimuchi*," and "Victory of Kimchi over *Kimuchi*" seems to support that impression. However, if one looks closely, what the CAC actually accepted was a joint proposal by Korean and Japanese officials after a long consultation process. Insofar as *kimuchi* is the Japanese pronunciation of "kimchi," the two terms were simply two different pronunciations of the same word, meaning the same thing. However, in the mid-1990s, *kimuchi* came to mean ersatz or Japanese-style kimchi for many Koreans — kimchi without the salty and distinctive sour taste produced by fermentation and the use of fermented fish, shrimp, shellfish, squid, or fish guts. In 1995, Korea pointed out the need to set international standards for kimchi and submitted a draft proposal, which, if accepted, would have classified Japanese *kimuchi* as not up to standard.[10] Japan expressed the desire to participate in the drafting of the standardization proposal. In 1997, Korea and Japan held working-level talks four times to draft a joint proposal. It did not matter to these Koreans that the Japanese in general were not as interested in the outcome of this war. In the eyes of many Koreans, Japan's sinister attempt to snatch away their kimchi had failed.[11]

In the 1980s, Koreans had been delighted that the Japanese had begun to appreciate kimchi at last, whatever the style. When kimchi began to be served and sold widely throughout Japan in the 1980s, the Japanese called it *kimuchi* whether it was Korean- or Japanese-style kimchi. *Kimuchi* was still simply regarded as the Japanese word for kimchi. Just as kimchi was becoming popular in Japan, Korean kimchi producers were losing their market in the Middle East as the construction boom came to an end. Korean kimchi producers were confident that they could succeed in the Japanese market, not simply because they had experience and technology, but also because their kimchi was "authentic."

But as the Japanese market grew rapidly,[12] Koreans became increasingly anxious, because their market share of "authentic" kimchi was not increasing as expected.[13] Koreans realized that Japanese-style *kimuchi* was doing extremely well. To add insult to injury, *kimuchi* was declared to be different from kimchi and considered a Japanese invention. Korean newspapers even ran articles with such titles as "Kimchi Is Defeated by *Kimuchi*" and "The Japanese Table So Far: Kimchi Is Surpassed by *Kimuchi*." In this way "kimchi" and *kimuchi* came to mean two different things in the mid-1990s.

To the dismay of Koreans, many Japanese were enjoying what Koreans might call kimchi salad, instead of the rich taste of ripened and properly seasoned kimchi. Koreans expected the arrival of the "Korean wave" *(hallyu)* — the vogue of Korean popular culture — to boost sales, but the result was less than satisfactory. For Koreans, *kimuchi,* the ersatz kimchi, was driving out good, authentic kimchi. What was more shocking was that Japanese producers were trying to export this Japanese-style kimchi to the world.

Korean producers as well as the government were alarmed at the prospect of losing not only the Japanese market but also the entire global market for kimchi to Japanese *kimuchi* producers.[14] This fear was not entirely groundless; there was widespread concern that Japanese manufacturers were diligently registering internationally the microorganisms used in traditional foods. Some writers warned that Koreans might lose their sovereign rights over traditional foods and become a colony again, this time of Japanese food.[15]

This conspiracy theory was easily spread because it confirmed the stereotype of Japanese "ingratitude" and "cunning." It is widely believed in Korea that Koreans "taught civilization" to the Japanese and that the Japanese not only refused to acknowledge this debt but invaded Korea in 1592 and then colonized it in 1910. According to popular belief, all the splendid things in Japan are there because Koreans passed them on or taught them in the past. The problem, it is believed, is that cultural advances originating in Korea are now better known in their "made in Japan" form. It is also widely believed in Korea that the Japanese are not very creative but are extremely good at copying, their imitation of the American automobile industry being one of the best examples. Even though the word *kimuchi* was only the Japanese way of expressing "kimchi," many Koreans began to consider *kimuchi* to be an adulteration of the sacred name of kimchi.

The Japanese seemed to be appropriating kimchi and claiming it was of Japanese origin.

During this alleged Kimchi War, a certain Mr. Hwang, a Korean citizen, succeeded in registering in his name Internet domain addresses that had "kimchi" and "kimuchi" in them. When the Korean media learned that such domain addresses as www.kimchi.com, www.kimuchi.com, www.kimchi.net, www.kimuchi.net, www.kimchi.org, and www.kimuchi.org were in the hands of a Korean, a reporter was immediately sent to interview him. Mr. Hwang proudly declared that he had done this in order to thwart Japanese efforts to sell or advertise *kimuchi* on the Internet. The reporter happily ended his report by remarking that the Japanese were now deprived of the chance to open a "*kimuchi* site" on the Internet.

Koreans were satisfied with the CAC decision, which they interpreted as a victory over Japan, and celebrated their triumph. However, this was a victory in name only. Nothing had really changed in the Japanese market. Use of the word *kimuchi* was still permitted and in fact the word could be written only that way in the Japanese katakana syllabary, and whether fermented or not, *kimuchi* was recognized as a kind of kimchi and continued to sell well in the Japanese market, while the "real" kimchi was not making much progress even after this great victory.

Korean producers were keenly aware that they needed to change the authentic, traditional taste of kimchi to make it more palatable to foreigners, reducing its saltiness and omitting *chŏtkal* (pickled fish) if they wanted to increase sales and profits. But they also needed to make kimchi that differed from both *kimuchi* and Chinese kimchi.[16] To the surprise of Korean producers, the supposed advantage of authentic Korean-made kimchi sometimes turned out to be a liability. However, if they made kimchi in the *kimuchi* style, they would lose the distinctiveness of Korean kimchi. This was a big dilemma: Korean kimchi producers were faced with changing the taste of kimchi and losing the claim of authenticity, or retaining kimchi's identity and losing their customers.

The Kimchi War with China:
For the health and wealth of the people

The Kimchi War with China broke out by accident in the autumn of 2005. It started with the October 20 announcement by the Korean Food and Drug Administration that it had found parasite eggs in nine samples of sixteen Chinese kimchi products. Imports from China were banned briefly. Headlines hit the familiar chord that food imported from China was unsafe and that Koreans should eat Korean produce. Many other incidents drew attention to the safety of food imported from China. In 2005 alone there were at least six incidents in which such food was found to be unsafe. National Assemblywoman Kyeong-Hwa Koh made food safety a major issue in her political career, and in September 2005 she was successful in bringing attention to the high lead content in kimchi imported from China. She then asked the agency whether Chinese kimchi was free from parasite eggs. Her motivation was apparently food safety, but one agenda in emphasizing safety and cleanliness in 2005 was to encourage the consumption of domestic agricultural produce.

And kimchi is no ordinary food. Because it is so uniquely Korean and so closely related to national identity, many Koreans found it galling to have to eat kimchi made in China. Thus, even though nobody had planned this war, Koreans were ready for a fight when it broke out. But to their surprise, Chinese authorities also got infuriated and took several measures clearly indicating their displeasure. The Chinese government shut down kimchi factories and prohibited the export of kimchi. It also announced that it had found parasite eggs in many Korean brands of kimchi. The news that one could not trust Korean kimchi as well as Chinese kimchi created a "food scare" in Korea (cf. Beardsworth and Keil 1997). China slapped an import ban on South Korean–made kimchi and several side dishes at the end of October and even threatened to ban Korean cosmetics. The Korean government was alarmed at this strong response and immediately tried to calm the situation by announcing that they, too, had found parasite eggs in kimchi produced in Korea. However, they added that these eggs were harmless, a statement that could be interpreted as a confession that Chinese kimchi was not actually harmful either.

The public was first angered, then puzzled, and then infuriated. When they learned that the whole fuss had been much ado about nothing, they criticized the government for making the announcement too hastily, misleading the public and spreading groundless fear, ruining businesses, and damaging the good name and image of kimchi as a health food. This Kimchi War, started by a salvo of the Korean government and mass media, ended in a hurried attempt to hush up the incident. The result was a loss of trust in commercially produced Korean kimchi and damage to its reputation. The hidden aim of the war, if there was any, was to curb the increase in the import of Chinese agricultural produce; but this strategy backfired, revealing that domestic brands could not be trusted either. A survey conducted immediately after the incident showed that about 46 percent of all respondents said that they planned to make their own kimchi, and only about 9 percent answered that they would buy kimchi in the market. The others said that they would make kimchi together with their relatives.[17]

Ironically, this Kimchi War with China destroyed the Korean share in the Japanese kimchi market rather than the Chinese share in the Korean market. Korean imports of kimchi from China began a steep increase half a year after the war, but because Japanese restaurants and mess halls could afford to serve the more expensive domestic *kimuchi,* Korean exports to Japan fell drastically and failed to recover quickly, owing to the reports of unhygienic Korean kimchi. In South Korea the public response was quite emotional because of the importance of kimchi to Korean identity and the outrage of housewives who felt guilty about having fed their families substandard kimchi.

Conclusion

Behind the emergence of kimchi as part of the national image of Korea lies national anxiety about a globalizing world. Underlying this anxiety is the power of this kind of consumer good to serve as cultural "ballast" and as an "object-code" (McCracken 1990). If there is a "certain crucial nexus of unease about culture itself and its transmission and stability in Japan" (Ivy 1995, 9), then in Korea, a nation that experienced a number of traumas in its recent history, such anxiety can only be more profound and complex.

This dispute with Japan, focused on the authenticity of Korean-made kimchi over Japanese-made *kimuchi,* took shape against a history of Korea's former colonization by Japan and in a contemporary context of globalization, where Koreans hoped to dominate the emerging kimchi market in Southeast Asia, America, and Europe. Less apparent, but perhaps more important, was the desire to defend ethnic intellectual copyright claims over kimchi. However, as we saw, Koreans were soon faced with the disturbing question of whether kimchi's authentic Korean taste could be compromised in order to gain markets outside Korea. The Kimchi War with China, centered on a food safety scare, gained enormous emotional support from the press as well as from housewives who felt betrayed, angry, and guilty. This war that started with much sound and fury ended rather abruptly and was hushed up by the government. Koreans could not mobilize "culturalism" as they had in the Kimchi War with Japan. Instead they had to resort to relative "civilization" by emphasizing hygiene and safety. Korean kimchi, once expected to dominate the emerging world market because of its "authenticity," wound up not only fighting a protracted, if not a losing, battle against *kimuchi* (ersatz kimchi) in the Japanese market but also being driven out of the domestic market by cheap Chinese imports.

What has happened on the "home front" before, during, and after these "wars" has involved not only questions of international trade, national identity, health, and food safety but also changes in lifestyle, class identities, women's work, and consumption patterns in modern Korean homes. Ever since kimchi became a national symbol in the affluent and internationalized Korea of the 1980s, Korean mothers and housewives have often been faulted for no longer making kimchi and instead buying Chinese imports. Thus Korea, the "suzerain state of kimchi," seems to be in a crisis: Korean women are abandoning the ancient art of kimchi making, Korean children prefer hamburgers and pizza to kimchi, Korean families no longer consume homemade kimchi full of motherly love and affection *(chŏng),* kimchi is losing its original taste and regional diversity, the Korean kimchi market is being invaded by "unsanitary" Chinese imports endangering health, and Korean kimchi producers are going out of business. Pessimists claim that when kimchi is driven out of the Japanese and world markets by *kimuchi,* the world might "little note nor long remember" that kimchi is Korean.

The Kimchi Wars were part of a moral panic over Korean family life, Koreans' health, the Korean economy, and Korean identity itself. Through these two disputes, Koreans were forced to confront the extremely complex and sometimes arbitrary relationship between national identity and authenticity in cultural tradition, as well as the enormous power of globalized production and distribution. Even something so clearly and distinctively Korean as kimchi is undergoing a profound transformation in its production and consumption as well as its identity and taste.

Notes

1. According to a report by the Korea Rural Economic Institute, the per capita consumption of kimchi in Korea decreased from 35.1 kilograms in 1991 to 32.4 kilograms in 2004 (*Yonhap News* 2005).

2. *Kimuchi* is the Japanese reading of "kimchi." The Japanese writing system (kana) is a syllabary, rendering *ki-mu-chi* the closest approximation to "kimchi" in Japanese.

3. Koreans have been consuming kimchi imported from China since the late 1990s. In 1998 the import volume was 10 tons. It grew to 92 tons in 1999 and 407 tons in 2000 and then decreased to 392 tons in 2001. In 2002 it again grew, to 1,041 tons. Since then it has increased dramatically, to 28,701 tons in 2003 and 72,605 tons in 2004 (*Yonhap News* 2006).

4. According to Manjo Kim (2001), it was during the Korean War (1950–1953) that the first non-homemade kimchi was produced. The Korean government commissioned scientists to create kimchi rations to meet demand from the battlefield.

5. Kimchi refrigerators were widely used after 1995, when the Mando Gongjo company invented the Dimchae, which was claimed to be able to reproduce the taste of kimchi fermented in a jar buried in the earth (www.dimchae.co.kr).

6. The firm started as a member of the Doosan Group, a conglomerate in Korea that bottled and sold Coca-Cola in Seoul, Kyŏnggi, and Kangwŏn provinces until 1997. The Doosan Group sold Chonggajip to the Daesang Group in 2006.

7. Chonggajip, ever since it first began to produce and sell so-called "brand" kimchi in 1987, has claimed that its product was the result of scientific research, sanitation checks, and quality control, unlike the kimchi made by lesser-known smaller firms and sold at traditional markets. Its share in the brand kimchi market has been above 60 percent since 2000.

8. As a rough idea of the relative costs of *paech'u* (cabbage) kimchi (the most commonly served), "Hotel Kimchi" costs six times more than "Hong Jingyeong Kimchi," an average-priced brand kimchi. Some Korean "brand" kimchi is priced 20 to 30 percent higher, others are priced 10 to 20 percent lower, and less well-known brands at even 40 to 50 percent lower than Hong Jingyeong Kimchi. At 30 or 40 percent more than the price of Hong Jingyeong Kimchi, it is possible to order kimchi supposedly made in a more or less traditional way. The cost of Chinese imports is 20 to 30 percent that of average-priced Korean "brand" kimchi, or 50 percent that of lesser-known "brand" kimchi. Middle-class households can afford to purchase "brand" kimchi at department stores and supermarkets or on the Internet. More economically minded people will buy kimchi of lesser-known or no brand, usually made by small firms. When they do not see much difference, they will buy Chinese imports. It is estimated that the production cost for one kilogram of Chinese imports is 700 Korean won, while that of the domestic kimchi is 1,800 Korean won.

9. Laurel Kendall, who came to Korea first as a Peace Corps worker and then as an anthropologist, says that she "cannot remember how many times" she was asked, after years of experience in Korea, whether she had ever "tried kimchi."

Kendall, like many other foreign residents in Korea, had to make efforts to convince Korean friends that she really liked the taste of kimchi, and she says that liking kimchi was a badge of pride and distinction for Americans in Korea in the 1970s (pers. comm.).

10. Chong Dae Sung (2004) points out that the Korean proposal to set the international standard for kimchi was intended to make Japanese *kimuchi* below standard. Although the official reason for needing an international standard was food safety, it was clear that the real reason was economic.

11. In fact, this is far from the truth. The final joint proposal recognized Japanese *asazuke kimuchi* in the category of kimchi.

12. According to one survey, as much as 95 percent of the food stores in Japan were already selling kimchi in 1992. Managers of these stores felt that they had to have kimchi on their shelves in order to be considered a proper food store (http://k.daum.net/qna/openknowledge/view.html?qid=3HpNW).

13. The total sales of Korean kimchi in Japan reached 23,861 tons in 1999 but decreased to 22,261 tons in 2000 (Cheon 2000). However, the sale of Japanese-style *kimuchi,* produced by Japanese firms with cabbage and red pepper imported from China, increased by more than 30 percent annually from 1997 to 1999 (Cheon 2000). The fierce price competition among Korean producers, which adversely influences the quality and taste of kimchi, might also cause lower sales.

14. The export of kimchi accounted for 5 percent, or $100 million, of the total of exported South Korean agricultural products in 2000 (Korea Agro-Fisheries Trade Corporation, www.kati.net).

15. The importance of rights over microorganisms was easily understood because Koreans were already familiar with the selling of domestic seed plant companies to American businesses during the so-called IMF Crisis (more broadly known as the Asian Financial Crisis of 1997).

16. In October 2004, KOTRA (Korea Trade-Investment Promotion Agency) announced that Japan's import of kimchi from China had increased 30 percent over that of the previous year, making China the largest supplier of kimchi in the Japanese market (*Joongang ilbo* 2004).

17. Survey conducted by Brand Stock, a brand evaluation firm (*Korea Times* 2005).

Part IV

Korea Performed

The metacultural outcome — heritage, both the designated masterpieces and the heritage enterprise itself — is intended, if not designed, to be better adapted to the social, political, and economic conditions of our time than the endangered practices themselves (even were they not endangered). This is why heritage is a mode of metacultural production that produces something new, which, though it has recourse to the past, is fundamentally different from it. — Barbara Kirshenblatt-Gimblett, "World Heritage and Cultural Economics"

South Korea has been at the vanguard of efforts to preserve and protect intangible cultural heritage. South Korea's model would subsequently influence UNESCO's creation of a system for designating and preserving World Intangible Heritage. Such projects are not without critics, both within South Korea (C. Choi 1991, 54) and internationally (Kirshenblatt-Gimblett 2006), who see such practices as freezing once-innovative forms and for encouraging conformity to universal standards and protocols that may make awkward fits with local practice. Barbara Kirshenblatt-Gimblett argues that any effort to preserve and foster exemplary and endangered cultural practices "alters the relationship of practitioners to their practices" (2006, 196), a phenomenon well documented in Keith Howard's studies of traditional South Korean performing arts and their modern fate (1989, 1998) and Chungmoo Choi's account of how heritage designations intensified rivalry and competition among a community of shamans (1991). At the same time, it should be recognized that without the intervention of folklorists and bureaucrats, what we know today as "Korean culture" would undoubtedly be flatter, narrower, and far less fun.

The two chapters in this section share concerns with the slippery category of "authenticity" in the performance of old forms for new audiences. Judy Van Zile describes an early twentieth-century performer of "new dance" whose turn to Korean forms was widely criticized as inauthentic, but with the fullness of time, Ch'oe Sŭng-hŭi's work has become the basis of what are now regarded as signature traditional Korean dances. Keith Howard describes an ongoing argument among performers and connoisseurs of traditional Korean music, between purists and adherents of commercially more successful fusion. These chapters suggest that the debates themselves are the stuff of significant engagement with the performance of culture and are themselves a proper subject of ethnographic inquiry.

Blurring Tradition and Modernity

The Impact of Japanese Colonization and
Ch'oe Sŭng-hŭi on Dance in South Korea Today

To many people, Korea's modernization in the twentieth and twenty-first centuries has meant Westernization. For some dancers, turning away from the sedate dances of the court and the satirical stories of village masked dance-dramas in favor of the *pointe* shoes of European ballet or the contraction-release technique of US modern dancer Martha Graham has been the path to modernity. For other dancers, becoming modern has not meant creating a dichotomy between what had been traditional and what was being done in the West. Instead, a tension developed between reconciling the past and the present. The dilemma became, How can one be modern in a uniquely Korean way?

This dilemma still provides a creative tension in dance in Korea today, but its seeds were solidly planted during Japanese colonization, with the dancer Ch'oe Sŭng-hŭi (1911–1964?) playing an important role in its establishment. The nature and style of dances she created contributed to shaping what scholars today describe as *shinmuyong*, or new dance.[1] The term *shinmuyong* paralleled *shinbuyō* (also meaning new dance), which came into use in Japan in the 1920s, and reflected terminology being applied to many things in Korea; as the country increasingly tried to modernize, Koreans began to speak of new poetry (*shinshi*), new education (*shin'gyoyuk*), new theater (*shin'gŭk*), and even new women (*shinyŏsŏng*).[2] The emphasis was on "the new," and Ch'oe Sŭng-hŭi sought to create a new kind of dance, one that was different from the kinds common prior to the twentieth century — the dances performed for entertainment in the royal courts, the dance-dramas of the villages, the dances of shaman, Confucian, and Buddhist rituals.

Despite their development during the early- and mid-twentieth century as something "new," and the use of "new" in today's terminology for identifying them, many of these dances have come to be considered, for general consumption, as representative of "traditional" Korea. The terms "tradition" and "traditional" are fraught with conflicting definitions and understandings. I use them here as they are generally translated from the Korean *(chŏnt'ong)*, and to refer to the kinds of things many Korean dancers and dance scholars today identify as traditional. They are most typically associated with dances that are old and are visually recognizable as being Korean. As will be shown here, however, what constitutes old and Korean dance is constantly being redefined, and a modernized dance tradition has become a contemporary commodity intended to represent Korea both in the past and today.[3]

This chapter examines selected dance characteristics and experiences of Ch'oe Sŭng-hŭi, their relationship to the times in which she lived and performed, and their contribution to a kind of dance that serves, today, as a visual symbol of Korea. Ch'oe began her dance career and quickly rose to stardom during colonial times. Her explicit desire to be Korean but in a modern way, and to satisfy diverse audiences in the dances she choreographed and performed prior to relocating to what is now North Korea, are foregrounded in order to show the impact she had on dance in South Korea today. Ultimately her experiences and the kind of dance she pioneered point to issues involved in the ongoing redefinition of tradition and who defines it, and in the uses of tradition in modern times.

Throughout the discussion it is important to keep in mind that history is slippery and all too often leaves a trail of unanswerable questions. It is challenging to determine the so-called facts of what transpired, particularly when they relate to an intangible art form such as dance, or to motivations from a time when personal beliefs that served as the basis for actions were constantly shifting as political policies changed and individuals sought ways to navigate the intertwining webs of colonialism, modernity, and nationalism. Because of the volatile era in which she lived, her husband's and possibly her own political entanglements, emotions related to her eventual iconic status, and censorship that erased many people from Korea's history, including its dance history, there is often conflicting or missing information about the details of Ch'oe's life and work. Nonetheless, these challenges do not preclude examining the ironies involved in how modernity has contributed to defining tradition in dance and how a modernized tradition became a national symbol in Korea. The biographical sketch and information provided here chart selected landmarks in Ch'oe's life, but the discussion focuses on her activities during the colonial period, because the dances she created then left an indelible mark on dance in South Korea today.

Biographical sketch

Ch'oe Sŭng-hŭi was born into a wealthy upper-class *(yangban)* family in the city of Seoul on November 24, 1911, a little more than a year after Japanese colonization officially began.[4] The youngest of four siblings, she was still a child when circumstances changed abruptly — her family lost property they owned, and her father's penchant for drinking strained the family coffers.[5] Her personal life, as well as the political and social upheaval of the period, contributed to challenges that marked both her youth and her artistic career. It was "a time when cultural earthquakes rocked our country," as one Korean described it, and "the modern world knocked, pounded, and battered its way into our consciousness" (Kang Pyŏngju [Kang Byung Ju], quoted in Kang H. 2001, 6).

The impact of these "earthquakes" on Ch'oe began at the time of her graduation from Sukmyŏng Girls' School in 1925 and continued when, in 1926, her brother took her to see a performance in Seoul by the visiting Japanese modern dancer Ishii Baku (1886–1962).[6] Her fascination with what she saw performed on a Western-style theater stage was tempered by prevailing negative attitudes toward dancers. In an autobiography written when she was only twenty-five years old, she said, "I thought dance was something low and crude. But with the influence of my brother's words, as I watched the stage my whole being was quickly attracted . . . by some kind of powerful inspiration. . . . Ishii's famous works . . . have a powerful underlying feeling that evoked the spirit hiding at the bottom of my heart" (quoted in Hirabayashi 1977, 188).

Encouraged by her brother, Ch'oe met with Ishii to inquire about studying with him, and much to the chagrin of her family, particularly her mother, she followed Ishii back to Japan. She studied with him for about eight years, with several periods during which they severed their student-teacher relationship and then resumed it. Throughout those years, she performed in both Seoul and Tokyo, sometimes with Ishii's company and sometimes independently. She opened a dance studio in Seoul in 1929, but because of financial difficulties it was short-lived.

While continuing her dance studies and establishing a performing career, in 1931 Ch'oe married An Mak, a political activist who became a recognized socialist writer and played a major role in her dance career.[7] An completed a university degree in Russian literature, graduating in 1935 from Waseda University. In 1932 they had a daughter, who later became a dancer, and in 1945 (while in China), a son, who became a violinist. In 1935 Ch'oe signed a contract to star in the film *Hanto no Maihimei* (The dancing princess of the Peninsula), a phrase often used to describe her in later years.[8] Ch'oe's career began to escalate, and in addition to her success as a dancer, she became a popular female icon, appearing in newspaper advertisements for such things as stationery, makeup, and snacks.

From 1938 to 1940 Ch'oe toured and performed in North and South America and Europe. She returned to Japan at the end of 1940, just before the United States entered World War II. Prior to her tour Japan had become Ch'oe's primary home, but when she returned, she began to move back and forth between Japan, Korea, and China, sometimes to perform and sometimes to flee the rapidly changing political climate. In 1945 or 1946, first her husband and then Ch'oe and her children fled to P'yŏngyang, where they remained when the Peninsula was officially divided.[9]

Ch'oe performed in North Korea, set up a school, and eventually became a favored government officer.[10] Her school gained national support, and in the early 1950s she received government recognition for her role in the arts, including the title of Peoples' Actor for her contribution to "authentic art during the war against America" (Takashima and Chŏng 1994, 215). Her husband became increasingly involved in political activities but, because of his views, lost favor with the North Korean government. In 1986 a Japanese publication claimed Ch'oe, her daughter, and her husband had been arrested and executed, but gave no dates (ibid., 214). The same year, a Korean dancer resident in Japan reported that name lists published annually in North Korea had included Ch'oe until 1964, but not after that time (ibid.).[11] In February 2003, Ch'oe Sŭng-hŭi was one of twenty-two people reburied in the North Korean Cemetery of Patriots and was "rehabilitated" as a People's Actor (Park 2006, 632).

Dance training

Ch'oe describes her introduction to Korean dance as coming from her father: "When my father was in a good mood, he stayed at home relaxing, and when he drank too much, he got carried away and showed me a dance called *kutkŏri ch'um*. . . . In Korea this dance was presented at parties when people started getting drunk. While I watched him dance *kutkŏri ch'um*, I was memorizing it without even knowing it" (quoted in Hirabayashi 1977, 187). *Kutkŏri* refers to a particular drum rhythm, and *kutkŏri ch'um* identifies a kind of informal, improvised dance done, as Ch'oe describes, by untrained individuals at parties. People who do *kutkŏri ch'um* usually incorporate movements similar to some of those they have seen executed by trained performers, such as lifting and lowering the shoulders, extending the arms sideward at shoulder height, and inwardly rotating the arms and relaxing the wrists so the fingers point downward. Ch'oe's introduction to Korean dance, therefore, was as an "audience member" at an informal "performance." Although the movements were representative of many kinds of older Korean dance, what she saw was not a fixed choreography that used clearly codified movements, nor any of the dances performed for entertainment in the former royal court or on special occasions in villages.

Ch'oe's formal training, which was not in Korean dance, began in 1926, the year she followed Ishii Baku to Tokyo. Ishii was initially reluctant to take Ch'oe on as a student, because of her lack of dance training. But eventually he "began to think that it might be important to have an excellent dancer come from Korea to soften the relationship between two ethnic people, and also for the Korean people to be known in the world" (Hirabayashi 1977, 189). These words suggest the importance he gave to maintaining some kind of distinct Korean identity, despite the country's colonial status, an issue that became increasingly important in Ch'oe's dance aesthetic.

The focus of Ch'oe's training was the Italian-style ballet and Western-style modern dance Ishii had learned and subsequently adapted.[12] Despite his training in ballet, Ishii questioned its validity and favored modern dance, but he believed that directly importing Western dance was boring and that there was a limit to simply imitating its form. He wanted to create a new kind of Japanese dance that was not just an imitation of other forms and that was concerned with issues of humanity and modern society. His works were noted for being harsh, often dealing with themes of social injustice and poverty in a realistic manner.[13] Although at first he made a conscious effort to reject traditional Japanese dance, feeling it was trapped in the past, he eventually came to believe that his roots had subconsciously imbued his dance with both a Japanese feeling and originality and that one must "reconstruct one's own ethnic spirit using an international or universal technique" (quoted in Hirabayashi 1977, 193).

Ishii's desire to both retain a Japanese aesthetic and develop something original had a strong impact on Ch'oe, leading to a tension she felt as she developed her own dance style and moved through her career. On the one hand, she was pulled by what many considered "traditional"—the older dances of Korea that were believed to exhibit a uniquely indigenous aesthetic and had been performed in villages or the royal court before colonization and exposure to Western modern dance. On the other hand, she was keen to draw on the contemporary, Western-influenced concert dance of her training with Ishii Baku. These pulls were further tempered by her desire to please her audiences and be a successful performing artist, political tensions within Korea at the time, and the push for modernity, which often meant Westernization, within the country as a whole and particularly in the performing arts. What is ironic is that the tensions Ch'oe experienced increasingly throughout her dance life continue to be manifest in the Korean dance world in the twenty-first century, and that the kind of dance she created is now regarded as unambiguously "Korean."

Development as a dancer

Ch'oe originally choreographed dances in the modern style of her teacher.[14] Photographs of some of these dances are remarkably similar to those of what was known as *ausdruckstanz* (expressionist dance) or *neue tanz* (new dance) in Germany, a kind of dance that is generally believed to have begun at the end of World War I and that spread rapidly, becoming the hallmark of a modern trend in dance throughout Europe. It advocated a freedom in the use of the body that was uncharacteristic of older dances of Korea's court and villages, was concerned with expressing strong personal emotion through movement, and often dealt with social themes from the darker side of life (Manning 1993; Partsch-Bergsohn 1994). It was this style that was blossoming in a modernizing Japan and that had so deeply affected Ch'oe's teacher, Ishii Baku. Ch'oe originally began to choreograph her own dances in this style, declaring, "I like to express something that has social meaning and that is full of the feelings of life. Although it might be a little complex dramatically, I like to express something that has substance" (quoted in Takashima and Chŏng 1994, 58).[15]

A photograph of one of Ch'oe's early dances, *With No Path to Follow* (choreographed in the early 1930s), shows the dancer's tension-filled fingers spread widely and arched, both arms bent at the elbows in harsh angles, and a dramatically mournful expression on her face.[16] Her costume includes a tight-fitting dark skirt with a hem that descends diagonally from about hip level to halfway between her knees and ankles, the edge torn in long strips as if pulled from a rag bin, and a wide swatch of dark fabric, draped around her neck and pulled taut across her breasts, reveals a bare midriff. As she balances on the balls of her feet, reminiscent of ballet, and sports short, bobbed hair, this image clearly reflects the Westernizing trends in dance as well as assertive feminist attitudes becoming popular at the time in both Korea and Japan.[17]

When Ch'oe performed this and other similar kinds of dance in Korea, they generally were not well received. Whether because of then-current negative attitudes toward dancers, particularly women, or the newness of the style, many people could not find a connection to what they were seeing on stage. And some were troubled by a woman dancer performing in a public setting. In former times women dancers usually were either itinerant village performers or official court entertainers *(kisaeng)*. When the court-sponsored *kisaeng* system was abolished, the Japanese government established a legalized system of public prostitution that absorbed many former court entertainers (Ha 2005). Thus the public could not easily distinguish between "dancers" and "prostitutes," and being a female dancer brought with it a stigma that had to be fought against constantly. One recent writer describes Ch'oe as having to "endure the hostile gaze of the conservative milieu that did not understand her art and considered her to be just a single [unmarried] woman," people who were thus unable to focus on her as a performing artist (Young-hoon Kim 2006, 174). Some writers believe Ch'oe married An Mak to specifically counter this attitude, which considered a woman performing on stage, and hence calling attention to being physically observed, an open advertisement for her sexual availability (see Park 2006, 604).

In 1933 Ch'oe returned to Ishii Baku in Japan following her first solo performances in Korea. Ishii encouraged her to abandon the foreign contemporary aesthetic approach she was using and to go back to her own roots. At that time Han Sŏng-jun (1874–1942), a Korean dancer who was developing his own style based on traditional Korean forms, was in Japan. Han had begun his dance studies with his grandfather, learning traditional tightrope walking, drumming, and some southern styles of village dances, including shaman dances. During the early 1900s he re-created and rearranged many village dances for theatrical performance by female entertainers (H. Choi 1995, 173).[18] Ch'oe studied with Han, but only for a short time.[19] It is unclear whether the brevity of her study with him was due to his involvement with female entertainers and Ch'oe's concern with distancing herself from such people or to her interest in moving beyond the older-style Korean-flavored dance Han was doing in order to develop her own style. But her days with him planted seeds for her interest in the dance of her own people, leading to some further explorations of older dances when she returned to the place of her birth. Like both Ishii and Han, however, she became intent on developing a style of her own, one she described as being "Korean in essence but that was capable of responding to and expressing modern concerns" (Ch'oe Sang-cheul 1996, 211–212). Thus, as Ch'oe implemented her aesthetic philosophy, the tension between retaining a unique, specifically Korean identity and reflecting the growing trend toward a Western-influenced modernity intensified. Her challenge was not to be Korean *or* modern but rather to find a way to be modern in a particularly Korean way.

Ch'oe's concern with a Korean identity in her dance has been construed by some as capitulating to Japan's policies to foster, at times, things of Korean heritage, as reflected, for example, in the comments of her teacher, referred to earlier, when he articulated a rationale for taking on a Korean student.[20] When looked at from this perspective, her artistic choices can be interpreted as catering to Japanese authorities who were in a position to prohibit or censor performances. At the same time, however, this concern can be interpreted as demonstrating Ch'oe's own desire to maintain a visible Korean-ness in her dance. Ch'oe may have been joining some Korean cultural nationalists who, given the new opportunities afforded by the freer policies of the colonizer at times during the occupation period, returned to their older art forms in order to reestablish an identity distinct from that of Japan. In either case, her actions reflected conflicting trends between the modern and what was described as traditional, in the sense of being older and pre–Western influence, manifested in both Korea and Japan. Her actions also probably reflected her desire to satisfy the diverse expectations of her ticket-paying audiences, something she had to do if she was to continue her career.

As Ch'oe began to clarify her aesthetic focus, she created a piece titled

Ehea noara (choreographed in the early 1930s, after *With No Path to Follow*), which became a signature work for many years.[21] Early pictures of this dance, and film footage of her performing it much later in her life, show an image antithetical to her previous works. In *Ehea noara* we see a figure completely concealed in traditional-style Korean men's clothing — legs covered in baggy Korean pants *(paji)*, arms and torso concealed in a traditional-style long cloak *(turumagi, or top'o)*, feet covered in tight-fitting socks *(posŏn)*, and a short stovepipe-style hat *(kat)*. Her positions in various photographs of this dance show her arms extended sideward at shoulder height, her head tilted, and suggest shoulder actions often identified as stereotypical features of older ("traditional") Korean dance.[22] The lifted knee in many of the photographs, together with the broad smile on Ch'oe's face, suggest the joviality found in *kutkŏri ch'um*, the dance Ch'oe remembered her father doing when he had drunk too much and was relaxing, and whose movements she claimed to have memorized as a child. This kind of dance reflected the new direction her choreography had begun to take — toward a visual image recognizably linked to some older Korean dance forms at the same time that it deviated from them. The extroverted presentational nature of the dance and its lifted leg gestures would not have been appropriate for a "traditional Korean woman."

Despite the seeming Korean-ness of *Ehea noara,* it was harshly criticized by a Korean playwright and journal editor who described it as "co-opted with vulgar popularity" and further suggested that Ch'oe "study more deeply and show the rightness . . . of an elegant and solemn Chosen [Chosŏn, or Korean] dance" (Ham Dae-hun, quoted in Park 2006, 612). The reason for the severe critique was likely that a dance similar to those improvised by men at drinking parties had been performed by a woman, onstage, and had employed greatly exaggerated movements and facial expressions not typical of, for example, dances previously performed for court entertainment. But the views of Koreans varied; while some saw such dances as making a mockery of Korean culture, others considered them a source of national pride (Park 2006, 611). One Korean critic suggested that Ch'oe had been successful in her goal to modernize Korean dance when he commented that in *Ehea noara,* as well as another dance, "she melded the material of indigenous dance in her own artistic kiln and molded it in a new way" (quoted in Takashima 1959, 61). This critic, as well as some other early writers in both Japan and Korea, praised Ch'oe for creating new versions of older dances (e.g., Kim Ch'ŏng-uk 1999, 78–81). In-

Figure 8.1. Ch'oe Sŭng-hŭi in a pose from *Young Korean Bridegroom*, a dance that appears to have been similar in nature to *Ehea noara*. Photographer unknown (Jerome Robbins Dance Division, The New York Public Library for the Performing Arts, Astor, Lenox and Tilden Foundations).

terestingly, however, the Japanese tended to favor her Korean-style dances more than the Koreans did.[23]

Ch'oe continued to create new dances she claimed were rooted in older ones, with such titles as *Korean Festival Dance, Peasant Girl, Young Korean Bridegroom,* and *Drum Dance* (see Figure 8.1). In many of these she wore costumes readily discernible as adaptations of traditional Korean attire

Figure 8.2. A still of Ch'oe Sŭng-hŭi from the dance sometimes referred to as *Bodhisattva*. Photograph by Soichi Sunami (Jerome Robbins Dance Division, The New York Public Library for the Performing Arts, Astor, Lenox and Tilden Foundations). Courtesy of the Sunami family.

(hanbok), and many photographs suggest modifications of movements used in older dances considered to be traditional. One dance, however, stands out in sharp contrast to these and, like *Ehea noara*, became another signature piece. It was known, at various times, as *Kwanŭm posal, Posalmu, Pohyŏn posal, Kamu posal,* or simply *Bodhisattva* (Figure 8.2).[24] What made this dance distinctive were both its costume and its movements.[25] Although the costume changed at different times, its most common version was extremely revealing, to the extent that Ch'oe was sometimes described as being seminude (Mishima Yukio, quoted in Park 2006, 614). Small pieces

of fabric studded with beads and sequins concealed only the most feminine parts of Ch'oe's anatomy. A heavily beaded belt rested seductively on
her hips, bejeweled bracelets were the only adornments on her arms, and
her legs were revealed beneath drapes of beads and jewels. Her bare feet
were accentuated with colored polish on her toenails, and a large jewel-
studded crown rested on her head. Still photographs capture her hands
in highly articulated finger positions reminiscent of many forms of East
Indian dance, and film footage shows her executing movements not at all
typical of known older Korean dances.[26]

Bodhisattva generally received very favorable reviews in Korea, Japan,
and abroad, often noting Ch'oe's exquisite body and sensual movements.
Although images of a Bodhisattva figure are common in Buddhist paintings in Korea, some Koreans considered the dance not at all Korean.
Among the many things that make Bodhisattva intriguing is that it is
clearly antithetical to the so-called tradition-based dances Ch'oe was beginning to choreograph. It is possible she created it to cater to popular
appeal in order to enhance support for her career. It is likewise possible
that the way in which she so daringly revealed her body was an assertion
of women's rights. And Ch'oe's own words suggest yet another rationale
for this rather unusual dance that became a favorite in her repertoire. In
a printed program from a performance in 1941 she describes the *Painting of Bodhisattva,* which was likely some version of what is known today
as *Bodhisattva,* together with several other dances, as having been "taken
from oriental material in a broad sense" (quoted in Takashima 1959, 154).
We can only wonder if she took a broadly Asian approach as a way to express worldliness and hence, modernity, as well as to cater to an audience
becoming increasingly intrigued with other parts of the world. Given the
trend at the time toward asserting women's rights, and Ch'oe's concerns
with being a successful dancer and pleasing diverse audiences in order to
do so, it is likely that all of these factors were involved in her decision to
create such a dance.

Direct foreign influence

Until the mid-1930s the influence of Western culture on Ch'oe's dance had
been filtered through elements of modernity that came via Japan. But in 1936,
ten years after her formal introduction to dance and after she had gained
widespread popularity in both Korea and Japan, a more direct Western in-

fluence took on a much greater role in her development. In 1936, plans began to evolve for an international performing tour for Ch'oe, and on December 19, 1937, she set sail for the United States. In preparation for this unprecedented travel by a woman dancer from Korea, Ch'oe's efforts became centered on the content of her performances, with pleasing foreign audiences a focal point. In a newspaper interview just prior to her first performance abroad (in San Francisco, California), Ch'oe stated, "If I am a success here I am sure that I shall be successful on my present trip around the world" (*New World-Sun* 1938). She suggested some of the kinds of changes she likely made in her choreography, as well as her continuing concern with both tradition and modernity, when she further stated that some "traditional" dances were "too long to perform onstage or too short and simple to perform onstage" and that therefore she "wanted to create something original and new that fits this contemporary era" (Anonymous 1938).

Ch'oe's early performances in the United States were not entirely favorably received.[27] In San Francisco one reviewer stated that "anyone who expected deep revelations of the mystic East . . . was disappointed" (Fried 1938); another declared that the "program remained on an even keel of mildly pleasant, unexciting entertainment" (Frankenstein 1938); and a third described Ch'oe's debut as "slightly dull, slightly boring, slightly entertaining" (Fisher 1938). Ch'oe's foreign audience also seemed to desire something very specifically Korean, but what that meant to people who had never seen Korean dance is puzzling. One reviewer felt that the second half of the program she saw, which was "devoted to ancient court dances, had far more interest, intrinsically and artistically, than [the] opening folk dances, which had covered a wide variety of subjects . . . with too little variation in tempo" (ibid.). Another writer reflected the strong interest of the times in "the Orient" when noting that the performance "seemed more like the sort of thing a somewhat conventional and old-fashioned Occidental artist might bring back from the orient rather than the kind of thing one expected from an artist reared and trained in the traditions of the Far East" (Frankenstein 1938). The desire for something more "Korean" or "Far Eastern" is intriguing, given that Ch'oe is generally described as the first Korean dancer to perform in the United States and that her primary training in Western-style modern dance with Ishii Baku actually paralleled that of an "Occidental artist." It is likely that reviewers and members of the audience did not know what *was* Korean, but thought they knew what was *not* Korean. What they certainly did not appear to know was that the very notion of what constituted Korean dance was changing even in Korea.

As Ch'oe continued her US tour, went on to Europe, and then returned to the United States, she had the opportunity to see not only the contemporary developments in the countries she visited but also what was being performed by dancers visiting from other countries. In addition to classical ballet and the kinds of modern dance performed in both Europe and the United States, she saw performances of East Indian dancer Uday Shankar, who was engaged in some of the same kinds of experimentation she was.[28] Whether most strongly influenced by some of the negative comments about her early US performances, by new things she was seeing, or by a desire to create works that would be recognizable as Korean at a time when political turmoil was increasing, there were differences between Ch'oe's early US performances and those before she returned to Japan. These differences can be ascertained from the titles of dances she had not previously performed in the United States and their descriptions in printed programs and publicity materials, and from comments made by reviewers and Ch'oe herself. Just prior to her final US performance, Ch'oe specifically stated her concern with displaying a more readily recognizable Korean image: "My program . . . will be entirely Korean. . . . I have gained much experience since my appearance here two years ago and have modified my program to give an exclusively oriental tone" (quoted in *New World-Sun Daily* 1940). At the same time she believed she was presenting a uniquely Korean image, however, she was catering to the foreign critics' notions of what that meant. Among the dances Ch'oe introduced on her return performances in the United States — most of which she had choreographed prior to her first US tour but had not performed at that time, and which she had likely revised since their initial creation — were *Sleeve Dance,* described as originally being popular among waiting women in the court; *Three Traditional Rhythms,* described as being based on fundamental movements of Korean dance, and *Two Court Dances,* said to have been originally performed at royal ceremonies.

Ch'oe's stated concern with being accepted by her foreign audiences suggests that changes she made stemmed from her desire for uniqueness, which meant satisfying her audiences' (as represented by her reviewers') aesthetic preferences and imagined visions of what constituted either Korean or "Oriental" dance. This translated into making her dances more palatable to an Occidental audience that originally saw a sameness in what she did and could not see anything that suggested to them the "exotic other." Ultimately, while it moved her further in the direction of creating works that were both visibly Korean as well as in some way modern, the Korean-ness was defined, at least in part, by the expectations of her non-Korean audience. This is reflected, for example, in one review of her last major New York performance, which commented, "[Ch'oe] has not made the mistake of bringing Korean dances to us out of the whole cloth. Rather she has heightened them dramatically for Occidental eyes" (Anonymous 1939). This suggests that from the perspective of at least one foreign re-viewer, Ch'oe was, indeed, successful in being Korean in a modern way.

Various versions of the dances Ch'oe performed most frequently in the United States are still performed in Korea today. *Scarf Dance* (a predecessor of what is now known as *Salp'uri*), *Fortune Teller* (often known today as *Shaman Dance, Shaman Fortune Teller,* or *Mudang ch'um*), *Fan Dance* (*Puch'ae ch'um*), and *Drum Dance* (now usually referred to as *Changgo ch'um*) serve as icons of Korean dance in performances for visitors to Korea, as part of programs performed by Koreans and Korean Americans outside of Korea, and in popular-oriented performances within Korea (see Figure 8.3).[29] These dances also find their way into other media. An analysis of posters intended for tourists from the 1960s to the 1980s, for example, points out that among the most frequent images were those depicting women dancers performing a fan dance or a drum dance (Young-hoon Kim 2003, 95–96).

The kinds of "modern Korean" dances Ch'oe choreographed are part of the style of dance often identified today as *shinmuyong*, or new dance, of which Ch'oe is described as a major innovator.[30] Although originally choreographed and performed in Korea and Japan and modified during her tour abroad, the interest in Ch'oe's dances in the United States and other foreign countries undoubtedly contributed to their ongoing popularity upon her return to Korea. And it was the constructed view of "Korean" dance that evolved during Ch'oe's 1938–1940 foreign performances — the result of Ch'oe's own training, her views about modernizing dance while rooting it in past tradition, and her choices based on foreign responses — that contributed to a lasting set of Korean dance icons.

Constructed images of "the Orient" were common in the 1930s and 1940s. People in the United States and Europe fantasized about the "exotic other" even though they had little, if any, direct knowledge about faraway countries or their knowledge came through performances adapted

Figure 8.3. Ch'oe Sŭng-hŭi in a pose from *Court Lady of Shiragi*, a likely precursor to contemporary versions of *Fan Dance*. Photograph by Soichi Sunami (Jerome Robbins Dance Division, The New York Public Library for the Performing Arts, Astor, Lenox and Tilden Foundations). Courtesy of the Sunami family.

for world's fairs and the often culturally biased reports of travelers. Such images are reflected in the advance press coverage of Ch'oe in the United States as well as in reviews of her performances there. The practices of frequently billing her as an "exotic dancer," stereotyping broad expanses of the Asian world by describing her "dances of the Orient," and criticizing her for "characterizing" Korean dance rather than actually doing Korean dance all reflect an assumed concept of the "other." At the same time, however, there was acknowledgment that Ch'oe should, and indeed did, modify her presentations for her foreign audiences. Since she was purported to be the first Korean dancer to perform abroad, the basis for what constituted Korean dance in the eyes of American writers and audience members could only have been in the imaginations of those watching and writing.

Politics and dance

Views are divided on the political beliefs and allegiances of Ch'oe Sŭng-hŭi and how they may have affected her dance aesthetic.[31] Although a full examination of her politically related involvements is beyond the scope of this discussion, several occurrences show politics as an important contributor to the way in which her dance developed, how it was used by various constituencies, and the necessity of her making adjustments to her dance in order to satisfy her audiences and continue her career as the sociopolitical environment changed.

It is likely that support from both Japan and the United States for Ch'oe's foreign tour was related to cultural diplomacy. Prior to her 1937 departure, the US consul general sent a letter to the American secretary of state in Washington, D.C. (Marsh 1937). He enclosed with the letter a *Seoul Press* newspaper article indicating that Ch'oe's upcoming US tour "would by her presence there help promote the long-standing friendly relations between Japan and America" (*Seoul Press* 1937). And Sang Mi Park observes, "Japanese commentators agreed that a cultural figure like Choe [*sic*] would serve an intermediary role most appropriately as one who would solve the uneasy tension and conflict among the nation states" (2006, 610). Perhaps because the repertoire Ch'oe performed in the United States, unlike some of her early choreography, did not make explicit political statements, her dance was perceived as an innocent visual cultural ambassador. But the mere fact that what she did was described as "Korean dance" did make a political statement, at least for some people, as reflected in demonstrations outside some of the theaters where she performed.

Even Ch'oe's name proved to be a political statement for some. As she rose to stardom in Japan and Korea and embarked on travels abroad, she began to use "Sai Shōki," the Japanese pronunciation of her name, as was becoming mandated for Japan's Korean subjects.[32] Thus, while on tour she used the Japanese pronunciation of her name, was largely described as a Korean dancer, and was purported by those who did not know her own descriptions of her choreography to be doing traditional Korean dance. All of this demonstrates the different constituencies contributing to the use of Ch'oe and her dance, and the different ways in which individuals were constructing the definition of tradition.

Ch'oe returned to Japan in late 1940 from her international tour and shortly after went to the China front to perform for Japanese soldiers. Although the nature of the full repertoire she performed for the soldiers is uncertain, it is clear that while she continued to do some of the Korean-style dances she had performed previously in Japan, Korea, and the United States, her dances also began to change, sometimes displaying political themes.[33] It is her dances from the late 1930s, however, that had the greatest impact on dance in South Korea today.

One writer believes that because showing Korean ethnicity during some periods of the occupation was suppressed, *anything* Ch'oe did was a political statement, even though her only motivation was to dance (Chŏng Pyŏng-ho, quoted in Takashima and Chŏng 1994, 38). Consciously or subconsciously, Ch'oe simply may have been reflecting the complex issues dealt with by everyone at the time, when living under Japanese rule could not help but color one's choices.

Explicit political use, and nonuse, of Ch'oe and her dance occurred after her death. When the South Korean government wanted to completely efface knowledge about individuals who had gone to North Korea, censorship was imposed and Ch'oe was erased from dance history. When censorship was lifted in the 1980s, a controversial article in a 1989 issue of the Korean magazine *Kaeksŏk,* as well as a 1994 Japanese publication (Takashima and Chŏng) and a 1995 Korean publication (Chŏng P.), contributed to research that began to reinsert Ch'oe into the history of dance in South Korea. This effort escalated with a 1998 performance by Paek Hyang-ju, which fostered a virtual Ch'oe Sŭng-hŭi mania. A young dancer then residing in Japan, Paek studied with her dancer father, described as an adopted son of Ch'oe Sŭng-hŭi (Tedesco 1998). Paek's 1998 performance in Korea featured works said to have been reconstructed from those created by Ch'oe, and together with the removal of censorship, it led to numerous master's theses and doctoral dissertations, symposia, publications, additional performances, and television programs about Ch'oe, as well as to controversy over Ch'oe's repertoire, her political inclinations, and interpretations of her motivations.[34] Some of the publications, research, and activities were supported by government funding, and all contributed to establishing Ch'oe's place in the history of dance in South Korea and to further embedding her contributions to dances performed today. Thus a dancer once erased from history has now been reinstated, and works in a style she created have been labeled "traditional."

Ch'oe's impact on dance in South Korea

That Ch'oe identified herself, and was most often put forward, as a performer of *Korean* dance likely contributed to her becoming a female icon in both Korea and Japan, albeit for different reasons, as well as to her popularity abroad. And these reasons reflect different ways in which culture is consumed. Some may have seen her icon status as a Japanese effort to establish a physical symbol suggesting support of both something traditionally Korean and of the Korean people. But the physical symbol simply would have been the literal Korean body that was put onstage, since there were varying amounts of "traditional" Korean-ness in the dances Ch'oe choreographed and performed — or at least differences in the way tradition was being defined. This visibility, together with any potential Korean-ness in her dances, contributed to dividing the population of Korea who followed Ch'oe's career. Reaction to her modernizing of older forms, as described previously, was mixed; some felt it important to adapt older things to contemporary times, while others believed that only by adhering to older forms could a distinctive Korean identity be maintained. Ch'oe had fans and detractors in both Korea and Japan.

It should be clear by now that the dances Ch'oe performed and her experiences at home, in Japan, and abroad during the period of Japanese colonization constitute an anomaly. Was she conciliatory in allowing herself to be used by the Japanese for their own political purposes? Was she taking advantage of concerns, among both the Japanese and the Koreans, for modernizing by becoming educated in Western dance forms, modifying — in order to modernize — those of her own heritage, and traveling abroad to see and learn whatever she could from a part of the world considered the standard for modernization? Or did she adopt some of the things Japan advocated in order to turn them around and make her *own* statement of her *own* identity? Was she motivated by purely artistic concerns, despite unavoidable influences from the complex and changing events surrounding her? As one Korea specialist notes, it is important to remember that people continued to pursue their routine daily activities and "that Koreans in the 1920s and 1930s did not relate everything to nationalist projects, as if there were no other reference points in their lives than the fact of Japanese rule" (Wells 1999, 197). It is very possible that, to expand on the description referred to earlier, Ch'oe was simply a young woman dancer growing up and maturing as an artist at a time when cultural earthquakes rocked Korea; when the colonial and modern worlds "knocked, pounded, and battered their way" into the consciousness of people, whether the commitments of those people lay in farming, religion, politics, or dance. It is ironic that more than six decades after liberation, during times when Koreans have made a conscious effort to remove or distance themselves from things Japanese, and despite the presence in Korea, onstage and in social settings, of many quite different kinds of dance, the dance icons most often chosen to represent Korea today were formed during the colonial era, and with an explicit intent to modernize, but are identified as traditional.

Conclusion

If we look at Ch'oe's Sŭng-hŭi's career from the perspective of cultural consumption, we see various ways in which she used aspects of culture for her own purposes as well as ways in which different cultures and governments used her and her dance. Because of the times in which she lived, it is challenging to disentangle motivations related to colonization, nationalism, modernity, the need to please both indigenous and foreign audiences, and personal aesthetic preferences. In the end, all of these likely influenced Ch'oe's choices.[35] Some Koreans needed an icon with which to identify when so much of what was Korean was being taken away, something to help them maintain a sense of self. Some Japanese wanted to be able to show they were supporting the Koreans — despite their viselike grip on Koreans in many arenas. And some individuals from the Western world wanted an artistic representation of the "mysterious East." When both Korea and Japan were concerned with modernity, it was likely easy to support powerful visual images that might be more readily embraced than the political ideologies of a colonial era. And what more powerful image could there be than a young, attractive woman using her body as a vehicle of expression?[36]

Ch'oe's choices to use elements of the cultures that surrounded her were undoubtedly sometimes more and sometimes less consciously made. Though her husband and her teacher recommended that she use both uniqueness, in the form of older Korean dance, and contemporary Western dance trends in her artistic efforts to modernize that uniqueness, her choice to do so may have simply suited her own artistic preferences and what she felt she needed to do to satisfy the desires of some of her audience members and to practice her art in complex times. One historian suggests that Ch'oe, like many other educated women of the period, made a decision to place personal ambition over national interests (Jun Yoo, pers. comm., August 18, 2006). Regardless of the reasons for the artistic choices she made, the kinds of dance Ch'oe created blended the old and the new and contributed to the foundation of what became known as *shinmuyong* —as well as to traditional dance.

In the late twentieth and early twenty-first centuries, *shinmuyong* is sometimes considered a subcategory of traditional dance, and it is used in settings in which a distinct Korean identity is desired. Therefore, several important questions emerge: Just what is "traditional"? What is "Korean"? And who defines and uses things that are so labeled? Tradition is most often associated with things that are old, and sometimes with things that are indigenous. But how old is old, and what constitutes indigenous? Having begun to develop in the early 1900s, *shinmuyong* is now a century "old," but that is hardly as old as the court and village dances of former times, some of which are still performed, albeit in modified or reconstructed ways. And with current performances of postmodern concert dance, salsa, and hip-hop, whatever *shinmuyong*'s origins, it certainly "looks" more Korean than many other kinds of dance seen in Korea today. In the end, it is clear that dance, as one part of culture, constantly changes and that, at least for general consumption, what constitutes traditional dance also changes.[37]

Young-hoon Kim discusses Ch'oe's life and dance in relation to border crossings, which also posit dichotomies — the borders between tradition and modernity, and between nationalism and colonialism (2006). Park adds the borders between the metropolis and the colony, and between culture and politics, to those Ch'oe traversed (2006). We could further add the literal borders between diverse countries. The crossing of borders is an apt way to look at Ch'oe in relation to cultural consumption. But as she crossed these complex borders in her daily life and in her desire to be a recognized dancer, she blurred them and became adept at modifying what she did for the widest consumption in each setting. While she consumed elements of the cultures around her, the cultures around her also consumed her. Her dance confounds notions that tradition and modernity constitute a dichotomy, and contributes to what is today often assumed to be, or considered to be, traditional Korean dance — despite its relatively recent creation.

Notes

My research on Korean dance has been carried out over numerous residencies in Korea since 1979 and has been supported by many organizations, to which I am most grateful: the Korean Culture and Arts Foundation (known since 2005 as Han'guk Chung'ang Yŏn'guwŏn and previously as Han'guk Munhwa Yesul Chinhŭngwŏn), the Academy of Korean Studies (Han'guk Chŏngshin Munhwa Yŏn'guwŏn), the Korean-American Educational Commission (Fulbright Program), the International Cultural Society of Korea (Han'guk Kukche Munhwa Hyŏphoe), and the University of Hawai'i at Manoa's Research Council and Center for Korean Studies. Despite the historical nature of this chapter, my work is based heavily on in situ participant-observation and direct interaction with practitioners, scholars, historians, and individuals involved with dance in various ways. Portions of this essay are adapted from Van Zile (2008), and chapters in Van Zile (2001). I am grateful to Choe Yong-ho for clarifying certain details related to sociopolitical history, and to Naoko Maeshiba for translating portions of Japanese-language sources.

1. For a discussion of Korean dance terminology and categories used today, see Van Zile (2001, chaps. 1 and 2) and Kyoung-ae Kim (1995).

2. For several theories about the origin of the term *shinmuyong*, see Van Zile (2001, 39–41).

3. For a discussion of the use of tradition to establish uniqueness, its importance in globalizing trends, and examples from postcolonial situations, see Al-Sayyad (2001).

4. This biographical sketch is based on Van Zile (2001, chap. 8), which relies on some of the most commonly agreed-upon information available. For details on sources, see Van Zile (2001, 282 n. 2), and for further biographical information, see Ch'oe Sŭng-hŭi (1936, in Japanese; 1937, in Korean); Takashima and Chŏng (1994, in Japanese); Chŏng P. (1995, in Korean); Park (2006, in English); and Young-hoon Kim (2006, in English).

5. Takashima describes Ch'oe's father as an absentee landlord with many investments who led an easy life in Seoul while others worked his land. This was so, Takashima says, until he was deceived and lost all his assets, which had been given to him by his parents (1959, 21–22).

6. Ch'oe's brother, Ch'oe Sŭng-il, was a writer and a member of the Korean Artists Proletariat Federation.

7. An is said to have "programmed Choe Seung-hui's [sic] activities as a concert planner and wielded great influence over . . . [her] artistic views" (Young-hoon Kim 2006, 174–175).

8. *Hanto no Maihimei* was made by Japanese filmmakers and to my knowledge, there is no remaining copy. For a synopsis of the film and a review following its premiere, see Takashima (1959, 94–97).

9. Conflicting dates are given for when they each relocated to the North. See, for example, Takashima (1959, 206) and Takashima and Chŏng (1994, 216).

10. According to Takashima and Chŏng, she was elected to the senate and was a cultural leader in the Working People's Party (1994, 216). Scalapino and Lee indicate that she served as director of the Dance Institute in 1946, shortly after her arrival in P'yŏngyang, and subsequently of the State Dance Theatre, and was selected to chair the Dancers' League when it was formed in 1960 (1972, 524, 878, 885).

11. Official lists of participants in the government and the Working People's Party were published on various occasions, and individuals conducting research on North Korea often consult these lists as an indication of who is in political favor (Hugh Kang, pers. comm., April 13, 1998).

12. Ishii had studied Cecchetti-style ballet from an Italian resident in Japan, and his modern dance training was with a man influenced by early US modern dancer Isadora Duncan and the eurhythmics of the Swiss Émile Jaques-Dalcroze. Ishii also toured Europe and was greatly impressed by new developments in modern dance there, particularly the German expressionist works of Mary Wigman, and was later influenced by the works of US modern dancers Ruth St. Denis and Ted Shawn, whose Denishawn company performed in Japan in 1925 and 1926.

13. For example, his 1916 *Nikki no ichi-peji* (Page from a diary) dealt with an individual seeking liberation from a repressive society.

14. There is very little film footage of Ch'oe during her early dance years, and

the veracity of works performed today by individuals who claim to have reconstructed her early dances has yet to be established. In the 1990s a number of television shows about Ch'oe were produced, and many included dancing attributed to her. The 1995 Munhwa Broadcasting Corporation of Korea docudrama contains excerpts of many dances from Ch'oe's early career, but no indication of the basis for the choreography displayed. Arirang TV's 1998 production includes documentary footage of Ch'oe herself, with brief excerpts from her early career and lengthier excerpts from her later career. A second 1998 Arirang TV production documents performances by Paek Hyang-ju, a Japan-based Korean who is said to be a disciple of one of Ch'oe's students. One must therefore rely, particularly for suggestions of her early work, on the many still photographs available, on verbal comments of people who chose to write about her work, and on Ch'oe's own comments. It is possible some of her later works are most closely represented today by the style of Kim Baek-pong, her sister-in-law, who studied and performed with Ch'oe in North Korea before settling in South Korea.

15. According to Takashima and Chŏng, in 1931, following the arrest of her husband, Ch'oe created several anti-Japanese pieces (1994, 221).

16. It is difficult to date precisely the original choreography of Ch'oe's works. She frequently modified her choreography and may or may not have changed a dance's name when doing so. Further, in many sources it is unclear whether "first performance" means the first performance of a dance in a particular locale (e.g., Korea, Japan, the United States) or its first performance ever, and it is unclear whether dates on photographs refer to the date the photograph was taken, the date on which it appeared in a publication, or a date on which the dance was performed. For various authors' indications of when individual dances may have been choreographed, see, for example, Chŏng P. (1995), Takashima (1959), and Takashima and Chŏng (1994).

17. For an overview of the changing position of women during the early twentieth century in Japan and Korea, see Yoo (2005) and Hane (1988, introduction).

18. Some attribute the origins of the now iconic Korean dance *Salp'uri* to the choreography of Han Sŏng-jun, who is noted for retaining traditional movement characteristics while at the same time being innovative. For further possibilities of *Salp'uri*'s origin, see Van Zile (2001, 159–160).

19. There is some question as to how long Ch'oe studied with Han. For example, Kyoung-ae Kim states that Han's memoirs say she spent only one week studying with him (1995, 57). Ae-joo Lee indicates that Ch'oe's studies with him lasted forty-four days (1998, 50).

20. See, for example, some of the views expressed in Park (2006). Japanese policies toward "things Korean" fluctuated during the colonial era. There were times when they were prohibited and times when they were supported in various ways. See also Robinson (1988) and G. Shin and Robinson (1999a).

21. One author states that Ch'oe herself choreographed *Ehea noara* after her studies with Han Sŏng-jun (A. Lee 1998, 50). Based on Ishii Baku's memoirs, another suggests the dance was at least in part crafted by Ishii after Ch'oe had learned two "Korean" dances from Han (Takashima 1959, 69). There is no English translation for this title, which is most likely simply a sequence of mnemonic syllables.

22. For a discussion of the most commonly identified characteristics of traditional Korean dance, see, for example, Van Zile (2001, 12–14).

23. AlSayyad observes, "It is interesting to note that at the same time that colonial governments were involved in suppressing indigenous cultural traditions, their fascination with the traditional customs of the 'other' also generated the first impulses toward its preservation" (2001, 6). Although Ch'oe Sŭng-hŭi's choreography could be looked at as at least in part seeking to preserve traditional Korean dance, she did not do so in the same way as, for example, Kim Ch'ŏn-hŭng (see Kim Ch'ŏn-hŭng 2005; also see Van Zile 2001, chap. 7), and it was Japan's system for preserving traditional folk dance that contributed to Korea's system, established in the 1960s, for preserving its own traditional practices. For explanations of the latter, see J. Yang (2003) and Van Zile (2001, chap. 3).

24. Because of the many versions of a dance with related names (Takashima 1959, 181, refers to a Bodhisattva series), it is difficult to ascertain when the version closest to what is known today as *Bodhisattva,* was choreographed. A dance titled *Picture of Bodhisattva* was performed in Tokyo in 1937, and images of the dance as it is known today can be seen in those of her performances in the United States between 1939 and 1940.

25. Most of the television films about Ch'oe include the only extant brief excerpt of her performing this dance. For discussions of this dance, see, for example, Sang-cheul Ch'oe (1996, 220–250) and Van Zile (2001, 192–193, 214–216).

26. For detailed descriptions of these movements, see Sang-cheul Ch'oe (1996, 220–250) and Van Zile (2001, 215–216).

27. For an examination of Ch'oe's US performances, see Van Zile (2001, chap. 8) and portions of Park (2006).

28. For a discussion of some kinds of things he and other dancers from Asia were doing at the time, see Erdman (1996).

29. Because of the lack of adequate film footage, it is not possible to know precisely how similar some of the versions of these dances performed today are to the ones performed by Ch'oe. For a debate surrounding the origins of Korean fan dances, for example, see the 1989 issue of *Kaeksŏk* magazine.

30. Other contributors to this style included Cho Taek-wŏn, Han Sŏng-jun (one of Ch'oe's teachers), Han Yŏng-suk, Kim Baek-pong, Lee Mae-bang, and Pae Ku-ja.

31. In April 2008, KBS Global announced that in preparation for a diction-

ary to be published at a later date the Institute for Research in Collaborationist Activities had released names of thousands of Koreans considered to be pro-Japanese collaborators during the colonial period, indicating the list would be finalized "after a 60-day comment period." Among the names in the announcement was that of Ch'oe Sŭng-hŭi (KBS Global 2008).

32. Since passports were issued by the Japanese Governor-General's Office, it is likely she *had* to use this version of her name to obtain a passport to travel abroad (Choe Yong-ho, pers. comm., November 30, 2006; Park 2006, 610).

33. See Young-hoon Kim (2006, 176) and Brandon (2009, 178–179) for comments relating to her pro-Japanese choreography and performances upon her return from the United States.

34. For an overview of some of the works on Ch'oe that began to appear, see Young-hoon Kim (2006, 178–179).

35. While the residue of where individuals stood politically during the colonial era is still strong for many people today, and the impact of politics was unavoidable, some dancers of that era chose quite different paths and contributed in other ways to today's definitions of "traditional" Korean dance and the impact of modernity on it. While a full discussion of the political and aesthetic choices made by such individuals is beyond the scope of this chapter, it is important to acknowledge Kim Ch'ŏn-hŭng, as well as individuals identified in note 30.

36. For a discussion of images versus ideology in representing modernity, see Young-hoon Kim (2006, 181–182).

37. Interestingly, Ch'oe and her brother countered some of the early negative criticisms that her dance was not authentic or traditional by writing about these very issues (see Park 2006, 212–213).

Kugak Fusion and the Politics of Korean Musical Consumption

For the last one hundred years, the dominant music culture in Korea has been Western. Nonetheless, *kugak,* traditional Korean music, stands for "Korea" in tourist brochures and on countless Internet sites, in historical films and TV dramas, and in the great majority of academic articles and books by musicologists and ethnomusicologists.[1] *Kugak* has become the soundworld of an Appaduraian ideoscape, through which Koreans slot themselves into global music flows. *Kugak,* though, has not gone through a process of commoditization. Hence, its iconicity does not match the deterritorialization of postcolonial theory that Appadurai wrote about, but remains, more, an agent of state hegemony (Appadurai 1990). To a degree, it is still embedded within Adorno and the Frankfurt School's conceptions of centralized and centralizing power, and within Attali's channeling of music as the "politics of noise" (Adorno [1968] 1988; Massumi 1985).

At first glance, it appears that *kugak* is flourishing, that it is widely consumed, that it has achieved a considerable degree of popularity. But the reality is rather different, for *kugak* struggles in the marketplace. Here I explore how promoters and performers of a new genre, kugak fusion *(kugak p'yusyŏn),* are attempting to commodify *kugak* for new audiences, to make *kugak* more commercial, and to ensure that *kugak* remains a part of the local music industry. "Kugak fusion" is a new term. It indicates music performed by a young generation of musicians that has porous boundaries and, insofar as it features musicians trained in *kugak,* might be considered as traditional music made modern. Unlike in world music elsewhere, the fusion in kugak fusion is not a mix of indigenous and foreign but a mix of Korean and Korean. It appropriates, for Korean musical consumption, elements of Western music styles present in Korea, be they jazz, classical, or pop, coupling these to elements of *kugak.*

Kugak: The appearance of success

In contemporary South Korea, *kugak* has a high profile. It is used both nationally and internationally as a potent sonic symbol of identity but is bought and sold less than preserved and promoted. *Kugak* is a central part of the state preservation system and features prominently within almost half of the 109 Important Intangible Cultural Properties *(Chungyo muhyŏng munhwajae)* elected and funded by the South Korean state. Three Properties involving music — *Chongmyo cheryeak* (music for the Rite to Royal Ancestors), *p'ansori* (epic storytelling through song), and *Kangnŭng tanoje* (Spring Festival of Kangnŭng) — have also achieved international recognition through their appointment as UNESCO Masterpieces of the Oral and Intangible Heritage of Humanity.

More than four hundred musicians and dancers work at the National Center for Korean Traditional Performing Arts, the current incarnation of court institutes stretching back to at least the eighth century.[2] The center is funded by the state and hence is little concerned with commoditization; indeed, a legal bar prevents it from selling its products. The center has primary responsibility for court music and dance and thus for music for the Rite to Royal Ancestors and for six additional Properties, music for the *Sŏkchŏn taeje* (Rite to Confucius), *taech'wit'a* (royal military processional music), *taegŭm chŏngak* (aristocratic music for the transverse flute), *kasa* and *kagok* literati song genres, and *Ch'ŏyongmu* (a court mask dance). The center populates a complex of offices, performance halls, archives and a museum adjacent to the Seoul Arts Center, and four satellite centers in Namwŏn, Pusan, Cheju, and Chindo. The current center opened its doors in the Pusan enclave during the Korean War in 1951 with just thirteen musicians and three administrators.[3] The center was known in Korean as the Kungnip Kugagwŏn. As it grew and expanded beyond court and aristocratic music, it replaced its initial English name, the National Classical Music Institute, to become the Korean Traditional Performing Arts Centre in 1989 and the National Center for Korean Traditional Performing Arts in 1995.

Today a dedicated radio station broadcasts traditional and creative traditional music 24/7. GugakFM was inaugurated in 2001 as part of the center but is now independent. Funded by the Korean Broadcasting Commission and the Ministry of Culture and Tourism, this is not a commercial operation. The initial staff of eighteen grew to thirty-five by the time of divorce in spring 2007, at which time GugakFM moved to new facilities in the Digital Media City near Seoul's World Cup Stadium. The center's director general back in 2001, Yun Miyong, came out of retirement to become GugakFM's chairman. GugakFM still has low market penetration, although since its launch it has consistently broadcast a high proportion of kugak fusion, the genre I consider here. It does so precisely to develop a new and younger audience, as one producer, Lee Yun'gyŏng, has commented: "Do you know sugar coated pills? People cover bitter medicines with sugar and color in order to swallow them. To approach the young generation and to open their minds to *kugak*, [GugakFM] cannot help but broadcast the new generation's music, so they can accept traditional music" (quoted in Yoonhee Chang 2004, 47). This mantra is crucial to kugak fusion and also is the reasoning behind a number of recent CD and VCD releases from GugakFM and elsewhere. The 2004 VCD *Manp'ashik chŏk,* issued by the center, is but one example. Through a cartoon, it tells the legend of the invention of the core Korean flute, the *taegŭm*. Animation DVDs, similarly, were released to promote the 2004 and 2005 Kugak Festival *(Kugak ch'ukch'ŏn)* — a festival I shall return to below that mixed old and new *kugak* funded by the state lottery through the Korean Culture and Arts Foundation.[4]

In fact, when GugakFM went live in 2001, two mainstream broadcasters, KBS and MBC, cut their *kugak* programming, thereby further reducing the commercialization of *kugak*. Through the 1990s, KBS FM1 had devoted between 10 and 15 percent of its airtime to *kugak* (the 1989 airtime figures were 78.6 percent Western, 2.4 percent lyric songs, and 14.2 percent *kugak*[5]). Its *kugak* programs were, however, at inconvenient times — 5:00 a.m., 5:00 p.m., and midnight (Kim Sungmun 1993, 57) — reflecting low consumer demand. Today KBS TV still airs a regular *Kugak hanmadang* (Traditional Music One Place) program with some success. Both MBC and KBS issue occasional promotional CDs, but legislation prohibits either broadcaster from selling recordings, so the primary KBS recording series is distributed and sold through a commercial tie-up with Seoul Records, while MBC's celebrated mammoth 103-CD folk song compendium was abridged to a 12-disc set in 2001 and released by Kirin Music Publishing.

Starting with Seoul National University in 1959, several dozen universities today offer degree programs in *kugak*. *Kugak* graduates populate the increasing number of traditional orchestras in Seoul and in each province, and universities are also the sites of musicological scholarship. Tracked back to the Japanese colonial period (as has been done by Provine 1993), Korean musicology was systematized by Lee Hye-Ku (b. 1908), the founder of both the *kugak* degree program at Seoul National University and the Korean Musicological Society (Han'guk Kugak Hakhoe). By 1981, Song Pangsong could list 1,278 entries in a bibliography of Korean musicological publications (Song P. 1981), and the journal *Han'guk ŭmak yŏn'gu* (Journal of the Korean Musicological Society [1985], 15:215–228) listed 199 MA dissertations written on *kugak* by 1984. Kim Sŏnghye (1998), although not distinguishing *kugak* from Western music, listed 4,131 MA dissertations completed in Korea by 1995. The sheer volume of musicological work, and the successful mix of East and West in its methodology, has done much to catapult *kugak* into the public arena, putting pressure on government agencies to fund and promote it. This in turn has increased awareness at the government level, although musicology still tends to highlight the formerly elitist court and aristocratic genres.

As I have demonstrated elsewhere (Howard 2006, 38–46), consumption of *kugak* has remained largely passive. Hence, awareness does not equate to buying tickets for *kugak* concerts, listening to GugakFM, or watching *kugak* programs on television. Indeed, it could be argued that musicology has increased the insularity of *kugak*. Rather than making it more approachable to the majority of the population, circular networks of exchange have evolved: students form the core of audiences for recitals by their teachers; graduates populate ensembles and orchestras; graduate soloists, ensembles, and orchestras commission composers; many composers are university professors. Korea has many active composers; a three-volume compendium, *Han'guk chakkok kasajip* (Han'guk yesul yŏn'guso 1995–1997) lists the works of 834 of them. A minority of this number write *ch'angjak kugak* (creative traditional music), new music for traditional Korean instruments, rather than new music for Western instruments. The linkage to universities is most apparent in small-scale compositions for traditional instruments, which began to multiply in the early 1960s precisely because the Seoul National University *kugak* curriculum required performers to include new works in their graduation recitals. Compositions for orchestras of traditional instruments had begun earlier, first with works written by Kim Kisu (1917–1986) for the National Center, then with works commissioned from many others as new orchestras were formed in the 1970s and 1980s. In 1995, Yi Sanggyu (1995, 109–160) was able to list

2,239 creative traditional music compositions that had been performed; a year later, a book compiled by researchers at the National Center listed 2,821 works by 351 composers in its archive, the majority of which had been first performed at, and in many cases commissioned by, the center (Song H., Kim, and Sŏ 1996). Neither university recitals nor concerts at the state-funded center are commercial propositions.

Much as in Europe and America, many Korean composers are affiliated with universities. The academic locus of teaching new composers and, indeed, composing eliminates the need for commercial sponsorship, sitting well away from Soviet socialist realism (or any other Marxist interpretation); no consumer is required beyond examiners, students, and academics. Thereby, Théophile Gautier's nineteenth-century idea of "art for art's sake" is given ample credence. Not surprisingly, composers in today's Europe are celebrated in the public imagination as the dead creators of sacralized scores, rather than the living (see, e.g., Lebrecht 1996), while music sociologists focus on the creation of jazz or pop more than art music composers (e.g., DeNora 2000). In Korea, much the same increasingly applies in respect to *ch'angjak kugak,* where ignoring musical consumption is enabled as universities, or collectives of composers employed by universities, provide subsidies for composition and sponsor performance venues. Influential composer coalitions include the Society for New Composition in Korean Traditional Music (Han'guk Ch'angjak Ŭmak Yŏn'guhoe), the Korean Society of Woman Composers (Han'guk Yŏsŏng Chakkokkahoe), and the Contemporary Music Society in Seoul (Ch'angakhoe), while the Korea National University of Arts (Han'guk Yesul Chonghap Hakkyo) takes on the role of a national conservatory. Arguably, *ch'angjak kugak,* even more than *kugak,* is marginal in terms of musical consumption.[6]

The effect of binding musicology to composition within university music departments further raises *kugak* on a pedestal. Hence, considerable debate ensues as to what should constitute *ch'angjak kugak.* Should it match "composition" *(chakkong),* mirroring the Western Enlightenment understanding of a celebrated artist creating music from individual inspiration, a concept that was imported to Korea with Western music (Byeon 2001a, 2001b; Ch'ae H. 1996, 2000)? Should it retain elements of the way that *kugak* itself is assumed to have developed, being "formed" *(hyŏngsŏng)* over time as, for example, folk songs were adapted to become instrumental pieces in the court repertory (Yi Sŏngch'ŏn 1987, 4; 1992, 168)? Is "arrangement," "reorganization," or "recomposition" *(chaegusŏng;* Hesselink 2004,

413–414) or "weaving" or "stitching together" (*chakch'ang*; Killick 1998, 403–404) acceptable, as occurs with contemporary percussion quartets, *samullori*, or among contemporary *p'ansori* singers? Scholars have been at the forefront of this debate (K. S. Lee 1977; 1980, 71; Yi Kangsuk 1985; Yi Kŏnyong 1987, 60–74). Their pronouncements, wherein Western classical music, jazz, or pop becomes Korean simply by being created or performed in Korea, partially match accounts of appropriation and assimilation elsewhere (e.g., Chou 1967, 1971; Born and Hesmondhalgh 2000; Everett and Lau 2004) but nod, gently, in the direction of musical consumption.

None of this is to deny that concerts of *kugak* have mushroomed. Between 1988 and 2001 they increased almost tenfold, according to yearbooks of the Korean Culture and Arts Foundation (Han'guk Munhwa Yesul Chinhŭngwŏn), from 282 to 2,076 annual events. Concerts that include creative traditional music and, more recently, kugak fusion, have also grown rapidly, so that 392 (18.9 percent) were devoted to new music alone and 595 (28.7 percent) mixed old and new in 2001; 511 (24.6 percent) featured *kugak* alone. The circular network of student-graduate-professor exchange pertains, particularly at regular weekday National Center concerts, while students preparing coursework assignments make up the bulk of the audience at the center's regular Saturday concerts. Concerts are heavily subsidized by national, city, or provincial governments, and many offer free admission.[7] *Kugak* aficionados remain rare, apart from those who are themselves performers or graduates of *kugak* programs, and it is reasonable to suggest that the public at large still has little awareness of *kugak* and oftentimes has negative impressions of it; indeed, many associate *kugak* with disliked folk song classes in school.

Kugak fusion: Steps on the road

Composers writing new music for Korean instruments have been encouraged to respect tradition. Critics have derided avant-garde adventures into "abstract madness" (Heyman 1985, 60) that "play havoc on the eardrums and leave faces of onlookers with the most awful grimaces" (Wade 1965, 36). In the 1960s the composer Yi Sŏngch'ŏn (1936–2003) was criticized by both musicologists and performers, who told him that his "compositions would damage traditional music." He observed, "My music was not considered Korean, yet my acceptance as a composer depended on how much I retained the tradition" (interview with the author, July 1991). Byungki

Hwang (b. 1936) found his most abstract piece, *Migung* (Labyrinth; 1975), effectively blacklisted. Lee Sanggyu (b. 1944), as a student of the National Traditional Music High School and a performer at the National Center, toed the line: "I think we need to be aware of our roots. I believe that if we change traditional music too much, we lose touch with the past" (interview with the author, August 1990).

It is a given that, as society evolves, so culture changes. Therefore, since artists are often held to reflect the contemporary zeitgeist, some composers have sought to escape the straitjacket of *kugak*. Young Dong Kim (b. 1951) was perhaps the first. While studying at Seoul National University, he produced incidental music for a drama, *Hanne ŭi sŭngch'ŏn* (The life of Hanne; 1974), and songs that captured the student movement for democracy. These were followed by music for television and film dramas that set melodies played on traditional Korean instruments (notably, his own instrument, the *taegŭm* transverse flute) with guitar, keyboard, or synthesizer harmonic fills. Kim recognized that the iconicity of *kugak* was vested by the public in melody and melodic ornamentation, aspects best captured with traditional instruments and vocal timbres, while the widespread familiarity of Western music meant that harmony, provided by Western diatonic instruments, was expected. Kim Soochul (b. 1958), who started as a pop musician and actor, followed the lead. He achieved moderate commercial success during the 1980s with music for dramas, in particular *Hwangch'ŏn kil* (The road to Hades) for Korean shawm and Western strings and *We kil* (Forked road) for *p'iri* oboe and synthesizer, but it was his 1993 soundtrack for the celebrated film directed by Im Kwon-taek (Im Kwŏnt'aek), *Sŏp'yŏnje,* that created a sensation, selling two million copies — an unheard-of figure in the *kugak* world.[8] He, too, took melodies from *kugak* — a *taegŭm* flute, three *p'ansori* singers — and framed them with synthesizer harmonies.

The *kugak* straitjacket was further loosened by the Third Generation, an informal 1980s group who wrote primarily for Western instruments. Led by Yi Kangsuk and Yi Kŏnyong, critics and composers, and former and current presidents of the Korean National University of the Arts, the Third Generation were little concerned with commercial success, although they acknowledged that both *kugak* and contemporary composers had failed to win a broad audience. Much in the spirit of a musical democracy, particularly following the Kwangju citizens uprising of May 1980 and its brutal suppression, they conceptualized "Korean music" as both *kugak* and all Western music performed or created in Korea: "We musicians should create a national music that overcomes foreign influence, pursues our desire for unification and is relevant to daily life . . . bringing together and unifying all music . . . as our national music" (Yi Kŏnyong 1990, 10). A group of *ch'angjak kugak* composers who at one time worked at Chung-Ang University, among them Baik Dae-woong (b. 1943), Park Bum-hoon (b. 1948), Kim Yŏngjae (b. 1947), and Yi Byung-wuk (b. 1952), took up Third Generation ideas. They abandoned critiques of appropriation as they mixed traditional court and folk source materials in an attempt to reinvigorate *kugak*. Baik's *Namdo kutkŏri* (1992), for example, is based on the movement of the same name in the old literati suite *Hyangje chul p'ungnyu*, Important Intangible Cultural Property 85; his *Pukch'ŏng saja norŭm* (1992) is an arrangement of a haunting flute melody taken from the accompaniment to a North Korean mask drama preserved as Property 15, and his *Sangju moshimgi norae* (1988) is a folk song rewritten as an instrumental piece within a strong diatonic frame. The distinction to make here is that melodies of *kugak* became diatonic, while Korean traditional instruments were harnessed to provide protodiatonic harmonic frames.

Vocalists explore similar territory in a more consumer-driven environment. Consider the "national" folk song[9] "Arirang," of which a large number of recordings exist. Rather than just slotted into the "traditional" bins of Korean record stores, one album, *The Heart of Corée in Cool Jazz*, offers a folk song set with versions of "Arirang" at beginning, middle, and end (Synnara NSC-057, 2002); another transports listeners to a smoke-filled bar, jazz quatrains setting a text about Korean unification in "T'ongil Arirang" (Samsung Music SCO-165KYW, 1998); another collects "Arirang" versions from across the Peninsula and adds gongs and Buddhist temple blocks, launching the solo career of the former SamulNori percussionist Kwang Soo Lee (b. 1951) (Samsung SCO-100CSS, 1996); yet another, by pop singer Kang Sanae, offers social commentary on the downside of contemporary urban life (Seoul Records SRCD-3495, 1998); while the pop megastars SG Wannabe open their fourth album, *The Sentimental Chord*, with a commercial pop version (Poibus/CJ Music DYCD-1255, 2007). "Arirang," played by the Yoon Tohyun Band, became the theme song for the 2002 World Cup, and GugakFM's January 2003 retrospective of soccer triumphs featured eight versions, including Yoon's, an opera rendition by Sumi Jo, a blues track by Jack Lee and the Shin Kwanung Trio, and a four-part choral setting. The Kugak Festival has its own compilation of "Arirang" updates (2004; issued as *Endless Song, Arirang* with English notes, 2005), featuring DJs, rap, punk, and even a tango version; in 2006, Korean consulates worldwide distributed a double CD, *Arirang, the Most Popular Korean Folk Song for All* (GugakFM/Munhwa Net), mixing local folk songs with rap and more.

During the last decade, one voice has been famously linked to updates of folk songs, Yong Woo Kim (b. 1968), and he too sang "T'ongil Arirang." He learned one track on his first album, *Pongjiga* (Seoul Records SRCD-1354, 1996), from Cho Ŭlsŏn (1915–2000) in Cheju, the former holder of Property 95, Cheju folk songs. The song was once used when weaving horsehair hats, but Kim slows the pace down, adding synthesized harmonies and removing all sense of any work activity. On another track, he takes the iconic southwestern women's song-and-dance genre, *Kanggangsullae,* Property 8, learned from the Chindo singer Cho Kongnye (1930–1997). Now, though, there are no women, just a male chorus adding a harmonic second part unknown in the countryside of old. In addition to the jazzy "T'ongil arirang," a cappella singing features on his second album (Samsung Music SCO-165-KYW, 1998), and on the third, *Mogaebi* (Seoul Records SRCD-1454, 1999), a southwestern folksong, "Ŏnggŏngk'wiya," is arranged for guitar, *haegŭm* two-stringed fiddle, and voice. His fourth album, *Yongchŏn'gŏm* (Universal DK0403, 2003), went to the top of the pop charts for an old milling song, again learned from Cho Ŭlsŏn but now accompanied by chorus and piano, bass guitar, *haegŭm* fiddle, *p'iri* oboe, *changgo* drum, and *kkwaenggwari* gong.

Linking Young Dong Kim to Yong Woo Kim is the group Seulgidoong, formed by Hojoong Kang (b. 1960) in 1985. Seulgidoong created a standard instrumental ensemble to fill out updated songs. In 1999, Kang told me:

> When I was in my second year of university, I took a simple pentatonic folk song from North Chŏlla Province and sang it for the University Song Festival *(Taehak kayoje)* on MBC TV. I accompanied myself on guitar and added a *tanso* flute. This was how I created my first hit. I established Seulgidoong with some alumni friends and colleagues. We felt we could not make successful careers if we just kept faithfully to the tradition. We wanted to make music that was easier to listen to and decided the way forward was to generate a style of songs based on traditional melodies, but with guitars and synthesizers as well as Korean instruments. We called this style *kugak kayo.*

Kugak fusion and the music industry

The realities of commercial promotion sidestep debates about the appropriateness of creativity and about respect for the iconicity of *kugak*. Today the Korean music industry is in meltdown, and this affects niche players who record and distribute local *kugak* and its derivatives far more than multinational companies who market titles globally. In 1997, Korea was the thirteenth-largest market for recorded music in the world, with domestic sales of 210 million albums.[10] By 2002, Korea was the second-largest music market in Asia after Japan, and domestic turnover, primarily from CD sales, reached $300 million. But 2002 was also the year when sales of cell phone ringtones outpaced CD sales for the first time. The peer-to-peer download site Soribada (Sea of Sound) had opened back in 2000 and by 2002 had six million users; other sites competed for netizens, bypassing royalty and copyright payments to push the average cost of custom-tailoring an album down to a nominal 50 won (5 US cents) in subscription fees. Sales of sound recordings fell year-on-year 7.7 percent in 2001, 31.4 percent in 2002, 31.2 percent in 2003, and 28.4 percent in 2004.[11] By 2004 the 14.2 million total units sold were valued at just $133 million, and 80 percent of the four thousand record stores open nationwide in 2000 had closed.

Korea's domestic record companies remain small. Matching the centralized economic planning model, the 1980s licensing agreements and the 1990s distribution agreements with foreign labels allowed some growth.[12] The relaxation of foreign ownership rules following the late 1990s economic collapse allowed foreign companies such as EMI to buy into the market without needing local partners. Local companies became marginalized. Three local labels dominated *kugak* recordings during the 1990s: Samsung, Seoul Records, and Synnara.[13] Samsung dissolved its labels after the economic collapse, although a number of its albums have since been reissued by the boutique E-One label. Seoul Records, part of a small conglomerate that controls the English-language school Si-sa-yong-o-sa, has retrenched, closing much of its central high-rise headquarters on Chongno (along with its retail subsidiary, Musicland, which had its flagship store in the same building) and moving in 2006 to small offices above a Volkswagen dealership in southern Seoul. Synnara, still a major local distributor, continues to affirm its commitment to traditional music in press releases (including one by Kim Kisun, the founder of its affiliated new religion[14]) but has reduced its output, moved its headquarters out of Seoul, and closed many retail stores.

Kugak albums are slow sellers. Seoul Records shifts an average of 300 copies of each of its several hundred titles annually.[15] The profit model is based on recouping initial costs over many years and does not fit the anticipated short life span of pop albums. Top pop albums no longer match the heyday of the local industry — the boy band H.O.T. sold 10 million albums in its seven-year existence to 2003 — but can notch up 100,000 or more sales a year. Kugak fusion fits, in terms of sales, somewhere between *kugak* and pop. In early 2007, two albums each sold more than 2,000 copies within a month of their release: Kim Kyung A's *P'iri,* in which the traditional Korean oboe is supported by piano, guitars, bass, and drum kit (SRCD-1633), and Kang Ŭnil's *Mirae ŭi kiŏk* (Remembering the future), with *haegŭm* two-stringed fiddle backed by an ensemble of Western and Korean instruments (SRCD-1636).

In 2006 the top-selling kugak fusion album was *For You* (SRCD-1627). This album garnered 20,000 sales and started an annual cycle of releases by the Sookmyung Kayagŭm Ensemble, led until 2006 by Kim Il-ryun and based at Sookmyung Women's University. The ensemble has proved immensely popular, becoming the model for others (see Song H. et al. 2005). In terms of market penetration and copies sold, its greatest success is also, from an outsider's perspective, its most dubious creation — namely, the 2003 album *Let It Be,* featuring five Beatles classics arranged by Pak Kyŏnghun for the eponymous *kayagŭm* zither (SRCD-1524). *For You* occupies the same territory, offering four more Beatles songs.[16]

Before the Sookmyung Kayagŭm Ensemble, arrangements for Korean instruments of repertoire designed for Western instruments began in the late 1980s, as traditional music orchestras rapidly expanded. Kugak fusion, then, effectively began both with the mixed compositions of Young Dong Kim and others and with commissioned arrangements and compositions for traditional orchestras. The orchestras struggled for acceptance among cosmopolitan consumers to whom Western music had become synonymous with urban life. In 1988, Yi Haeshik (b. 1943) was commissioned by the state broadcaster KBS to arrange Vivaldi's *Four Seasons* for zither ensemble. Chaesuk Lee (b. 1941), today one of the most senior zither performers and scholars, and the sole female *kugak* member of the prestigious Korean Academy of Arts, writes,

I was given the arrangement, designed for playing on one 21-stringed *kayagŭm* and three 12-stringed instruments. It was extremely difficult, and I felt that the sound was not good, because these zithers used silk strings and since, although tuned to a pentatonic scale, they were being required to play Western diatonic scales . . . I suggested we postpone the performance until we had a Korean *kayagŭm* with Western characteristics. In 1994, I set up the Korean Zither Musicians Association, and in 1998, when we held our first concert in Seoul, we finally premiered "Autumn," one of the four concertos that comprise Vivaldi's "Four Seasons." It now worked well, because we could use the new 25-stringed *kayagŭm.* The arrangement became something of a "hit" because it suited youthful tastes, and one result was that four of my zither students created a quartet named Sagye (Four Worlds).[17] (C. Lee, Howard, and Casswell 2008, 31)

Lee alludes to one reason why kugak fusion has become a reality: traditional twelve-stringed *kayagŭm,* the structure and tonal characteristics of which date back at least 1,500 years, have in recent years been modified. The traditional instrument is pentatonic, with a range of less than three octaves, using wound silk strings plucked by the soft fleshy part of fingers (and occasionally by the fingernails). Modifications allow the instrument to more closely approach the soundworld of Western music. In 1985 a twenty-one-stringed instrument commissioned from the maker Ko Hŭnggon by the composer Yi Sŏngch'ŏn increased the range by adding three additional bass strings and six higher-pitched strings. Yi had in mind creating a Korean equivalent to the piano, capable of simultaneously playing treble melodies and bass harmonies. In the same year, the composer Pak Pŏmhun asked the maker Pak Sŏnggi to create a trio of instruments, adding a larger bass version and a narrower soprano version. The trio was used by the Saeul Ensemble, allowing Chung-Ang University composers a halfway house between Western trios and a Korean ensemble.[18] A year later Hwang Pyŏngju commissioned the same maker to produce a seventeen-stringed instrument that used more resonant polyester strings rather than the traditional wound silk strings, for use by the KBS Traditional Music Orchestra. Pak Pŏmhun enlarged this as a twenty-two-stringed instrument with a bigger resonator for his composition *Sae sanjo* (New Sanjo). Kim Il-ryun premiered his piece in 1995 but found the instrument problematic, so he asked another maker, Cho Chŏngsam, to redesign this as a twenty-five-stringed version capable of being tuned to the Western hep-tatonic major and minor scales.

Kayagŭm ensembles have been central to the development of kugak fusion. Sagye was one of the first, with its members marketed as virtual pop stars. Their first album, *Sagye* (Polymedia, 2001), included arrange-ments of Baroque masters and contemporary music such as Astor Piaz-zolla's "Oblivion." It reached the nineteenth spot in the domestic album charts, selling 10,000 copies within two months of release.[19] The trio Gaya Beauty, whose name alludes to the legendary invention of the zither in the fifth century, are a product of the rival university, Chung-Ang, play-ing, twenty years beyond the Third Generation, folk song arrangements on twenty-five-stringed zithers. The mother-and-daughters trio Lee Rang have a more conservative image, not least since the mother, Mun Chaesuk, is holder of Property 23, the folk-art genre of *kayagŭm sanjo*. One daugh-ter of Lee Rang was crowned Miss Korea in 2006, presenting a golden marketing opportunity, but *Family Ensemble Lee Rang* (Synnara NSC-172, 2006) still falls back on Mun's career, starting with traditional *sanjo*, part of *kugak* proper, and ending with a medley of Christmas carols reworked from Mun's earlier *Gayagum X-Mas* (Synnara NSC-071, 2003).

When instrumental textures are pared back for hymns and carols, as in the Lee Rang album, shortcomings of the *kayagŭm* in imitating West-ern instruments become apparent. Players of nonamplified old and new *kayagŭm* struggle to produce sustained melodic tones because, lacking plectra, plucking a string entails a long contact with the unresonant fin-ger. Again, the instrument cannot produce resolutely steady pitches, since the individual bridges under each string constantly shift, minutely alter-ing the pitch. The quartet Yeoul offers one way forward, adding electric pickups that sustain resonance and allow additional timbres imitative of slide guitars and sustained strings.[20] This is well suited to their arrange-ments of "Fly Me to the Moon" and "Stairway to Heaven" on the album *Haengbokhan iyagi* (Happy story; C&L Music/EMI CNLR-624-2). Yeoul mixes stereotypical *kugak* girl-next-door images with the commercial-ized and showy, and although the album also includes Schubert, Mozart, and samba, it comes packaged with a bonus video much like many pop releases.

An even more iconic instrument in terms of its sonic characteristics is the *haegŭm*, a two-stringed fiddle with roots in Central Asia and imported to Korea almost a thousand years ago. The *haegŭm*'s nasal timbre is generated by its structure; silk strings pass across a bridge of hardwood resting on a paulownia softwood soundboard, with earth pasted inside the sound box to dampen resonance and cancel out high frequencies. There is no fingerboard, so pitches are produced by pushing strings with the fingers along the neck. Hence, steady pitches are difficult, and the timbre is unlike the clean sound of many Western instruments. If I compare it with the violin, the violin uses more resonant gut strings amplified through thin hardwood soundboards and reflective hardwood sound boxes tuned by carefully positioned sound posts. The violin's sonic attack, as the bow agitates a string, produces a chaotic harmonic spectrum similar to that of the *haegŭm,* but this soon resolves onto a steady tone of consonant harmonics and rich higher partials. The apparent *haegŭm* shortcomings when used to play Western melodies match those of the *kayagŭm,* but the *haegŭm* is distinct in one way — exciting the strings with a bow allows tones to be sustained at will.

The *haegŭm* catapulted to popularity with Seulgidoong's second-generation lineup player, Soonyon Chung, and by the end of the 1990s it had overtaken the *kayagŭm* as the most popular instrument for students at the National Traditional Music High School. Chung has been joined by others, including Kang Ŭnil, Kim Chŏngnim, and Ccotbyel (Kkotpyŏl). While Kang's album *Mirae ŭi kiŏk* (Remembering the future) sticks to piano and guitar backings in easy-listening programmatic tracks by Korean composers, Kim's third album, *Happy Haegeum* (Seoul Records SRCD-1638, 2006), offers a medley of Korean and foreign children's songs mixed with folk songs about kittens, flowers, and puppets, with an accompaniment of piano, guitar, accordion, bass, and bongos. Ccotbyel's 2006 *Fly, Fly, Fly* (Ponycanyon Korea, PCKD-20189) is the most cosmopolitan offering I have encountered, mixing Korean songs, Italian film themes, Spanish gypsy music, blues, and more.

I suggest that the *haegŭm* has proven popular in kugak fusion for two reasons. First, the sustained nature of *haegŭm* melodies allies it to the voice. This was ably demonstrated by former Seulgidoong member and composer Wŏn Il (b. 1967) in his soundtrack to the 1996 film *Kkonip* (A petal). The film, directed by Jang Sun Woo, tells of the brutal suppression of the 1980 Kwangju civilian uprising, from the perspective of a fifteen-year-old girl. The theme song begins with pizzicato strings and a single *ching* (large handheld gong), damped after each note in deference to southwestern shaman gongs. Above this, the *haegŭm* intones a lament, gradually fusing with the strings. The same theme returns at the end, sung by the heroine to an accompaniment of electric guitars, synthesizers, and high-hat cymbals, what began as a *haegŭm* melody being transformed into a pop song. The album sold a very creditable 40,000 copies before the demise of its label (Samsung Music SCO-088WIN, 1996). Second, lacking frets or fingerboard, the *haegŭm* need not be confined to pentatonic tuning. It can easily accommodate Western scales without sacrificing anything of its typical Korean timbre.

This second aspect of the *haegŭm* introduces a further factor in the success of kugak fusion, taking us forward from Seulgidoong and its pre millennial contemporaries to today's young artists. Until the 1980s, *kugak* musicians had lower status than those who specialized in Western music. No musician trained in both *kugak* and Western music. Neither of those former truisms applies today, and newly graduating *kugak* performers also know Western soundworlds. They have been brought up on a diet of Western pop and Western art music, and their ears accommodate both Korean pentatonic tunings and Western diatonic scales. Because of this, solo kugak fusion has become the equal of orchestral kugak fusion and — returning to Appadurai's notion of ideoscapes — it is much easier to promote the glamorous images of soloists and small groups than it is full orchestras.[21]

Park Sŭngwŏn at Seoul Records explained the generational shift to me in April 2007: "In the old days, *kugak* musicians had limited modal and playing skills and found it difficult to play anything that used Western tunings. But young people today know Western diatonic tuning, and they have modified traditional instruments at their disposal, so they find it natural to play fusions of Western and Korean musics." Park's comment incorporates an important observation about identity, as music consumption has moved from tradition to pop: identity has lost its nationalistic edge. Ch'ae Hyun-kyung (1998, 293) usefully notes how marking ownership with the term *uri* is no longer defensive but has become a normal and conventional way of expressing that something is Korean (*uri* food, *uri* country, *uri* music). Hence, for the majority of Koreans today, the juxtapositions between old and new — or Korean and Western — cause little or no difficulty.[22]

This is most apparent in mixed kugak fusion ensembles of Korean and Western instruments. The audience sought is one for whom "Korean" has meaning, but the emphasis on image is designed to appeal to teenagers and university students. The Lim, for example, deftly uses its website to generate a fan base. On its first album, the title being simply the name of the group (Yedang YDGC-003, 2003), the Lim evokes images of the Korean idyll and the communal past yet shows little interest in maintaining the world of traditional music in tracks such as "Morning Scenery" ("Nature will sing a morning song, and the morning sunshine reveals . . . a world of liveliness and brilliance rather than of secrecy and tenderness") and "Déjà vu" ("They don't believe that memories exist until one day their shadows return and tell them about their past days"). Musicore, consisting of four traditional instrumentalists and a pianist, uses Korean percussion and the shawm to retain sonic links back to old Korea. As the album notes put it, "They try to make [*kugak*] for the present age with the modern and contemporary feeling. This young group wants to enjoy Korean music with many people more easily" (AkdangEban ADCD-503, 2005). Vinalog, on its album, combines traditional *taegŭm* flute with Western accordion and guitar yet rarely signals any traditional identifiers (Synnara VLD-001, 2005).[23] The members of IS (Infinity of Sound), a trio of *kayagŭm*, *haegŭm*, and the *kŏmun'go* six-stringed zither, dress in virginal white, like China's Twelve Girls Band or the Angels from the Eastern Heavens (their first album, *Step One*, appeared in 2007; Seoul Records SRC-3959). The trio's biggest hit has been "Paengmansongi changmi" (A million roses), a track arranging Alla Pugachova's 1983 Russian song of the same name that is here merely credited to Wŏn Il as composer. Sorea, a made-to-measure girl band, similarly plays on image. And there are many more.

The backlash

Despite its commercial success, kugak fusion remains controversial. Its performers are blamed for the decline in concerts and recitals devoted solely to traditional music over the last few years, as more and more concerts mix the old with the new. Kugak fusion albums have multiplied, but this has decreased the number of *kugak* recordings produced by Korea's music industry. In recent discussions with composers and performers of *kugak* I have often heard the following sentiments (here reported without naming names):

- I have no interest in kugak fusion. It is not Korean, and it has no real connection to our music. Those who create music need to have a greater understanding of tradition.

- It's not that kugak fusion is bad, but the performers often sacrifice quality of playing for approachability. They want audience appeal rather than quality.
- Kugak fusion won't work in the international marketplace until we have developed quality. At the moment, we don't have deep understanding of both the Eastern and Western music cultures that are used.
- It is true that composers make things too complicated, so there is a role for music that is simple. But too much of kugak fusion is about being pretty and sexy. It is about trying to get quick fame. It is closer to pop than to kugak.

In 2004 the Kugak Festival opened shop, directed by music critic and broadcaster Yun Chunggang and composer and kugak performer Byungki Hwang. It published two CDs, one of "Arirang" versions (mentioned above) and one of creative traditional music (Seoul Records SRCD-8933, 2004). Both mixed rap, hip hop, and kugak, featuring a diverse range of kugak fusion groups and more. In 2005 the festival toured Vietnam as well as Korea, repeating the formula. Then a backlash began. Hwang became critical.[24] Yun was ousted, replaced by a former director of the National Center, Han Myŏnghŭi. Han took the festival back to its roots, replacing the new with traditional kugak. In 2006 the festival was held in Mongolia as well as Korea, but, fed with a diet of preserved sounds from the past rather than kugak fusion, audiences rapidly shrank. Han was ousted. A legal challenge was issued that threatened the very future of the festival, and as I write this, fiery debates continue.

Conclusion

Kugak, traditional music, is not a commercial proposition. It is iconic at home and abroad and is a major part of music production in Korea, funded, preserved and promoted by the government and other agencies. The audience for kugak remains limited and, in many cases, is founded on a circular network of exchange between students, graduates, and professor-performers. Kugak fusion emerged from compositions and arrangements within the genre of creative traditional music that introduced a mix of Korean and Western instruments and structures, but in recent years it has been championed by a young generation who reflect the contemporary Korean glocalized soundworld. Kugak fusion is marketed much like pop, through image and familiarity; as Hobsbawm might have argued (1990; Hobsbawm and Ranger 1983), kugak fusion appropriates a set of constructs to create a shared identity both traditional and modern. This works in Korea for a young audience aware that contemporary culture is in flux (after Marcus and Fischer 1986; Clifford 1988) and familiar with the "cultural traffic" (Alvesson 1996, 80) that characterizes their situation.

That theoretical perspectives from beyond Korea can be introduced indicates that kugak fusion can be considered a local manifestation of something more global.[25] In Europe and America, we have classical pops, dressed-up snazzy versions of Beethoven and Mozart performed by the spiky-haired, streetwise Nigel Kennedy, by slinky Vanessa-Mae, or by the voluptuous Bond Quartet. We have imaginary classics, such as *Adiemus,* begun as an advertisement for Delta Airlines in 1993 and expanded on the 1995 album *Songs of Sanctuary,* and Sony Classical's top-selling album ever, the theme music to *Titanic.* In Britain we listen to interminable "cool" bite-size classical pops on Classic FM; in America the Boston Pops plays Madison Square Garden. Worldwide we — depending on one's perspective — suffer or adore the Three Tenors. Folk songs remain a part of the urbanized modern world in versions that Dave Harker (1985) once pithily tagged as "fakelore." Easy listening, which in a sense is what all of these represent, surely equally captures the essence of kugak fusion, for, as GugakFM's chairman, Yun Miyong, told me in April 2007:

> Young people find *kugak* difficult. Kugak fusion is much simpler to understand. Older musicians complain if we give too much airtime to kugak fusion and tend to want more traditional *kugak.* But this has never worked for ordinary Koreans, who, just like the young, find kugak fusion much easier to listen to. It is in the GugakFM charter to broadcast to the many ordinary Koreans, rather than to merely cater for a few specialists.

Kugak fusion reflects rapid changes in global technology that are transforming the local music industry. Technological change influences musical consumption, while ongoing shifts in sponsorship increase the concentration on ideoscapes as image becomes more important than content. This is seen as governments and corporations move from elite arts toward the popular, and as products are marketed by industry through the familiar faces of popular musicians. As this happens, so music is increasingly consumed by the masses but produced and performed by a few.

Korea has moved in the last two decades from state censorship, control, and promotion — the world that valued *kugak* — to a deterritorialization in which the multinational music industry seeks commercialization and commodification without boundaries. Kugak fusion is but one contemporary reaction to change, designed to satisfy domestic demand, to sell recordings, and to promote artists who play *kugak* instruments or sing *kugak* songs to as broad an audience as possible. It is, then, a strategy to create work as well as profits. It is a strategy for survival, a flexible and evolving genre created by young performers and sponsored by a small, undercapitalized, local music industry.

Notes

Throughout this essay, I give CD and DVD catalogue numbers and dates of publications only where these are provided on the recordings or publications.

1. *Kugak* would more accurately translate as "national music," referring to indigenous court, aristocratic, and folk genres. So far as is known, *kugak* was used as a term for the first time in 1907 (No 1989, 13), specifically to separate the local from Western music. In contrast, Koreans largely associate the more general Korean (or, rather, East Asian) term for music, *ŭmak,* with Western music. I use "tradition" to translate the Korean notion of *chŏnt'ong,* that is, something premodern and preindustrial that, at least when preserved or documented within scholarship, emphasizes the maintenance of archetypes *(wŏnhyŏng)* — authentic and original forms supposedly kept without change.

2. For discussions of the center's history and development, see Chŏn Yŏngjo (1982), Kungnip kugagwŏn (1991), and Yun Miyŏng (2001).

3. Note that, after a fifty-year absence in the city, the center opened a new Pusan facility in autumn 2008.

4. The 2005 DVD was produced by the Arts Council Korea and was titled *Tŭnnŭn kugak, ponŭn kugak* (Listen to traditional music, look at traditional music).

5. Figures provided by Pak Ch'anghan at KBS, August 1990.

6. Two commercial companies, Seoul Records and Synnara, still produce some CDs of creative traditional music, but they do so very selectively, featuring, for example, the works of Pak Pŏmhun, Hwang Ŭijong, Kim Dae-Seong, and Gyewon Byeon (Synnara SYNCD-033, -049, -050, -065, -074, -075, -096, -110, -116; NSSRCD-007, -038, -039; Seoul Records SRCD-1621–1628). In addition, the works of Byungki Hwang are featured on a number of discs originally released by Sung Eum.

7. The trend toward free events is seen elsewhere, in, for example, London's

South Asian Melas, community festivals, and free foyer music in concert halls and theaters.

8. Seoul Records SRCD-3215 (1993); Samsung Nices SCO-046KSC (1994), SCO-057KSC (1994).

9. After McCann (1979).

10. 155 million cassettes and 55 million CDs (Han'guk yŏngsang ŭmban hyŏphoe 1998, 39, 43).

11. Figures are from IFPI and Han'guk yŏngsang ŭmban hyŏphoe.

12. No imports of foreign albums were allowed until late in the Roh Tae Woo regime. All LP/cassette/CD production was therefore local, with local repressings of albums originally produced abroad controlled by Ministry of Culture and Information licensing.

13. Howard (1999) lists releases by these and other labels; Kim Yŏngjo (2005; discussed at www.ohmunews.com/articleview/article_view.asp?at_code=146658) offers an annotated Synnara catalogue.

14. "Shinnara Kim Kisun hoejang ŭi kugak munhwa saŏp inyŏm kwa kongjŏk hyŏnhwang," undated press release issued in early 2007.

15. This paragraph is based on a discussion with Park Sŭngwŏn in April 2007.

16. *For You,* unlike *Let It Be,* gives full publisher and originator credits, which is unusual in the world of kugak fusion to date. Although Korea signed the pertinent international copyright convention in 1985, it is only recently that major international labels, now that they have operations in Korea, have begun to police the local market.

17. Four worlds of music: old, new, court, and folk.

18. See the Saeul Ensemble album, SKC SKCD-K-0436 (1992).

19. www.asiaweek.com/asiaweek/magazine/nations/0,8782,165862,00.html. Sagye's second album maintained the same formula, mixing arrangements and compositions (Tae Kwang Records/EMI, 2004).

20. The guitar in its many forms has come to epitomize the harmonic support instrument of acoustic pop. Hence, kugak fusion advocates seek ways to transfer its functions to the *kayagŭm* — Pak Hyeyun outlines the argument (2005).

21. Recent notable examples of solo *kayagŭm* albums within the kugak fusion genre include Seulgi's *In the Green Café* (Synnara NSC-156, 2006) and Jung Gilseon's *Kŭnyŏ ŭi sarang* (A story of her love; Seoul Records SRCD-1637, 2007).

22. This shift in identity has begun to be charted by Korean anthropologists. See *Cross-Cultural Studies (Pigyo munhwa yŏn'gu)* 4 (1998), in Korean and *Korea Journal* 43, no. 1 (2003) [in English].

23. One member of Vinalog is the son of the Chung-Ang composer Yi Byung-wuk.

24. At the 2005 conference of the Society for Ethnomusicology, Hwang played the festival's theme music, questioning whether it could be considered Korean.

25. This should not be taken to indicate that kugak fusion can work in the global marketplace. If kugak fusion incorporates simple harmonic and melodic structures based on Korean takes on Western classical, jazz, and pop music, then these will not readily match European or North American jazz and pop. At the time of writing, it is somewhat unfortunate to see that Korean funding agencies, although aware of far-from-positive reviews of a number of recent attempts, continue to push kugak fusion abroad while limiting support for *kugak*.

Bibliography

Abelmann, Nancy. 1996. *Echoes of the past, epics of dissent: A South Korean social movement.* Berkeley: University of California Press.

———. 2002. Women, mobility, and desire: Narrating class and gender in South Korea. In Kendall 2002, 25–54.

———. 2003. *The melodrama of mobility: Women, talk, and class in contemporary South Korea.* Honolulu: University of Hawai'i Press.

Abelmann, Nancy, and Jung-ah Choi. 2005. "Just because": Comedy, melodrama and youth violence in *Attack the gas station.* In *New Korean cinema,* ed. Chi-Yun Shin and Julian Stringer, 132–143. Edinburgh: Edinburgh University Press.

Adorno, Theodor W. [1968] 1988. *Introduction to the sociology of music.* New York: Continuum.

Akiba, Takashi. 1957. A study on Korean folkways. *Folklore Studies* 16:1–106.

AlSayyad, Nezar. 2001. Global norms and urban forms in the age of tourism: Manufacturing heritage, consuming tradition. In *Consuming tradition, manufacturing heritage,* ed. Nezar AlSayyad, 1–33. London: Routledge.

Alvesson, Mats. 1996. *Cultural perspectives on organizations.* New York: Cambridge University Press.

Anagnost, Ann S. 1994. The politics of ritual displacement. In *Asian visions of authority: Religion and the modern states of East and Southeast Asia,* ed. C. F. Keyes, L. Kendall, and H. Hardacre, 221–254. Honolulu: University of Hawai'i Press.

Anonymous. 1938. Hantō no minyo odori wo sekaiteki buyō ni: Bijin maihime, Sai Shōki san Chaku Sō [Making folk dance of the Peninsula into a universal dance: Beautiful dancing Princess Sai Shōki arrives in San Francisco]. *Shinsokai Asahi,* January 13.

———. 1939. Review and captioned photograph. *Dancing Times* (London), January 13, 510–511.

Appadurai, Arjun. 1986a. Introduction: Commodities and the politics of value. In Appadurai 1986b, 3–63.

———, ed. 1986b. *The social life of things: Commodities in cultural perspective.* Cambridge: Cambridge University Press.

———. 1990. Disjuncture and difference in the global economy. *Public Culture* 2 (2): 1–24.

———. 1996. *Modernity at large: Cultural dimensions of globalization.* Minneapolis: University of Minnesota Press.

Ariyama Teruo. 2002. *Kaigai kankō ryokō no tanjō* [The birth of foreign travel]. Tokyo: Yoshikawa kōbunkan.

Babcock, Barbara. 1986. Modeled selves: Helen Codere's "little people." In *The Anthropology of Experience,* ed. V. W. Turner and E. M. Bruner, 316–343. Urbana: University of Illinois Press.

Backes, Nancy. 1997. Reading the shopping mall city. *Journal of Popular Culture* 31 (3): 1–17.

Bak, Sangmee. 1997. McDonald's in Seoul: Food choices, identity, and nationalism. In Watson 1997, 136–160.

———. 2004. Negotiating national and transnational identities through consumption choices: Hamburgers, espresso, and mobile technologies among Koreans. *Review of Korean Studies* 7 (2): 33–52.

———. 2005. From strange bitter concoction to romantic necessity: The social history of coffee drinking in South Korea. *Korea Journal* 45 (2): 37–59.

Bank of Chōsen. 1919. *Pictorial Chōsen and Manchuria.* Compiled in commemoration of the decennial of the Bank of Chōsen. Seoul: Bank of Chōsen.

Baudrillard, Jean. 1983. *Simulations.* New York: Semiotext(e).

———. 1987. Modernity. *Canadian Journal of Political and Social Theory* 11 (3): 63–73.

———. 2001. Simulacra and simulations. In *Selected writings,* ed. M. Poster, 166–184. Stanford, CA: Stanford University Press.

Beardsworth, Alan, and Teresa Keil. 1997. *Sociology on the menu: An invitation to the study of food and society.* London: Routledge.

Beaulieu, Jill, and Mary Roberts, eds. 2002. *Orientalism's interlocutors: Painting, architecture, photography.* Durham, NC: Duke University Press.

Bendix, Regina. 1997. *In search of authenticity: The formation of folklore studies.* Madison: University of Wisconsin Press.

Benjamin, Walter. 1969. The work of art in the age of mechanical reproduction. In *Illuminations: Essays and reflections,* ed. H. Arendt, 217–251. New York: Schocken.

Bennet, Tony. 1988. The exhibitionary complex. *New Formations* 1:73–102.

Bergman, Sten. 1938. *In Korean wilds and villages.* Trans. Frederick Whyte. London: John Gifford Ltd.

Berman, Marshall. 1983. *All that is solid melts into air: The experience of modernity.* London: Verso.

Bloch, Peter H., Nancy M. Ridgway, and Scott A. Dawson. 1994. The shopping mall as consumer habitat. *Journal of Retailing* 70 (1): 23–42.

Born, Georgina, and David Hesmondhalgh, eds. 2000. *Western music and its others: Difference, representation, and appropriation in music.* Berkeley: University of California Press.

Bourdieu, Pierre. 1984. *Distinction*. Trans. Richard Nice. Cambridge, MA: Harvard University Press.

———. 2000. *Pascalian meditations*. Trans. Richard Nice. Cambridge, MA: Polity.

Boym, Svetlana. 2001. *The future of nostalgia*. New York: Basic Books.

Brandon, James R. 2009. *Kabuki's forgotten war, 1931–1945*. Honolulu: University of Hawai'i Press.

Brody, Alyson. 2006. The cleaners you aren't meant to see: Order, hygiene and everyday politics in a Bangkok shopping mall. *Antipode* 38 (3): 534–556.

Byeon Gyewon. 2001a. *Ch'angjak kugak*: Writing new music for Korean traditional instruments. PhD diss., University of London.

———. 2001b. The concept of composition in Korean music. Paper presented at the Sixth International Asian Music Conference, Seoul.

Callon, Michel. 1998a. An essay on framing and overflowing: Economic externalities revisited by sociology. In *The laws of the markets,* ed. Michel Callon, 244–269. Oxford: Blackwell.

———. 1998b. Introduction: The embeddedness of economic markets in economics. In *The laws of the markets,* ed. Michel Callon, 1–57. Oxford: Blackwell.

Callon, Michel, Cécile Méadel, and Vololona Rabeharisoa. 2002. The economy of qualities. *Economy and Society* 31 (2): 194–217.

Campbell, Colin. 1992. The desire for the new: Its nature and social location as presented in theories of fashion and modern consumerism. In *Consuming technologies: Media and information in domestic spaces,* ed. R. Silverstone and E. Hirsch, 48–62. London: Routledge.

Causey, Andrew. 2003. *Hard bargaining in Sumatra: Western travelers and Toba Bataks in the marketplace of souvenirs*. Honolulu: University of Hawai'i Press.

Cavendish, Captain A. E. 1894. *Korea and the sacred White Mountain: Being a brief account of a journey in Korea in 1891*. London: George Philip and Son.

CGK (Government-General of Chōsen — Chōsen Sōtokufu). 1915–1935. *Chōsen koseki zufu* [Album of ancient Korean sites and monuments]. 15 vols. Seoul: CGK.

———. 1929. *Chōsen of today*. Compiled in commemoration of the vicennial of the Government-General of Chōsen. Seoul: CGK.

———. 1938. Bukkokuji to Sekkutsuan [Pulguk Temple and Sokkuram Cave in Keishū]. Vol. 1 of *Chōsen hōmotsu koseki zuroku* [Album of Korean antiquities]. Kyoto: Bunseido.

CGR (Chōsen Government Railways — Chōsen tetsudo). 1923. *Chōsen tetsudō ryokō henran* [Guidebook to Chōsen railways]. CGR.

———. 1932. *Chōsen Kongosan* [Kŭmkangsan in Chōsen]. CGR.

———. 1936. *Keishū* [Guide to Kyŏngju]. CGR.

———. 1938. *Keijō, Jinsen, Suigen, Kaijō* [Seoul, Inch'ŏn, Suwŏn, Kaesŏng]. CGR.

———. n.d. *Chōsen no hanashi* [Stories of Korea]. Tokyo: CGR.

Ch'ae Hyun-kyung. 1996. *Ch'angjak kugak:* Making Korean music Korean. PhD diss., University of Michigan.

———. 1998. *Ch'angjak kugak* (Newly composed Korean music): Making Korean music Korean. *Tongyang ŭmak/Journal of the Asian Music Research Institute* 20: 289–316.

———. 2000. Newly-composed Korean music: Westernization, modernization, or Koreanization? *Tongyang ŭmak/Journal of the Asian Music Research Institute* 22:141–151.

Ch'ae Man-Sik. [1938] 1993. *Peace under heaven*. Trans. K.-J. Chun. Armonk. New York: M. E. Sharpe.

———. 1998. A ready-made life. In *A ready-made life: Early masters of modern Korean fiction,* trans. Kim Chong-un and Bruce Fulton, 55–80. Honolulu: University of Hawai'i Press.

Chakrabarty, Dipesh. 1998. Afterword: Revisiting the tradition/modernity binary. In *Mirror of modernity: Invented traditions of modern Japan,* ed. Stephen Vlastos, 285–296. Berkeley: University of California Press.

Chamberlain, Basil Hall, and W. B. Mason. 1907. *Handbook for travelers in Japan, including the whole empire from Saghalien to Formosa.* 8th ed. London: John Murray.

———. 1913. *Handbook for travelers in Japan, including Formosa.* 9th ed. London: John Murray.

Chang, Yoonhee. 2004. Promoting traditional music through radio in South Korea: An ethnography of GugakFM, a media institution. MA thesis, Indiana University.

Chaplin, Sarah, and Eric Holding. 1998. Consuming architecture. *Architectural Design* 131:7–9.

Cheon, Hong-Beom. 2000. Current status of Korean kimchi export and the means to expand kimchi export. Paper presented at the 12th Kimchi Symposium, Kimchi Research Institute, Pusan University.

Cho Hae-joang (Cho Han Hae-joang). 1994a. Chŏntong kwa han'guk munhwa e taehan tamnon punsŏk [An analysis of the discourses on Korean tradition and culture]. *Tongbanghakji* 96:175–210.

———. 1994b. *T'al singminji sidae chisigin ŭi kŭl ilgi wa salm ilgi 3: Hanoi esŏ Sinch'ŏn kkaji* [A postmodern era intellectual's reading of text and reading of life 3: From Hanoi to Sinch'ŏn]. Seoul: Tto hana ŭi munhwasa.

———. 1998. Constructing and deconstructing "Koreanness." In *Making majorities: Constituting the nation in Japan, Korea, China, Malaysia, Fiji, Turkey, and the United States,* ed. Dru C. Gladney, 73–91. Stanford, CA: Stanford University Press.

Cho Hung-yŏn. 1990. *Mu wa minjok-munhwa* [Mu and folk culture]. Seoul: Minjok munhwa sa.

Ch'oe, Sang-cheul (Ch'oe Sang-ch'ŏl). 1996. Seung-hee Choi [*sic*], pioneer of Korean modern dance: Her life and art under Japanese occupation, 1910–1945. PhD diss., New York University.

Ch'oe Hyŏng-bŏm. 1993. *Changseang* [Changsŭng]. Seoul: Tosŏch'ulp'an ŭnhyesa.

Ch'oe Kilsung (Ch'oe Kilsŏng). 1974. Misin t'ap'ae taehan ilgoch'al [A study of the destruction of superstition] *Han'gugminsokhak* [Korean folklore] 7:39–54.

———. 2003. *War and ethnology/folklore in colonial Korea: The case of Akiba Takashi.* Vol. 65 of *Wartime Japanese anthropology in Asia and the Pacific.* Osaka: National Museum of Ethnology.

Ch'oe Sŭng-hŭi. 1936. *Watakushi no jijoden* [My autobiography]. Tokyo: Nihon Shosō.

———. 1937. *Naŭi chasŏjŏn* [My autobiography]. Kyŏngsŏng: Imundang.

Choi, Chungmoo. 1991. Nami, Ch'ae, and Oksun; Superstar shamans in Korea. In *Shamans of the twentieth century,* ed. R. I. Heinze, 51–61. New York: Irvington.

———. 1993. The discourse of decolonization and popular memory: South Korea. *Positions* 1 (1): 77–102.

———. 1995. The Minjung culture movement and the construction of popular culture in Korea. In *South Korea's minjung movement: The culture and politics of dissidence,* ed. K. M. Wells, 105–118. Honolulu: University of Hawai'i Press.

Choi, Haeree (Ch'oe Hae-ri). 1995. *Ch'angjak ch'um:* History and nature of a contemporary Korean dance genre. MA thesis, University of Hawai'i.

Ch'ŏn Puk-hua. 2001. *Mudang naeryŏk* [Mudang chronicles]. Seoul: Minsogwŏn.

Chŏn Yŏngjo, ed. 1982. *Kugak yŏnhyŏk* [History of *kugak*]. Seoul: Kungnip kugagwŏn.

Chŏn Yu-sŏng. 1997. *Nam ŭi munhwa yusan tapsagi 1* [The chronicle of my field study of other people's cultural remains 1]. Seoul: Gaseowon.

Chŏng Chae-jŏng. 1999. *Ilche ch'im nyak kwa Han'guk ch'ŏldo* (1892–1945). Seoul: Taehakkyo ch'ulp'anbu.

Chong Dae Sung. 2004. *Yakiniku, mikuchi to nihonjin* [Seasoned and sliced grilled beef, *kimuchi,* and the Japanese]. Tokyo: PHP Shinsho.

Chŏng Hye-kyŏng and Yi Chŏng-hye. 1996. *Sŏul-e umshik munhwa: Yŏngyang hakkwa illyuhak-e mannam* [Culinary culture of Seoul: Nutritional science meets anthropology]. Seoul: Sŏulhak yŏn'guso.

Chŏng Pyŏng-ho. 1995. *Ch'umch'unŭn Ch'oe Sŭng-hŭi — Segyerŭl hwiachabŭn Chosŏn yŏja* [The dancing Ch'oe Sŭng-hŭi — The Korean woman who captivated the world]. Seoul: Deep-Rooted Tree Publishing House.

Chou, Wen-chung. 1967. Towards a re-merger in music. In *Contemporary composers on contemporary music,* ed. Elliott Schwartz and Barney Childs, 308–315. New York: Holt, Rinehart and Winston.

———. 1971. Asian concepts and twentieth-century Western composers. *Music Quarterly* 57 (2): 211–229.

Chun, Kyung-Soo. 2002. Anthropology of colonialism and war during Imperial Japan: Scholars and scholarship at Taihoku Imperial University (Taiwan) and Keijo Imperial University (Korea). *Cross-Cultural Studies* 8 (2): 135–167.

Clark, Charles Allen. 1961. *Religions of old Korea.* Seoul: Christian Literature Society.

Clifford, James. 1988. *The predicament of culture: Twentieth-century ethnography, literature, and art.* Cambridge, MA: Harvard University Press.

Clunas, Craig. 1991. *Superfluous things: Material culture and social status in early modern China.* Cambridge, MA: Polity Press.

Cohen, Eric. 1995. Contemporary tourism- trends and challenges: Sustainable authenticity or contrived post-modernity? In *Change in tourism: People, places, processes,* ed. R. Butler and D. Pearce, 12-29. London: Routledge.

Cohen, Erik. 1973. Nomads from affluence: Notes on the phenomenon of drifter-tourism. *International Journal of Comparative Sociology* 14:89–103.

———. 2003. Backpacking: Diversity and change. *Tourism and Cultural Change* 1 (2): 95–110.

Cohen, Nicole. 2006. Children of empire: Growing up Japanese in colonial Korea, 1876–1946. PhD diss., Columbia University.

Cohn, Bernard S. 1996. *Colonialism and its forms of knowledge: The British in India.* Princeton, NJ: Princeton University Press.

Comaroff, Jean. 1985. *Body of power spirit of resistance: The culture and history of a South African people.* Chicago: University of Chicago Press.

———. 1996. The empire's old clothes: Fashioning the colonial subject. In *Cross-cultural consumption: Global markets, local realities,* ed. D. Howes, 19–38. London: Routledge.

Connerton, Paul. 1989. *How societies remember.* Cambridge: Cambridge University Press.

Cook, Thomas, and Son. 1998. *Letters from the sea and from the foreign lands: Descriptive of a tour round the world (1873).* The History of Tourism Series 3. London: Routledge.

Crawford, Margaret. 1992. The world in a shopping mall. In *Variations on a theme park: The new American city and the end of public space,* ed. M. Sorkin, 3–30. New York: Hill and Wang.

Creighton, Millie. 1997. Consuming rural Japan: The marketing of tradition and nostalgia in the Japanese travel industry. *Ethnology* 36 (3): 239–254.

Cwiertka, Katarzyna J. 2006. *Modern Japanese cuisine: Food, power and national identity.* London: Reaktion Books.

Cybriwsky, Roman. 1999. Changing patterns of urban public space: Observations and assessments from the Tokyo and New York metropolitan areas. *Cities* 16 (4): 223–231.

Davis, Susan G. 1996. The theme park: Global industry and cultural form. *Media, Culture and Society* 18:399–422.

Debord, Guy. 1983. *Society of the spectacle.* Detroit: Black and Red.

de Certeau, Michel. 1984. *The practice of everyday life.* Trans. S. Rendall. Berkeley: University of California Press.

Deering, Mabel Craft. 1933. Chosen: Land of morning calm. *National Geographic* 44 (July–December): 421–448.

Delissen, Alain. 2001. The aesthetic pasts of space. *Korean Studies* 25 (2): 243–260.

———. 2004. Frustrations centripètes et pays cachés: Retour sur le régionalisme Coréen et la question du cheolla, 1925–1993 [Centripetal frustrations and hidden regions: A return to Korean regionalism and the question of Chŏlla, 1925–1993]. In *La Corée en miettes: Régions et territoires* [Korea in fragments: Regions and territories]. Géographie et cultures [Geography and cultures] 51, ed. Valérie Gelézeau, 15–31. Paris: Éditions L'Harmattan.

DeNora, Tia. 2000. *Music in everyday life.* Cambridge: Cambridge University Press.

Deuchler, Martina. 1992. *The Confucian transformation of Korea: A study of society and ideology.* Cambridge, MA: Harvard University Press.

Duranti, Alessandro, and Charles Goodwin, eds. 1992. *Rethinking context: Language as an interactive phenomenon.* Cambridge: Cambridge University Press.

Durkheim, Emile. 1915. *The elementary forms of the religious life.* Trans. Joseph Ward Swain. New York: Free Press.

Duus, Peter. 1995. *The abacus and the sword: The Japanese penetration of Korea, 1895–1910.* Berkeley: University of California Press.

Eckert, Carter J. 1991. *Offspring of empire: The Koch'ang Kims and the colonial origins of Korean capitalism, 1876–1945.* Seattle: University of Washington Press.

———. 1993. The South Korean bourgeoisie: A class in search of hegemony. In *State and society in contemporary Korea,* ed. Hagen Koo, 95–130. Ithaca, NY: Cornell University Press.

Eco, Umberto. 2002. *Travels in hyperreality: Essays.* San Diego, CA: Harcourt.

Editorial. 1934a. Mitsukoshi, Chōjiya, Minakai shokudō gassenki [Record of the Battle between Mitsukoshi, Chōjiya, and Minakai]. *Chōsen oyobi Manshū* [Korea and Manchukuo] 317:86–88.

———. 1934b. Shokudō haiken [Looking into canteens]. *Chōsen oyobi Manshū* [Korea and Manchukuo] 319:87–89.

———. 1935. Saero naksŏng toen ochu'ŭngu paekhwajŏm kugyŏnggii [Record of a visit to the newly completed five-story Hwasin department store]. *Samch'ŏlli* 7 (9): 388–390.

Edwards, Elizabeth. 1992. *Anthropology and photography (1860–1920).* New Haven, CT: Yale University Press.

Edwards, Elizabeth, Chris Gosden, and Ruth B. Phillips, eds. 2006a. *Sensible objects: Colonialism, museums and material culture.* Oxford: Berg.

———, eds. 2006b. Introduction. In Edwards, Gosden, and Phillips 2006a, 1–31.

Edwards, Walter. 2003. Monuments to an unbroken line: The imperial tombs and the emergence of modern Japanese nationalism. In *Politics of archaeology and identity in a global context,* ed. S. Kane, 11–30. Boston: Archaeological Institute of America.

Epstein, Stephen. 2000. Anarchy in the U.K., solidarity in the R.O.K.: Punk rock comes to Korea. *Acta Koreana* 3:1–34.

Epstein, Stephen, and Timothy R. Tangherlini. 2002. *Our nation: A Korean punk rock community.* Documentary film. New York: Filmakers Library.

Erdman, Joan L. 1996. Dance discourses: Rethinking the history of the "Oriental Dance." In *Moving words: Re-writing dance,* ed. Gay Morris, 288–305. London: Routledge.

Everett, Yayoi Uno, and Frederick Lau, eds. 2004. *Locating East Asia in Western art music.* Middletown, CT: Wesleyan University Press.

Fisher, Marjory. 1938. Sai Shōki is acclaimed in debut. *San Francisco News,* January 24.

Forshee, Jill. 2001. *Between the folds: Stories of cloth, lives, and travels from Sumba.* Honolulu: University of Hawai'i Press.

Frankenstein, Alexander. 1938. Korean dancer makes debut. *San Francisco Chronicle,* January 23.

Freeberg, David. 1989. *The power of images: Studies in the history and theory of response.* Chicago: University of Chicago Press.

Fried, Alexander. 1938. Korean dances of Sai Shoki lack variety. *San Francisco Examiner,* January 23.

Fukuzawa Yukichi. 1934. *The autobiography of Fukuzawa Yukichi.* Trans. Eichii Kiyooka. Tokyo: Hokuseido Press.

Gale, James S. 1898. *Korean sketches.* New York: Fleming H. Revell.

———. 1911. *Korea in transition.* New York: Missionary Education Movement of the United States and Canada.

Garcia, Marie-France. 1986. La construction sociale d'un marché parfait: Le marché au cadran de Fontaines-en-Sologne [The social construction of a perfect market: The declining bids auction market of Fontaines-en-Sologne]. *Actes de la Recherche en Science Sociales* 65:2–13.

Gelezeau, Valerie. 1999. Habiter un grand ensemble á Seoul: Formes contemporaines du logement et pratiques de l'espace résidentiel en Corée du Sud [Living in a large apartment building in Seoul: Contemporary residential forms and spatial practices in South Korea]. Thesis, Université de Paris IV-Sorbonne.

———. 2003. *Seoul, ville géante, cités radieuses* [Seoul, giant city, radiant cities]. Paris: CNRS Editions.

Gell, Alfred. 1998. *Art and agency: An anthropological theory.* Oxford: Clarendon Press.

Gifford, Daniel L. 1898. *Every-day life in Korea: A collection of studies and stories.* Chicago: Fleming H. Revell.

Goffman, Erving. 1974. *Frame analysis: An essay on the organization of experience.* Cambridge, MA: Harvard University Press.

Gottdiener, Mark. 1998. Consumption of space and spaces of consumption. *Architectural Design* 131:12–15.

Graburn, Nelson H. H. 1976. *Ethnic and tourist arts: Cultural expressions from the fourth world.* Berkeley: University of California Press.

———. 1995. The past in the present in Japan: Nostalgia and neo-traditionalism in contemporary Japanese domestic tourism. In *Change in tourism: People, places, processes,* ed. Richard Butler and Douglas Pearce. London: Routledge.

———. 1997. Tourism and cultural development in East Asia and Oceania. In *Tourism and cultural development in Asia and Oceania,* ed. S. Yamashita, K. H. Din, and J. S. Eades, 178–193. Bangi: Penerbit Universiti Kebangsaan Malaysia.

Grajdanzev, Andrew J. 1944. *Modern Korea.* New York: John Day Co.

Griffis, William Elliot. 1911. *Corea: The hermit nation.* New York: Charles Scribner's Sons.

Grinker, Roy Richard. 1998. *Korea and its futures: Unification and the unfinished war.* New York: St. Martin's Press.

Gwon, Hyeok Hui (Kwŏn Hyŏk-hŭi). 2005. *Chosŏnesŏon sajinyŏpsŏ* [Postcards from Chosŏn]. Seoul: Minumsa.

———. 2007. Iljesigi "chosŏnp'ungsoginyŏng" kwa Chosŏninŭi sigakchŏk chaehyŏn [A study of "Joseon folk dolls" and visual reproduction of Koreans during the period of Japanese imperialism]. Kungnimminsokpangmulguan [National Folk Museum of Korea], no. 12:7–29.

Ha, Ju-yong. 2005. Korean Kisaeng and their performing traditions under the impact of Japanese colonialism. Paper presented at the annual conference of the Society for Ethnomusicology, Atlanta, GA.

Hamada Kōsaku and J. G. Andersson. 1932a. The Far East. *Museum of Far Eastern Antiquities* 4:9–14.

———. 1932b. *Keishu Kingan tsuka* [Tomb of the Gold Crown]. Tokyo: Keishū koseki hozonkai [Kyŏngju Preservation Society].

Han, Kyung-Koo (Han Kyŏng-gu). 1994. Ŏttŏn ŭmsik ŭn saenggak hagi e chot'a: Kimch'i wa Han'guk minjoksŏng ŭi chŏngsu [Some foods are good to think: Kimchi and the essence of Korean nationality]. *Han'guk munhwa illyuhak* 26:51–68.

———. 2000. Some foods are good to think: Kimchi and the epitomization of national character. *Korean Social Science Journal* 27 (1): 231–235.

Handler, Richard. 1988. *Nationalism and the politics of culture in Quebec.* Madison: University of Wisconsin Press.

Handler, Richard, and Jocelyn Linnekin. 1984. Tradition, genuine or spurious. *Journal of American Folklore* 97 (385): 273–290.

Hane, Mikiso, trans. and ed. 1988. *Reflections on the way to the gallows.* Berkeley: University of California Press.

Han'guk munhwa yesul chinhŭngwŏn [Korean Culture and Arts Foundation]. 1992, 1995, 2002. *Munye yŏn'gam 1992, 1995, 2002* [Yearbook of arts and culture, 1992, 1995, 2002]. Seoul: Han'guk munhwa yesul chinhŭngwŏn.

Han'guk yesul yŏn'guso [Korean Arts Research Institute], ed. 1995–1997. *Han'guk chakkok kasajip* [Collection of Korean compositions], vols. 1–3. Seoul: Han'guk yesul chonghap hakkyo [Korean National University of Arts].

Han'guk yŏngsang ŭmban hyŏphoe [Korean Video and Record Association], ed. 1998. *Han'guk ŭmban, pidioyŏn'gam 1998* [Yearbook of Korean record and video, 1998]. Seoul: Han'guk yŏngsang ŭmban hyŏphoe.

Hannerz, Ulf. 1992. *Cultural complexity: Studies in the social organization of meaning.* New York: Columbia University Press.

Harker, Dave, 1985. *Fakesong: The manufacture of British "folksong" from 1700 to the present day.* Milton Keynes, UK: Open University Press.

Hart, Dennis. 2001. *From tradition to consumption: Construction of a capitalist culture in South Korea.* Seoul: Jimoondang.

Hatsuda Tōru. 1993. *Hyakkaten no tanjō* [The birth of the department store]. Tokyo: Sanseidō.

Hayashi Hiroshige. 2003. *Maboroshi no Minakai hyakkaten: Chōsen o sekken shita Ōmi shōnin hyakkatenō no kōbō* [The phantom of Minakai department store: How Ōmi merchants conquered Korea, or ups and downs of a department store]. Tokyo: Banseisha.

Heidegger, Martin. 1962. *Being and time.* Trans. John Macquarrie and Edward Robinson. San Francisco: HarperSanFrancisco.

Hendry, Joy. 2000a. Foreign country theme parks: A new theme or an old Japanese pattern? *Social Science Japan Journal* 3 (2): 207–220.

———. 2000b. *The Orient strikes back: A global view of cultural display.* Oxford: Berg.

Hesselink, Nathan. 2004. *SamulNori* as traditional: Preservation and innovation in a South Korean contemporary percussion genre. *Ethnomusicology* 48 (3): 405–439.

Heyman, Alan C. 1985. Hwang Pyŏng-gi Korean masterpieces. *Korea Journal* 25 (5): 58–60.

Hindman, Heather. 2009. Shopping in the bazaar/bizarre shopping: Culture and the accidental elitism of expatriates in Kathmandu, Nepal. *Journal of Popular Culture* 42 (4): 663–679.

Hirabayashi, Hisae. 1977. Sai Shōki to Ishii Baku [Sai Shōki and Ishii Baku]. Special issue, *Zainichi Chōsenjin no genjō* [The present state of Korean residents in Japan], no. 12 (November 1): 186–192.

Hobsbawm, Eric. 1990. *Nations and nationalism since 1780.* Cambridge: Cambridge University Press.

Hobsbawm, Eric, and Terence Ranger, eds. 1983. *The invention of tradition.* Cambridge: Cambridge University Press.

Hochschild, Arlie Russell. 2003. *The commercialization of intimate life: Notes from home and work.* Berkeley: University of California Press.

Hoffenberger, Peter H. 2001. *An empire on display: English, Indian, and Australian exhibitions from the Crystal Palace to the Great War.* Berkeley: University of California Press.

Howard, Keith. 1989. *Bands, songs, and shamanistic rituals: Folk music in Korean society.* Seoul: Royal Asiatic Society, Korea Branch.

———. 1998. Preserving the spirits? Rituals, state sponsorship, and performance. In *Korean shamanism: Revivals, survivals, and change,* ed. K. Howard, 187–207. Seoul: Royal Asiatic Society, Korea Branch.

———. 1999. *Korean music: A listening guide.* Seoul: National Center for Korean Traditional Performing Arts.

———. 2006. *Perspectives on Korean music 1: Preserving Korean music.* Aldershot, UK: Ashgate.

Hower, Ralph M. 1946. *History of Macy's of New York, 1858–1919: Chapters in the evolution of the department store.* Cambridge, MA: Harvard University Press.

Howes, David. 1996. *Cross-cultural consumption: Global markets, local realities.* New York: Routledge.

Huang Hyŏnman, Yi Chong-ch'ŏl, et al. 1988. *Changsŭng.* Seoul: Yŏlhuadang.

Hutcheon, Linda. 1988. *A poetics of postmodernism: History, theory, fiction.* New York: Routledge.

Hwang Wŏn-uk. 1997. Yŏhaeng ŭn "what" i anira "how" [Not the "what" but the "how" of travel]. *Paenang yŏhaeng* 2 (1): 128.

Hyakkaten shōhōsha, ed. 1933. *Nihon hyakkaten sōran* [Guide to Japanese department stores]. Tokyo: Hyakkaten shōhōsha.

IFPI. 2005. *The recording industry: World sales.* London: IFPI.

Im, Tong-gwŏn. 1999. *Taejanggun sinangŭi yŏn'gu* [Research on beliefs regarding the great general]. Seoul: Minsogwŏn.

Inoue Shigeo. 1933. Keijō depāto gassen [The battle of Keijō department stores]. *Chōsen oyobi Manshū* [Korea and Manchukuo] 310:81–83.

Ivy, Marilyn. 1988. Tradition and difference in the Japanese mass media. *Public Culture Bulletin* 1 (1): 21–29.

———. 1995. *Discourses of the vanishing: Modernity, phantasm, Japan.* Chicago: University of Chicago Press.

Jager, Sheila Miyoshi. 1996. Women, resistance and the divided nation: The romantic rhetoric of Korean reunification. *Journal of Asian Studies* 55 (1): 3–21.

Jameson, Fredric. 1984. Postmodernism, or the cultural logic of late capitalism. *New Left Review* 123:53–92.

———. 1991. *Postmodernism, or, The cultural logic of late capitalism.* Durham, NC: Duke University Press.

Janelli, Roger L., and Dawnhee Yim Janelli. 1982. *Ancestor worship and Korean society.* Stanford, CA: Stanford University Press.

Japan Imperial Government Railways (JIR). 1926. *Pocket Guide to Japan.* Ed. Frederic De Garis. JTB.

Japan Tourist Bureau (JTB). 1917. *Tsūristo* [The tourist]. No. 27. Tokyo: Japan Imperial Government Railways.

———. 1926. *Guide to Japan.* Tokyo.

———. n.d., ca. 1930s. *The Chosen Hotel: Keijo (Seoul).* Chosen: Japan Tourist Bureau.

———. 1982. *Nihon Kōts kōsha nanajūnen shi* [Seventy years of the Japan Tourist Bureau]. Tokyo: JTB.

Japan Tourist Bureau (JTB) Chōsen Branch. 1939. *Heizyō, Tyōsen branch* [How to see Heizyō (P'yŏngyang)]. JTB.

———. n.d. *How to see Keishū, Chōsen.* Toppan Printing Co.

Jonaitis, Aldona. 1999. Northwest Coast totem poles. In Phillips and Steiner 1999b, 104–121.

Jones, George Heber. 1902. The spirit worship of the Koreans. *Transactions of the Royal Asiatic Society, Korea Branch* 2:37–58.

Joongang ilbo. 2004. Chinese kimchi gets ahead of Korean kimchi in Japan. October 15.

Kanda Koji. 2003. Landscapes of national parks in Taiwan during the Japanese colonial period. In *Representing local places and raising voices from below,* ed. Toshio Mizuuchi, 112–119. Osaka: Osaka City University.

Kang, Hildi. 2001. *Under the black umbrella: Voices from colonial Korea, 1910–1945.* Ithaca, NY: Cornell University Press.

Kang, Sŏk-kyŏng. [1986] 1989. A room in the woods. In *Words of farewell: Stories by Korean women writers,* by Kang Sŏk-kyŏng, Kim Chi-wŏn, and O Chŏng-hŭi, trans. Bruce Fulton and Ju-Chan Fulton, 28–147. Seattle: Seal Press.

Kang Nae-hŭi. 1995. Monopoly capital and "cultural space": A reading of Lotte World. *Muae* 1:34–59.

KBS Global. List of pro-Japanese collaborators announced. April 29, 2008. http://english.kbs.co.kr/news/news print.php?key=2008041911

Keijŏ shŏkŏ kaigisho. 1939. *Keijŏ shŏkŏ meiroku* [The register of commerce and industry of Keijŏ]. Keijŏ: Keijŏ shŏkŏ kaigisho.

Keishū Koseki Hozonkai zaidan (Kyŏngju Preservation Corporation). 1922. *Keishū koseki annai* [A guide to ancient remains in Kyŏngju]. Keishū.

———. 1929. *Keishū koseki zu: Silla Gyūdo* [Illustrated old capital of Silla]. Keishū.

———. 1935. *Keishū koseki annai* [A guide to ancient remains in Kyŏngju]. Rev. ed. Keishū.

Kelly, William. 1986. Rationalization and nostalgia: Cultural dynamics of new middle-class Japan. *American Ethnologist* 13 (4): 603–618.

Kendall, Laurel. 1998. Who speaks for Korean shamans when shamans speak of the nation? In *Making majorities: Constituting the nation in Japan, Korea, China, Malaysia, Fiji, Turkey, and the United States,* ed. D. Gladney, 55–72. Stanford, CA: Stanford University Press.

———, ed. 2002. *Under construction: The gendering of modernity, class, and consumption in the Republic of Korea.* Honolulu: University of Hawai'i Press.

———. 2008. Of hungry ghosts and other matters of consumption in the Korean shaman world. *American Ethnologist* 35 (1): 1–17.

Killick, Andrew. 1998. The invention of traditional Korean opera and the problem of the traditionesque. PhD diss., University of Washington.

Kim, Kwang-ok. 1988. A study on the political manipulation of elite culture: Confucian culture in local level politics. *Korea Journal* (November).

———. 1992. Socio-political implications of the resurgence of ancestor worship on contemporary Korea. In *Home bound: Studies in East Asian society,* ed. Nakane Chie and Chien Chao, 179–203. Tokyo: Center for East Asian Cultural Studies.

———. 1994. Rituals of resistance: The manipulation of shamanism in contemporary Korea. In *Asian visions of authority: Religion and the modern states in East and Southeast Asia,* ed. Charles F. Keyes, Laurel Kendall, and Helen Hardacre, 195–219. Honolulu: University of Hawai'i Press.

————. 1996. The reproduction of Confucian culture in contemporary Korea: An anthropological study. In *Confucian traditions in East Asian modernity: Moral education and economic culture in Japan and the four mini-dragons,* ed. Tu Wei-Ming, 202–227. Cambridge, MA: Harvard University Press.

————. 2001. Contested terrain of imagination: Chinese food in Korea. In *Changing Chinese foodways in Asia,* ed. D. Y. H. Wu and C. B. Tan, 201–218. Hong Kong: Chinese University Press.

Kim, Kyoung-ae. 1995. Development of Korean dance since liberation. *Koreana* (Autumn): 56–61.

Kim, Manjo. 2001. Development of kimchi in global village and the half century history of industrialization of kimchi production in Korea. Paper presented at the 13th Kimchi Symposium, Seoul, Korea.

Kim, Young-hoon. 2003. Self-representation: The visualization of Koreanness in tourism posters during the 1970s and the 1980s. *Korea Journal* 43 (1): 83–105.

————. 2006. Border-crossing: Choe Seung-hui's life and the modern experience. *Korea Journal* 46 (1): 170–197.

Kim Chin-man. 1995. *X: Orae toen choŭn kŏt poda saeroun nappŭn kŏt i chot'a* [X: New bad things are better than old good things]. Seoul: Kyŏre.

Kim Ch'ŏng-uk, ed. 1999. Tonggŏng e issŏso ŭi Ch'oe Sŭng-hŭi che il-hoe palp'yohoe Insanggi [Written impressions of Ch'oe Sŭng-hŭi's first performance in Tokyo]. *Ch'um* (April): 76–81.

Kim Ch'ŏn-hŭng. 2005. *Simso Kim Ch'ŏn-hŭng sŏnsaengnimŭi uri ch'um iyagi* [Stories of our (Korean) dance by Master Simso Kim Ch'ŏn-hŭng]. Seoul: Minsogwŏn.

Kim Jin-song. 1999. *Sŏul e ttanssŭhol ŭl hŏhara: Hyŏndaesŏng ŭi hyŏngsŏng* [Dance halls in Seoul: Creating the contemporary]. Seoul: Hyŏnsil Munhwa Yŏn'gu.

Kim Sŏnghye, ed. 1998. *Han'guk ŭmak kwallyŏnhak ŭi nonmun ch'ongmok* [Full text of treatises on Korean music related studies]. Seoul: Minsogwŏn.

Kim Sŏng-yŏl. 1996. Kalmaegi Chonadan i toeja [Let's become Jonathan Seagull]. *Paenang yŏhaeng* 1 (11): 12.

Kim Sungmun. 1993. *Die geschichte, struktur and politische funktion der Koreanische medien* [The history, structure and political function of Korean media]. Frankfurt: Peter Lang.

Kim T'ae-su. 2005. *Kkot kach'o p'iŏ maehokkke hara* [May women bloom like flowers]. Seoul: Hwangso Chari.

Kim Tu-ha. 1990. *Pŏksuwa changsŭng* [Pŏksu and changsŭng]. Seoul: Chimmundang.

Kim Tu-ha, Yun Yŏl-su, Song Pong Hwa, Kang Hyŏn-gu, and Yi T'ae-wan. 1991. *Changsŭnggua pŏksu* [Changsŭng and *pŏksu*]. Seoul: Taewŏnsa.

Kim Won-mo. 1996. Misŭ Sont'ak kwa Sont'ak hot'el [Miss Sontag and the Sontag Hotel]. *Hyangt'o Sŏul* [Old Home Seoul] 56:175–220.

Kim Yŏngjo. 2005. *Han'guk ŭi sori* [The sounds of Korea]. Seoul: Synnara.

Kin Sei-do. 1928. *Rakurō koseki annai* [Guide to the ancient remains of Rakurō]. Shiritsu Mie Gakkō.

Kincaid, Jamaica. 1988. *A small place.* New York: Farrar, Straus and Giroux.

Kirshenblatt-Gimblett, Barbara. 1998. *Destination culture: Tourism, museums, and heritage.* Berkeley: University of California Press.

———. 2006. World heritage and cultural economics. In *Museum frictions: Public cultures/global transformations,* ed. Ivan Karp and Corinne A. Kratz, 161–202. Durham, NC: Duke University Press

Kita, Sadakichi. 1921. Nissen ryōminzoku dōgenron [The common origins of the two races — Japanese and Koreans]. *Chōsen* 6:3–69.

Knez, Eugene I., and Chang-su Swanson. 1968. *A selected and annotated bibliography of Korean anthropology.* Seoul: National Assembly, Republic of Korea.

Kōgo Eriko. 2003. Teishinshō hakkō nichirosen'eki kinen hagakisho: Sono jissō to igi [The Ministry of Communications series of commemorative postcards of the Russo-Japanese War issued in the 1900s: Their background and significance]. *Bijutsushi Kenkyū* 41:103–124.

Kopytoff, Igor. 1986. The cultural biography of things: Commoditization as process. In Appadurai 1986b, 64–91.

Korea Ministry of Tourism and Culture. 1999a. *Han'guk kwan'gwang t'onggye 1998* [Korean Tourism Statistics for 1998]. Seoul: Han'guk Kwan'gwang Kongsa.

———. 1999b. *Kwan'gwang Pijŏn 21* [The vision for Korean tourism in the 21st century]. Ed. Kwan'gwang Chinhŭnghoe. Seoul: Munhwa Kwan'gwang-bu [Ministry of Tourism and Culture].

Korea Times. 2005. Making your own kimchi. November 4.

Korea Travel Newspaper. 1999. Han'guk kwan'gwang oshipnyŏn pisa [The secret fifty years history of Korean tourism].

Kowinski, William Severini. 1985. *The malling of America: An inside look at the great consumer paradise.* New York: W. Morrow.

Kungnimminsokpangmulguan [National Museum of Folklore]. 1988–1997. *Chibang changsŭng sottae sinang* [Survey of regional changsŭng and sottae belief]. 8 vols. Seoul: Kungnimminsokpangmulguan.

———. 2003. *Sajinŭro ponŭn minsokŭi ŏjewa onŭl, 1950–2000: Nyŏndae, Chang Chu-gun Paksa Kijŭngsajin charyujip* [Folklore's yesterday and today as seen through photographs, 1950–2000: Photographic data donated by Professor Chang Chugun]. Seoul: Kungnimminsokpangmulguan .

Kungnip kugagwŏn [Korean Traditional Performing Arts Center]. 1991. *Yi wangjik aakpuwa ŭmagindŭl* [Musicians of the Court Music Bureau of the Yi King]. Seoul: Kungnip kugagwŏn.

Kungnip Kyŏngju Pangmulgwan. 1994. *Kyŏngju pangmulgwan hakkyo 40-nyŏn: Hanŭl to nae kyosil, ttang to nae kyosil* [Forty years of the Kyŏngju Museum School: The sky too is my classroom, the earth too is my classroom]. Kyŏngju: Kungnip Kyŏngju Pangmulgwan.

Lancaster, Bill. 1995. *The department store: A social history.* London: Leicester University Press.

Lankov, Andrei. 2007. *The dawn of modern Korea: The transformation in life and cityscape.* Seoul: EunHaeng NaMu.

Latour, Bruno. 1986. The powers of association. In *Power, action and belief: A new sociology of knowledge,* ed. John Law, 264–280. London: Routledge and Kegan Paul.

———. 2005. *Reassembling the social: An introduction to actor-network-theory.* New York: Oxford.

Leach, William R. 1984. Transformation in a culture of consumption: Women and department stores, 1890–1925. *Journal of American History* 71 (2): 319–342.

———. 1993. *Land of desire: Merchants, power, and the rise of a new American culture.* New York: Pantheon Books.

Lebrecht, Norman. 1996. *When the music stops: Managers, maestros and the corporate murder of classical music.* London: Simon and Schuster.

Lee, Ae-joo. 1998. Spirit in Korean dance with reference to Han Sŏng-jun's dance. In *The spirit in Asian dance,* Proceedings of the International Conference on Asian Music, ed. National Center for Korean Traditional Performing Arts and Korean Traditional Music Promotion Association, 37–52. Seoul.

Lee, Chaesuk, Keith Howard, and Nicholas Casswell. 2008. *Korean Kayagŭm Sanjo: A traditional instrumental genre.* Aldershot, UK: Ashgate.

Lee, Kang Sook (Yi Kangsuk). 1977. Korean music culture: Genuine and quasi-Korean music. *Korea Journal* 20 (11): 4–10.

———. 1980. Today's Korean music. *Korea Journal* 20 (11): 70–77.

Lee, Myeong-hwa. 1991. Row between church and community over Korean totem poles. *Newsreview,* November 23.

Leheny, David. 1998. Tours of duty: The evolution of Japan's outbound tourism. PhD diss., Cornell University.

Lett, Denise Potrzeba. 1998. *In pursuit of status: The making of South Korea's "new" middle class.* Cambridge, MA: Harvard University Asia Center.

Levine, Amy. 2004. The transparent case of virtuality. *PoLAR* 27 (1): 90–113.

Lévi-Strauss, Claude. 1966. *The savage mind.* Chicago: University of Chicago.

Lockyer, Angus. 2000. Japan at the exhibition, 1867–1877. In *Japanese civiliza-*

tion in the modern world: Collection and representation, Senri Ethnological Series, vol. 17, ed. Tadao Umesao, 67–76. Osaka: National Museum of Ethnology.

Lofgren, Orvar. 1999. On holiday: History of vacationing. Berkeley: University of California Press.

MacCannell, Dean. 1999. The tourist: A new theory of the leisure class. Berkeley: University of California Press.

MacPherson, Kerrie L., ed. 1998. Asian department stores. Richmond: Curzon Press.

Makerji, Chandra. 1983. From graven images: Patterns of modern imperialism. New York: Columbia University Press.

Manning, Susan. 1993. Ecstasy and the demon: Feminism and nationalism in the dance of Mary Wigman. Berkeley: University of California Press.

Marcus, George, and Michael Fischer. 1986. Anthropology as cultural critique. Chicago: University of Chicago Press.

Marsh, O. Gaylord. 1937. Unpublished letter to American Consulate, February 23. U.S. National Archives Document 123 M 351/452. Washington, DC.

Marx, Karl. 1977. Capital. Vol. 1. Trans. Ben Fowkes. New York: Vintage.

Massumi, Brian, trans. 1985. Noise: The political economy of music. Minneapolis: University of Minnesota Press.

Matsuda Isao. 1972. Watashi no rirekisho [My curriculum vitae]. Tokyo: Mitsukoshi Mita Kai.

Mauss, Marcel. 1967. The gift: Forms and functions of exchange in archaic societies. Trans. Ian Cunnison. New York: W. W. Norton.

———. 1969. The gift. London: Routledge and Kegan Paul.

———. 1973. Techniques of the body. Economy and Society 2:70–88.

Maxwell, Anne. 1999. Colonial photography and exhibitions: Representations of the "native" and the making of European identities. London: Leicester University Press.

McCann, David R. 1979. Arirang, the national folksong of Korea. In Studies on Korea in transition, ed. David R. McCann, J. Middleton, and E. J. Shultz, 43–56. Honolulu: Center for Korean Studies/University of Hawaiʻi Press.

McCracken, Grant. 1990. Culture and consumption: New approaches to the symbolic character of consumer goods and activities. Bloomington: Indiana University Press.

Miller, Daniel. 1994. Modernity: An ethnographic approach; Dualism and mass consumption in Trinidad. Oxford: Berg.

———, ed. 1995a. Acknowledging consumption: A review of new studies. London: Routledge.

———. 1995b. Consumption as the vanguard of history. In Miller 1995a, 1–57.

———, ed. 1995c. *Worlds apart: Modernity through the prism of the local.* London: Routledge.

———. 1998. *A theory of shopping.* Ithaca, NY: Cornell University Press.

———. 2002a. Consumption. In *The material culture reader,* ed. Victor Buchli, 237–263. Oxford: Berg.

———. 2002b. Turning Callon the right way up. *Economy and Society* 31 (2): 218–233.

Miller, Michael B. 1981. *The Bon Marché: Bourgeois culture and the department store, 1869–1920.* London: George Allen and Unwin.

Mimesisŭ. 1993. *Sinsedae, ne mŏt taero haera: Tŏ isang t'anwŏn ŭn ŏpta, tolp'a hara!* [New generation, do as you like: There's no asking anymore, break through!] Seoul: Hyŏnsil munhwa yŏn'gusa.

Mitchell, Timothy. 1989. The world as exhibition. *Comparative Studies in Society and History* 31 (2): 217–236.

Mitsukoshi honsha, ed. 2005. *Kabushikigaisha Mitsukoshi 100 nen no kiroku* [The 100-year record of Mitsukoshi Co. Ltd.]. Tokyo: Kabushikigaisha Mitsukoshi.

Moeran, Brian. 1984. Making an exhibition of oneself: The anthropologist as potter in Japan. In *Unwrapping Japan: Society and culture in anthropological perspective,* ed. E. Ben-Ari, B. Moeran, and J. Valentine, 117–139. Honolulu: University of Hawai'i Press.

———. 1997. *Folk art potters of Japan: Beyond an anthropology of aesthetics.* Honolulu: University of Hawai'i Press.

———. 1998. The birth of the Japanese department store. In MacPherson 1998, 141–176.

Moon, Okpyo. 1997a. *Han'gugin ŭi sobi wa yŏgasaenghwal* [Consumption and leisure in contemporary Korea]. Sŏngnam: Academy of Korean Studies.

———. 1997b. Tourism and cultural development: Japanese and Korean contexts. In *Tourism and cultural development in Asia and Oceania,* ed. S. Yamashita, K. H. Din, and J. S. Eades, 178–193. Kebangsan, Malaysia: Penerbit University.

———. 1998. Ancestors becoming children of God: Ritual clashes between Confucian tradition and Christianity in contemporary Korea. *Korean Journal* 38 (3): 148–177.

———. 2000. Kwangwangŭl tonghan munhwaŭi saengsan kwa sobi: Hahoe maŭlŭi saryerŭl sungsimŭro [The production and consumption of culture through tourism: The example of Hahoe village]. *Han'guk munhwa illyuhak* 33 (2): 79–110.

———. 2005. Hahoe: The appropriation and marketing of local cultural heritage in Korea. *Asian Anthropology* 4:1–28.

Moon Okpyo, Pak Pyŏng-ho, Kim Kwang-ok, Ŭn Ki-su, and Yi Chung-gu.

2004. *Chosŏn yangban ŭi saenghwal segye* [The life world of Korean scholar gentry]. Seoul: Baeksansŏdang.

Moose, Robert J. 1911. *Village life in Korea.* Nashville, TN: Methodist Church South, Smith and Lamar Agents.

Morphy, Howard. 1995. Aboriginal art in a global context. In D. Miller 1995a, 211–239.

Morse, Anne Nishimura, J. Thomas Rimer, and Kendall Brown. 2004. *Art of the Japanese postcard: The Leonard A. Lauder collections at the Museum of Fine Arts.* Boston: Museum of Fine Arts Publications.

Murray, David. 1894. *Japan.* 5th ed. London: T. Fisher Unwin.

Myers, Fred R., ed. 2001a. *The empire of things. Regimes of value and material culture.* Santa Fe, NM: School of American Research Press.

———. 2001b. Introduction: The empire of things. In Myers 2001a, 3–61.

———. 2001c. The wizards of Oz: Nation, state, and the production of Aboriginal fine art. In Myers 2001a, 165–204.

Namigata Shoichi, Kenji Nimura, and Noritake Sunaga. 2004. *Tōa ryokōsha Manshū shibu jūnen shi: Shashin de miru Nihon keizaishi shokuminchihen* [Ten years of the Manchuria branch of the Tōa Travel Agency: The economic history of Japan: Colonial era]. Vol. 31. Yumanishobō.

Nava, Mica. 1996. Modernity's disavowal: Women, the city and the department store. In *Modern times: Reflections on a century of English modernity,* ed. M. Nava and A. O'Shea, 38–76. London: Routledge.

Nelson, Laura C. 2000. *Measured excess: Status, gender, and consumer nationalism in South Korea.* New York: Columbia University Press.

———. 2006. South Korean consumer nationalism: Women, children, credit, and other perils. In *The ambivalent consumer: Questioning consumption in East Asia and the West,* ed. S. Garon and P. L. Maclachlan, 188–211. Ithaca, NY: Cornell University Press.

New World-Sun. 1938. Sai Shoki is truly beautiful. January 13.

New World-Sun Daily. 1940. Sai Shoki, premier Korean dancer, to give concert today at Curran. April 7.

Nippon. 1939. Chosen travel guide. No. 18.

No Tongŭn. 1989. *Han'guk minjok ŭmak hyŏndan'gye* [Current state of Korean national music]. Seoul: Segwang ŭmak ch'ulp'ansa.

Nora, Pierre. 1989. Between memory and history: Les lieux de mémoire. *Representations* 26 (Spring): 7–25.

Oak, Sung-Deuk. n.d. A genealogy of an "other": Early Protestant missionaries' discourse on Korean "shamanism." Unpublished; courtesy of the author.

Oh, Se-Mi. 2008. Consuming the modern: The everyday in colonial Seoul, 1915–1937. PhD diss., Columbia University.

Oh Jin-sŏk. 2004. Ilcheha paekkwajŏm ŏpke ŭi tonghyang kwa kwankeindŭl ŭi saenghwal yangsik [The department store business under Japanese colonial rule and everyday life of its relations]. In *Ilche ŭi sinminchipae wa ilsang saenghwal* [Japanese colonial rule and everyday life], ed. Yŏnse taehakkyo kukhak yŏn'guwŏn, 123–188. Seoul: Hyean.

Oppenheim, Robert. 2008a. Kyŏngju Namsan: Heterotopia, place-agency, and historiographic leverage. In *Sitings: Critical approaches to Korean geography,* ed. Timothy Tangherlini and Sallie Yea, 141–156. Honolulu: University of Hawai'i Press.

———. 2008b. *Kyŏngju things: Assembling place.* Ann Arbor: University of Michigan Press.

Oppert, Ernest. 1880. *A forbidden land: Voyages to the Corea.* New York: G. P. Putnam's Sons.

Osgood, Cornelius. 1951. *The Koreans and their culture.* New York: Ronald Press Co.

Paenang yŏhaeng. 1998. IMF kŭkbok ŭl wihan chip'ijigi paenang yŏhaeng [Backpack trips for inspiration in overcoming the IMF]. *Paenang yŏhaeng* 3 (2): 47–59.

Pai, Hyung Il. 1994. The politics of Korea's past: The legacy of Japanese colonial archaeology in the Korean peninsula. *East Asian History* 7:25–48.

———. 2000. *Constructing "Korean origins": Archaeology, historiography, and racial myth.* Harvard/Hallym Series. Cambridge, MA: Harvard University Press

———. 2001. The creation of national treasures and monuments: The 1916 Japanese laws on the preservation of Korean remains and relics and their colonial legacies. *Journal of Korean Studies* 25 (1): 72–95.

———. 2006. Shinhwa sok kot'o bokwŏn ul wihan yujŏk t'amsaek: Meiji shidae Hanbando e sŏŭi kokohak kwa misulsahakjok chosa (1900–1916) [Reclaiming the ruins of imagined imperial terrains: Meiji archaeology and art historical surveys in the Korean peninsula (1900–1916)]. In *Ilbon ŭi pallmyŏng kwa kŭndae* [The discovery of "Japan" and modernity], ed. Yoon Sang-in and Park Kyu-tae, 247–284. Seoul: Yeesan.

———. 2009. Capturing visions of Japan's prehistoric past: Torii Ryūzō's field photographs of "primitive" races and lost civilizations (1896–1915). In *Looking modern: East Asian visual culture from treaty ports to World War II,* ed. J. Purtle and H. Thomsen, 258–286. Chicago: Center for the Art of East Asia and Chicago University Press.

———. Forthcoming. Resurrecting the ruins of Japan's mythical homelands: Colonial archaeological surveys in the Korean peninsula and heritage tourism. In *The handbook of post-colonialism and archaeology,* ed. Jane Lydon and Uzma Rizvi. World Archaeological Congress Research Handbook Series. Walnut Creek, CA: Left Coast Press.

Pai, Hyung Il, and Timothy R. Tangherlini. 1998. Nationalism and the construction of Korean identity. Korea Research Monograph 26. Berkeley: Institute of East Asian Studies.

Pak Hyeyun. 2005. *25-hyŏn kayagŭm kich'o yŏnsŭp ch'egye kaebal yŏn'gu:* Guitar *chubŏp kwa yŏnsŭp ch'egyerŭl ch'amgohayŏ* [Research on the development and basic practice system for the 25-stringed zither, referring to the art of playing the guitar and its practice system]. In *Kayagŭmŭl wihan ch'angŭijŏk kyosubŏp* [Creative instruction for the Korean zither], ed. Song Hyejin, Kim Sŏngjin, Yi Chihyŏn, Pak Hyeyun, and Ch'ŏn Kyŏngwŏn, 149–207. Seoul: Minsogwŏn.

Pak Il-yŏng. 1999. *Han'gugmugyoŭi ihae* [Understanding Korean shamanism]. Seoul: Pundo ch'ulp'ansa.

Pak Ŭn-gyŏng. 1997. Sunhwa ŭi ttang kwan'gwang ŭn "modok" [In a pure land tourism is "blasphemy"]. *Paenang yŏhaeng* 2 (4): 53–55.

Pak Wan-sŏ. 1997. *Modok* [Desecration]. Seoul: Hakkojae.

Park, Sang Mi. 2006. The making of a cultural icon for the Japanese Empire: Choe Seung-hui's U.S. dance tours and "new Asian culture" in the 1930s and 1940s. *Positions* 14 (3): 597–632.

Partsch-Bergsohn, Isa. 1994. *Modern dance in Germany and the United States: Cross currents and influences.* Philadelphia: Harwood Academic Publishers.

Pels, Peter. 1998. The spirit of matter: On fetish, rarity, fact, and fancy. In *Border fetishisms: Material objects in unstable spaces,* ed. P. Spayer, 91–121. New York: Routledge.

Pemberton, John. 1994. *On the subject of "Java."* Ithaca, NY: Cornell University Press.

Phillips, Ruth B., and Christopher B. Steiner. 1999a. Art, authenticity and the baggage of cultural encounter. In Phillips and Steiner 1999b, 1–19.

————, eds. 1999b. *Unpacking culture: Art and commodity in colonial and post-colonial worlds.* Berkeley: University of California Press.

Polanyi, Karl. 1944. *The great transformation.* New York: Farrar and Rinehart.

Poleax, Alexandis. 1895. Wayside idols. *Korea Repository* 2:143–144.

Poole, Janet. 2004. Colonial interiors: Modernist fiction of Korea. PhD diss., Columbia University.

Provine, Robert C. 1993. Korea. In *Ethnomusicology: Historical and regional studies,* ed. Helen Myers, 363–376. London: Macmillan.

Rappaport, Erika D. 1995. "A new era of shopping": The promotion of women's pleasure in London's West End, 1909–1914. In *Cinema and the invention of modern life,* ed. Lee Charney and Vanessa R. Schwartz, 130–155. Berkeley: University of California Press.

————. 1996. "The halls of temptation": Gender, politics, and the construction of the department store in late Victorian London. *Journal of British Studies* 35 (1): 58–83.

Riles, Annelise. 2000. *The network inside out*. Ann Arbor: University of Michigan Press.

Ritzer, George. 2004. *The McDonaldization of society*. Rev. new century ed. Thousand Oaks, CA: Pine Forge Press.

Robertson, Jennifer. 1988. *Furusato* Japan: The culture and politics of nostalgia. *Politics, Culture, and Society* 1 (4): 494–518.

———. 1998. Internationalization and nostalgia: A critical interpretation. In *Mirror for modernity: Invented traditions in modern Japan*, ed. Stephen Vlastos, 110–132. Berkeley: University of California Press.

Robinson, Michael Edson. 1988. *Cultural nationalism in colonial Korea, 1920–1925*. Seattle: University of Washington Press.

———. 2007. *Korea's twentieth-century odyssey: A short history*. Honolulu: University of Hawai'i Press.

Ruhlen, Rebecca N. 2003. Korean alterations: Nationalism, social consciousness, and "traditional" clothing. In *Re-orienting fashion: The globalization of Asian dress*, ed. Sandra Niessen, Ann Marie Leshkowich, and Carla Jones, 117–137. Oxford: Berg.

Ryan, James. 1997. *Picturing empire: Photography and the visualization of the British Empire*. Chicago: University of Chicago Press.

Salcedo, Rodrigo. 2003. When the global meets the local at the mall. *American Behavioral Scientist* 46 (8): 1084–1103.

Sandberg, Mark B. 2003. *Living pictures, missing persons: Mannequins, museums, and modernity*. Princeton, NJ: Princeton University Press.

Sandicki, Ozlem, and Douglas B. Holt. 1998. Malling society: Mall consumption practices and the future of public space. In Sherry 1998, 305–336.

Satow, Ernest, and A.G. S. Hawkes. 1881. *A handbook for travelers to central and northern Japan*. Yokohama: Kelly and Walsh.

Scalapino, Robert A., and Chong-sik Lee. 1972. *Communism in Korea*. Berkeley: University of California Press.

Schmid, Andre. 2002. *Korea between empires, 1895–1919*. New York: Columbia University Press.

Schwartz, Joan, and James Ryan, eds. 2003. *Picturing place: Photography and the geographical imagination*. London: Tauris and Co.

Selwyn, Tom, ed. 1996. *The tourist image: Myths and myth making in tourism*. Chichester, UK: John Wiley and Sons.

Seoul Press. 1937. Sai Shoki makes good. February 23.

Sherry, John F., Jr., ed. 1998. *ServiceScapes: The concept of place in contemporary markets*. Lincolnwood, IL: NTC Business Books.

Shin, Gi-Wook. 1995. Marxism, anti-Americanism, and democracy in South

Korea: An examination of nationalist intellectual discourse. *Positions* 3 (2): 508–534.

Shin, Gi-wook, and Michael Robinson, eds. 1999a. *Colonial modernity in Korea.* Cambridge, MA: Harvard University East Asia Center.

———. 1999b. Introduction: Rethinking colonial Korea. In Shin and Robinson 1999a, 1–18.

Shin Myŏng-jik. 2003. *Modŏn boi Kyŏngsŏng ŭl kŏnilda* [Modern boy strolls about Kyŏngsŏng]. Seoul: Hyŏnsil munhwa yŏn'gu.

Slater, Don. 2002. From calculation to alienation: Disentangling economic abstractions. *Economy and Society* 31 (2): 234–249.

Smith, Adam. 1976. *An inquiry into the nature and causes of the wealth of nations.* Ed. Edwin Cannan. Chicago: University of Chicago Press.

Song Hyejin, Kim Myŏngsŏk, and Sŏ Ŭn'gyŏng, eds. 1996. *Han'guk ŭmak: Ch'angjakkok chakp'um mongnokchip* [Korean music: Compositions and composition techniques]. Seoul: Kungnip kugagwŏn.

Song Hyejin, Kim Sŏngjin, Yi Chihyŏn, Pak Hyeyun, and Ch'ŏn Kyŏngwŏn. 2005. *Kayagŭmŭl wihan ch'angŭijŏk kyosubŏp* [About the performance practice of masters of the Korean zither]. Seoul: Minsogwŏn.

Song Pangsong. 1981. *Han'guk ŭmakhak nonjo haeje* [A bibliographical manual on Korean musicology treatises]. Sŏngnam: Han'guk chŏngshin munhwa yŏn'guwŏn [Academy of Korean Studies].

Sorkin, Michael. 1992. *Variations on a theme park: The new American city and the end of public space.* New York: Hill and Wang.

Spooner, Brian. 1986. Weavers and dealers: The authenticity of an Oriental carpet. In Appadurai 1986b, 195–235.

Steiner, C. 1994. *African art in transit.* Cambridge: Cambridge University Press.

Stewart, Kathleen. 1988. Nostalgia: A polemic. *Cultural Anthropology* 3 (3): 227–241.

Stewart, Susan. 1984. *On longing: Narratives of the miniature, the gigantic, the souvenir, the collection.* Durham, NC: Duke University Press.

Stocking, George W. 1991. *Colonial situations.* History of Anthropology Series, vol. 7. Madison: University of Wisconsin Press.

Sydow, C. W. von. [1932] 1948. Om traditionsspridning [On the spread of tradition]. In *Selected papers on folklore,* ed. Laurits Bødker. Repr. Copenhagen: Rosenkilde and Bagger.

Takashima Yusaburō. 1959. *Sai Shōki.* Japan: Sekai gakuhu shoin.

Takashima Yūsaburō and Chŏng Pyŏng-ho, eds. 1994. *Seiki no bijin buyōka Sai Shōki* [One of the most beautiful dancers of the century, Sai Shōki]. Japan: MT Publishing Co.

Tamilia, Robert D. 2005. *The wonderful world of the department store in histori-*

cal perspective: A comprehensive international bibliography partially annotated. http://faculty.quinnipiac.edu/charm/Docs/dept.store.pdf.

Tangherlini, Timothy R. 2008. Chosŏn memories: Spectatorship, ideology and the Korean folk village. In *Sitings: Critical approaches to Korean geography,* ed. T. R. Tangherlini and S. Yea, 61–82. Honolulu: University of Hawaiʻi Press.

TEA/ERA. 2009. *Attraction Attendance Report 2008.*

Tedesco, Frank. 1998. Korean dance legend video clips. http://koreaweb.ws/pipermail/koreanstudies_koreaweb.ws/1998-July/000942.html.

Terry, T. Phillip. 1933. *Terry's guide to the Japanese Empire including Chōsen (Korea) and Taiwan (Formosa).* Boston: Houghton Mifflin.

Thomas, Nicholas. 1991. *Entangled objects: Exchange, material culture, and colonialism in the Pacific.* Cambridge, MA: Harvard University Press.

Thompson, Frederic. 1907. The summer show. *Independent,* June 20.

Uchida, Jun. 2005. Brokers of empire: Japanese settler colonialism in Korea, 1910–1937. PhD diss., Harvard University.

Urry, John. 1990. *The tourist gaze: Leisure and travel in contemporary societies.* London: Sage.

———. 1995. *Consuming places.* London: Routledge.

Uzzell, David L. 1999. The myth of the indoor city. *Journal of Environmental Psychology* 15:299–310.

Van Zile, Judy. 2001. *Perspectives on Korean dance.* Middletown, CT: Wesleyan University Press.

———. 2008. We must be unique, we must be modern: Dance in Korea during Japanese colonization. *Taiwan Dance Research Journal,* no. 4 (May): 111–149.

Vester, H. G. 1996. The shopping mall — A tourist destination of postmodernity. *Gruppendynamik: Zeitschrift für angewandte sozialpsychologie* 27 (1): 57–66.

Vlastos, Stephen. 1998. Tradition: Past/present culture and modern Japanese history. In *Mirror of modernity: Invented traditions of modern Japan,* ed. Stephen Vlastos, 1–16. Berkeley: University of California Press.

Wade, James. 1965. Performance of new music. *Korea Journal* 5 (11): 36–37.

Wang, Ning. 1999. Rethinking authenticity in tourism experience. *Annals of Tourism Research* 26 (2): 349–370.

Warren, Stacy. 1996. Popular cultural practices in the "postmodern city." *Urban Geography* 17 (6): 545–567.

Watson, James L., ed. 1997. *Golden Arches East: McDonald's in East Asia.* Stanford, CA: Stanford University Press.

Weiner, Annette. 1992. *Inalienable possessions.* Berkeley: University of California Press.

Weinstein, Raymond M. 1992. Disneyland and Coney Island: Reflections on the evolution of the modern amusement park. *Journal of Popular Culture* 26 (1): 131–164.

Weisenfeld, Gennifer. 2000. Touring Japan as museums: Nippon and other Japanese imperialist travelogues. *Positions* 8 (3): 747–793.

Welcome Society of Japan (Kihinkai). 1908. *A guide book for tourists in Japan.* 4th ed. Tokyo: Chamber of Commerce.

Wells, Kenneth. 1999. The price of legitimacy: Women and the Kŭnuhoe movement, 1927–1931. In Gi-wook Shin and Michael Robinson 1999a, 191–220.

Williams, Rosalind H. 1982. *Dream worlds: Mass consumption in late nineteenth-century France.* Berkeley: University of California Press.

Yanagi, Soetsu. 1978. *The unknown craftsman: A Japanese insight into beauty.* Tokyo: Kodansha International.

Yang, Jongsung. 2003. *Cultural protection policy in Korea: Intangible cultural properties and living national treasures.* Seoul: Jimoondang International.

Yang Young-Kyun. 2005. *Jajangmyeon* and *Junggukjip:* The changing position and meaning of Chinese food and Chinese restaurants in Korean society. *Korea Journal* 45 (2): 60–88.

Yano, Christine R. 2002. *Tears of longing: Nostalgia and the nation in Japanese popular song.* Cambridge, MA: Harvard University Asia Center.

Yano Kanjō and Morikawa Seijin. 1936. *Shinhan dai Keijō annai* [A guide to great Keijō, new edition]. Keijō: Keijō toshi bunka kenkyūjo.

Yi Chin-Haeng. 2001. Kimch'iŭi sanŏphwawa matŭi sŏ [Industrialization of kimchi and the choice of taste]. Paper presented at the 13th Kimchi Symposium, Seoul, Korea.

Yi Chong-ch'ŏl. 1992. Changsŭng. In *Han'gugmunhwasangjingsajn* [Dictionary of Korean myths and symbols], 518–521. Seoul: Dong-a Publishing.

Yi Kangsuk. 1985. *Ŭmak ŭi ihae* [The understanding of music]. Seoul: Minŭmsa.

Yi Kŏnyong. 1987. *Han'guk ŭmak ŭi nolliwa yulli* [The logics and ethics of Korean music]. Seoul: Segwang ŭmak ch'ulp'ansa.

———. 1990. Ch'aegŭl naemyŏnsŏ [Introduction to volume]. *Minjok ŭmak* [People's music] 1:10–11.

Yi Kwan-ho. 2005. Maŭlŭi annyŏnggwa p'ungyorŭl chik'yŏ chunŭn maŭljik'imi [The village guardian who takes care of the village's peace and prosperity]. In *Ch'ŏngyech'ŏn pokwŏn chunggonginŏm t'uekpyŏlchŏn: Han'gungmiŭi chaebalkyŏn — Yigaragŭi changsŭng, sottaejŏn* [Special exhibition commemorating the opening of the Ch'ŏngye Stream: The rediscovery of Korean beauty — exhibition of Lee Garag's changsŭng and sottae], 4–5. Seoul: Sejongmunhwahoegwan.

Yi Kyŏng-hun. 2001. Missukkosi, kŭndae ŭi showindou: Munhak kwa p'ungsok

[Mitsukoshi as showcase of modernity: Literature and customs]. In *Han'guk kŭndae munhak kwa ilbon munhak* [Korean modern literature and Japanese literature], ed. Han'guk munhak yŏn'gu hakhoe, 107–146. Seoul: Kukhak charyowŏn.

———. 2003. *Oppa-ŭi t'ansaeng: Han'guk kŭndae munhak ŭi p'ungsoksa* [The birth of Older Brother: Modern Korean literature and the history of manners]. Seoul: Munhak kwaji sŏnsa.

Yi Pilyŏng. 1997. Changsŭnggwa sottae [Changsŭng and sottae]. In *Han'gungminsokŭi ihae, Kungnimminsokpangmulgwan* [Understanding Korean folklore, National Museum of Folklore], 267–277. Seoul: Kungnimminsokpangmulgwan.

Yi Sang. 1970. *Wings*. In *Modern Korean Short Stories and Plays*. Trans. Chu Yo-sup. Korean Centre, International PEN, 190–219. Seoul: Korean Centre, International PEN.

Yi Sanggyu. 1995. Ch'angjak hwaltong mit kugakki kaeryang ŭi sŏnggwawa munjejŏm [The products and problems of creative activity and the improvement of Korean traditional instruments]. In *Kwangbok 50-junyŏn kinyŏm haksul taehoe* [Proceedings of the Conference for the Fiftieth Celebration from Japanese Colonization], 109–160. Seoul: National Center for Korean Traditional Performing Arts.

Yi Sŏngch'ŏn. 1987. Han'guk ŭmak ch'angjak ŭi yŏksawa Kim Kisu ŭi ŭmak [The history of creating Korean music in Kim Kisu's music]. In *Han'guk ŭmak* [Anthology of Korean music] 23:3–4. Seoul: Kungnip kugagwŏn.

———. 1992. Han'guk chŏnt'ong ŭmak ŭi ch'angjak pangbŏbe kwanhan yŏn'gu [A study of the methods for creating and Korean traditional music]. In *Yŏnse nonmunjip* [Thesis collection of Yonsei University], 119–181. Seoul: Yŏnse taehakkyo.

Yi Sŏng-u. 1980. Umsikchŏm [Drinking and eating establishments]. In *Han'guk minjok munhwa taebaekkwa sajŏn* [Great encyclopedia of the culture of Korean people], ed. Han'guk Chŏngsin Munhwa Yŏn'guwŏn P'yŏnch'anbu [Compilation Department of the Academy of Korean Studies], vol. 17, 451–453. Seoul: Han'guk chŏngsin munhwa yŏn'guwŏn.

Yi Tu-hyŏn (Lee, Du-hyon). 1984. Changsŏng. In *Han'gugminsokhangnongo* [Vintage discussions of Korean folklore studies], ed. T.-h. Yi. Seoul: Haksosa.

Yŏm, Sang-Sŏp. 2005. *Three generations*. Trans. Yu Young-nan. New York: Archipelago Books.

Yonhap News. 2005. I cannot live without eating kimchi — Is this no longer true? November 2.

———. 2006. Figure: Change in the import of Chinese kimchi. July 31.

Yŏnse taehakkyo kukhak yŏn'guwŏn, ed. 2004. *Ilche ŭi sinminchipae wa ilsang saenghwal* [Japanese colonial rule and everyday life]. Seoul: Hyean.

Yoo, Theodore Jun. 2005. The new woman and the politics of love, marriage and divorce in colonial Korea. *Gender and History* 17 (2): 295–324.

Yoshii, Hideo. 2007. Ilche kangjŏmgi Sŏkkuram chosa mit haech'e suri wa sajin ch'wallyŏng e tahaesŏ [A photographic study of the reconstruction of Sŏkkuram during the Japanese colonial period]. In *Kyŏngju Silla Yujŏk ui ŏje wa onŭl: Sŏkkuram, Pulguksa, Namsan* (Exhibition catalog of glass-plate photographs of Silla remains in Kyŏngju), vol. 2, ed. Kim Tae-shik, Kim Chong-bok, and Kim Ch'ae-shik, 198–209. Seoul: Sŏngyunkwan University Museum.

Yoshino, Kosaku. 1999. Introduction to *Consuming ethnicity and nationalism: Asian experiences,* ed. Kosaku Yoshino, 1–7. Richmond, UK: Curzon.

Young, Louise. 1999. Marketing the modern: Department stores, consumer culture, and the new middle class in interwar Japan. *International Labor and Working Class History* 55:52–70.

Yu Hong-jun. 1993. *Na ŭi munhwa yusan tapsagi 1* [The chronicle of my field study of cultural remains 1]. Seoul: Ch'angjak kwa pip'yŏng sa.

———. 1994. *Na ŭi munhwa yusan tapsagi 2* [The chronicle of my field study of cultural remains 2]. Seoul: Ch'angjak kwa pip'yŏng sa.

———. 1997. *Na ŭi munhwa yusan tapsagi 3* [The chronicle of my field study of cultural remains 3]. Seoul: Ch'angjak kwa pip'yŏng sa.

———. 1998. *Na ŭi Pukhan munhwa yusan tapsagi sang* [The chronicle of my field study of North Korean cultural remains, part one]. Seoul: Chungang M&B.

———. 2001. *Na ŭi Pukhan munhwa yusan tapsagi ha* [The chronicle of my field study of North Korean cultural remains, part two]. Seoul: Chungang M&B.

Yun Miyŏng, ed. 2001. *Kŏnwŏn 1400-nyŏn, kaewŏn 50-nyŏn Kungnip kugagwŏn* [1400th anniversary of foundation, 50th anniversary of refounding the National Center for Korean Traditional Performing Arts]. Seoul: Kungnip kugagwŏn [National Center for Korean Traditional Performing Arts].

Contributors

Katarzyna J. Cwiertka is a lecturer in material culture at the School of Asian Studies, Leiden University, Netherlands. Her research to date has used food as a window into the modern history of Japan and Korea. Cwiertka is the author of *Modern Japanese Cuisine: Food, Power and National Identity* (2006) and coeditor of *Asian Food: The Global and the Local* (2002). She is currently completing a monograph on Japanese colonialism in Korea, also using food as the research focus.

Kyung-Koo Han taught anthropology at Kangwon National University and Japanese studies at Kookmin University before he moved to Seoul National University as professor at the newly established College of Liberal Studies. He has authored, coauthored, or edited many books and articles on Korea and Japan, including *Company as Community: An Anthropological Study of a Japanese Business Organization; Koreans in Asia and the Pacific Region; My First Encounter with Cultural Anthropology; Korean Anthropology;* "Two Deaths of Hirohito"; "The Politics of Network and Social Trust: A Case Study in the Organizational Culture of Korean Venture Industry"; and "The Archaeology of the Ethnically Homogeneous Nation-State and Multiculturalism in Korea."

Keith Howard is a professor of music at SOAS, University of London, and associate dean of the Sydney Conservatorium of Music. He is the author or editor of fifteen books, including *Preserving Korean Music* (2006), *Korean Pop Music* (2006), *Zimbabwean Mbira Music on an International Stage* (2007), and *Singing the Kyrgyz Manas* (2010) and has written more than one hundred articles on the music, dance, and shamanism of Korea, Nepal, Zimbabwe, and Siberia. Howard was the founder and licensee of OpenAir Radio, he founded and continues to run the SOASIS label of CDs and DVDs, and from 2002 to 2007 he directed the AHRC Research Centre for Cross-Cultural Music and Dance Performance.

Laurel Kendall, an anthropologist, is chair of the Division of Anthropology and curator of the Asian Ethnographic Collection at the American Museum of Natural History and is an adjunct (full) professor at Columbia University. She has authored many books and articles on gender, ritual, shamans, and popular religion in South Korea, most recently *Shamans, Nostalgias, and the IMF: South Korean Popular Religion in Motion* (2009). Her recent work concerns sacred objects, magic, and markets in contemporary East and Southeast Asia.

Okpyo Moon is a professor of anthropology at the Academy of Korean Studies. Her recent publications include *Yangban: The Life World of Korean Scholar-Gentry* (2004) and *Japanese Tourism and Travel Culture* (coedited with Sylvie Guichard-Anguis, 2009).

Robert Oppenheim, an anthropologist, is an associate professor in the Department of Asian Studies at the University of Texas at Austin. His book *Kyŏngju Things: Assembling Place* (2008) examines place-making and technical politics in the historic city. Other articles on various topics have appeared in the *Journal of Asian Studies, Anthropological Theory,* and *Histories of Anthropology Annual.*

Hyung Il Pai is an associate professor at the Department of East Asian Languages and Cultural Studies, University of California, Santa Barbara. She is the author of *Constructing "Korean" Origins: A Critical Review of Archaeology, Historiography, and Racial Myth in Korean State-Formation Theories* (2000) and a coeditor of *Nationalism and the Construction of Korean Identity* (1998) and has written on a wide range of topics related to the politics and history of East Asian archaeology, museum studies, heritage management, and culture contact and change. She is currently completing a book entitled *Reinventing Cultural Patrimony in Japan and Korea: Colonialism, Nationalism and Heritage Management.*

Timothy R. Tangherlini is a professor in the Department of Asian Languages and Cultures at UCLA. He is the coeditor, with Hyung Il Pai, of *Nationalism and the Construction of Korean Identity* (1998) and the coeditor, with Sallie Yea, of *Sitings: Critical Approaches to Korean Geography* (2008). He is also the coproducer, with Stephen Epstein, of the documentary film *Our Nation: A Korean Punk Rock Community* (2002).

Judy Van Zile is a professor emerita of dance at the University of Hawaiʻi at Mānoa. She has published widely on various aspects of dance in Korea, with her recent *Perspectives on Korean Dance* (2001) receiving an Outstanding Publication Award from the Congress on Research in Dance. Her research focuses on movement analysis and issues of change.

Index

Numbers in **bold** refer to figures. The letter *t* following a page number denotes a table.

Adorno, Theodor W., 195
advertising: of Japan Tourist Bureau, 75; of kimchi, 154–155, 156
Akiba Takashi, 136
American Museum of Natural History, 129, 147n2
amusement parks, 40–44, 45, 61. *See also* Lotte World; theme parks
An Mak, 171–172, 175
ancestral rites, 88–90, 99–100, 101–102, 103n2, 104n18
Andong, 92, 93–94, 95–99, 103n9. *See also* Chirye Artist Village; *yangban*
Appadurai, Arjun, 2, 114, 128, 146, 154, 195
"Arirang," 202–203
art: *changsŭng* as, 130, 131–132, 141–142, 143, 144; objects as, 133
Asahi Newspaper Company, 76
Asian financial crisis, 48, 111
authenticity: in backpack travel, 120; of experiences, 41–42, 89–90, 94, 98; inauthentic and, 41–42, 61–62, 168; of kimchi, 153, 155, 158–159, 161, 163, 164; of Lotte World, 61; nostalgia for, 154, 155; of performing arts, 14–15

Bachelard, Gaston, 57
Backpacker.net, 111–112, 119, 120, 121–122

backpack travel. See *paenang yŏhaeng*
Baik Dae-woong, 202
Baudrillard, Jean, 1, 61–62
Bergman, Sten, 136
Boher, J., 24
border crossings, 189–190
Bourdieu, Pierre, 114
Brody, Alyson, 43
Bureau of Cultural Properties Preservation, 97

CAC. *See* Codex Alimentarius Commission
Callon, Michel, 114–115, 116, 120, 123
capitalism, 5, 27, 155
caricature, 51, 52–53, 55
censorship, 170, 176, 186, 212–213
CGK. *See* Colonial Government-General of Korea Office
CGR. *See* Colonial Government Railways Company
Ch'ae Hyun-kyung, 209
Ch'ae Mansik, 1, 2, 23
ch'angjak kugak (creative traditional music), 198–200, 202, 211
changsŭng: as artworks, 130, 131–132, 141–142, 143, 144; carvers, 133–134, 137, 139, 141, 143–146; Chinese production, 131; commoditization, 136; contemporary, 130–133, 141–142; description, 133–134; faces, 130–131, 133, 143; in foreign museums, 129, 136–137, 147n2; frightening expressions, 134, **134**, 140–141, 143, 145; interest in, 138–140; interpretations

by outsiders, 134–136; multiple narratives, 130, 146; preservation, 138; protest, 139–140; regional styles, 138, 145; at restaurants, 129, 131, 144; scholarship on, 135, 139, 140–141; small souvenir versions, 129, 130, 131, 135, 136–137; sports and, 131, 139; surveys, 138–139, 148n17; as symbols of Korea, 129, 140; at tourist sites, 129–130, 139, 145; traditional functions, 133, 140–141; veneration, 133, 138, 145–146; in villages, 133–134, **134**, 137, 140–141, 147n5

China: *changsŭng* production, 131; consumption patterns, 27; department stores, 29; kimchi production, 156, 161–163, 165n3, 166n16; Kimchi War, 161–164; lineage brides and, 97

Chinsŏng Yi lineage house, 94

Chirye Artist Village (Chirye Ch'angjak Yesulch'on), **89**, 95–96, 98, 99–100, 101–102, 104n18

Cho Chŏngsam, 206–207

Cho Hae-joang, 107

Cho Kongnye, 203

Cho Ŭlsŏn, 203

Ch'oe Hyŏng-bŏm, 131–132

Ch'oe Sŭng-hŭi: biography, 171–172; career, 171, 172, 174–180, 187–190; choreography, 169, 174–175, 176–180, 181, 191n14, 193n21; costumes, 175, 177, 178–179; criticism of, 175, 177, 181–183, 185; dance training, 171, 172–174, 176, 192n19; influence, 183, 186–188; marriage, 171–172, 175; photographs of performances, 175, 177, **178**, **179**, 180, **184**; political beliefs, 185–186, 193n31; Western tour, 181–186

Choi, Chungmoo, 4

Chōjiya department store, 26, 30, 31

Chŏn Yu-sŏng, 111

Chonggajip company, 154–155, 156, 165n7

chongtaek. See lineage houses

chŏnt'ong. See traditions

Chōsen annaisho. See guidebooks to Chōsen

Chōsen Hotel, 24–25

Chōsen tetsudo. *See* Colonial Government Railways Company

Christians, 102, 134–135, 138

Chung, Soonyon, 208

classes: of department store customers, 36–38, 46; kimchi consumption and, 150, 155–156; of Lotte World visitors, 46–47, 48; performance of distinctions, 106; of tourists, 75. *See also* middle class

clothing, traditional, 88, 109, 111, 177, 178–179

Clunas, Craig, 27

Codex Alimentarius Commission (CAC), 158–159, 161

Cohen, Erik, 61

Colonial Government-General of Korea Office (CGK), 69, 81

Colonial Government Railways Company (CGR): guidebooks, 76, 83; headquarters, 78; hotels, **70**; Korea branch, 69, 75, 76, 86n10; magazines, 80–81

colonial period (1910–1945): capitalist development, 47–48; "civilizing mission," 24; collaborators, 193n31; consumer culture, 31; department stores, 29–33, 36–38; economic activity, 31, 68–69; folk museum representations, 58–59; Japanese

residents, 21–22, 23, 31, 32, 37, 69;
legacy, 163; leisure activities, 81;
modernity, 3, 24; music, 6–7; name
pronunciations, 186; postcards, 12,
76, 81; rural residents, 37–38, 81;
souvenirs, 12; tourism, 69, 71–73t,
74–81, **80**, 87n15, 137; transportation, 69, **70**; urban areas, 21–22, 24.
See also Ch'oe Sŭng-hŭi; Keijō
commercialization, of kimchi production, 151, 152–153, 157, 162–163
commodification of traditions, 3, 16,
94, 99–102, 136, 170, 213
commodities, 4, 13, 128. *See also* consumption; industrial production
Confucian culture: ancestral rites,
88–90, 99–100, 101–102, 103n2,
104n18; compatibility with modernity, 91; family relations, 100–101;
folk museum representations, 55;
Korean national identity and, 91,
99, 101, 102; revival in 1990s, 90–91;
tourism and, 88–90, 93–94, 98
consumer culture, 27–36, **37**, 153
consumption: of commodities, 13;
contexts, 113; cultural, 188–190;
definition, 4; department stores
and, 27–33; economic views, 113;
excessive, 112, 153–154; globalization and, 2–3, 7; mass, 27–28; modernity and, 1, 4; of objects, 105;
of places, 120–121; scholarship on,
106–107, 113; theme parks and, 42;
of traditions, 4–5, 7, 16–17, 109; as
transaction, 105, 114–115, 123; travel
as, 120–121, 123
court dance, 181, 182, 196
Crawford, Margaret, 45
Creighton, Millie, 94
cuisine. *See* food; restaurants

cultural consumption, 188–190
cultural inventory, 54
cultural properties. *See* intangible
cultural heritage assets; lineage
houses
Cybriwsky, Roman, 49

dance: Japanese, 173–174; *kutkŏri
ch'um*, 172–173, 177; modern, 169,
174, 182; "Oriental," 181–185; traditional, 169–170, 174, 176, 177, 180,
183, 187, 189. *See also* Ch'oe Sŭng-
hŭi
Dante, *Inferno*, 39
Davis, Susan G., 42, 49–50
Delissen, Alain, 12
department store restaurants: customers, 34–36; food preparation
for, 25–26; food styles, 25–26, 35–
36, 38n3; interiors, 26, **27**, 35, 36;
locations, 26; popularity, 25, 26–27;
prices, 25, 35, 37; waitresses, 26; in
West, 26, 34, 35
department stores (*paekhwajŏm*):
buildings, 26, 36; clientele, 31–33,
34, 36–38, 46; in colonial period,
29–33, 36–38; consumer culture
and, 27–33, 36; differences from
older stores, 28, 32; exotic décors,
28–29; Japan Tourist Bureau offices, 75, 76, 77–78; kimchi sales,
156, 165n8; Korean, 32–33, 38n3; as
leisure and tourist destinations, 29,
33, 38; marketing strategies, 28, 29;
modernity and, 36–38; popularity,
36; sales taxes paid, 31, 32t; services
and facilities, 34
desire, for new, 28
destination tourism, 48–49
devil posts. See *changsŭng*

dining-out. *See* restaurants
Disney theme parks, 44, 48, 63n3
dolls, 55–58

Eckert, Carter J., 48
Eco, Umberto, 61–62
Egypt, backpackers in, 121–122
entertainment: night life, 78; shopping as, 28, 33, 38, 41, 45; by women, 78, 175
Europe: backpack travel, 111, 119; Ch'oe Sŭng-hŭi's tour of, 182; composers, 199; department store restaurants, 26, 34; modern dance, 174, 182; packaged tours, 85n1; tourists from, 75
exoticism, 7, 28–29, 67, 129, 130, 183–185

families, 34–36, 94–95, 96–97, 100–101. *See also* mothers
festivals, 6, 140, 196, 197, 202–203, 211
fetishes, 135
field study travel. See *tapsa yŏhaeng*
films, 6–7, 15, 172, 208–209
folk dance. *See* dance
folklore, 6, 135, 136
Folklore Museum (Minsok Pangmulgwan), Lotte World, 53–60. See *also* National Folklore Museum
folk songs, 202–203, 207, 211, 212
Folk Village (Minsokch'on), Suwŏn, 6, 53, 55, 129–130
folk villages, Scandinavian, 42
food, traditional, 93, 150–151. See *also* kimchi; meals; nostalgia; restaurants
framing, 114–115, 118, 123
France: department store restaurants, 34; expositions, 136; strawberry market, 114
Friends of Silla Culture, 116
Fukuzawa Yukichi, 68

Gale, James S., 135
Gautier, Théophile, 199
Gaya Beauty, 207
gaze, 20, 66
Generation X, 110, 112–113
globalization, 2–3, 7, 17, 110, 158, 163. *See also* Korean wave
Goethe, Johann Wolfgang von, 47
Goffman, Erving, 114
Gottdiener, Mark, 42
GugakFM, 196–197, 198, 202, 212
guidebooks: to Japan, 74; Lonely Planet, 105, 119
guidebooks to Chōsen (*Chōsen annaisho*), 73, 76–77, 78, 80, 81–83
Gwon Hyeok Hui, 137

haegŭm (fiddles), 207–209, 210
Haetbahn, 154
Hahoe Village, 139
hallyu. *See* Korean wave
han, nostalgia of, 58–59
Han Myŏnghŭi, 211
Han Sŏng-jun, 175–176, 192nn18–19
hanbok (traditional Korean dress), 88, 109, 178–179
handicrafts. See *changsŭng*
Hanilgwan, 129
Hannerz, Ulf, 2
Hanto no Maihimei, 172, 191n8
Harker, Dave, 212
Hayashi Hiroshige, 31
Hendry, Joy, 4, 43, 48
heritage. *See* intangible cultural heritage assets; traditions

heritage tourism, 6, 88–90, 99–101, 102, 105
Hiddink, Guus, 131
Hine, Thomas, 136
Hirata department store, 30
historic sites. *See* heritage tourism; *tapsa yŏhaeng*
Hŏ Hŏn-sŏn, 57–58
Hobsbawm, Eric, 4–5, 212
hotels, 24–25, **70**, 74, 156
houses. *See* lineage houses
Howard, Keith, 4
Hower, Ralph M., 35
Hutcheon, Linda, 61
Hwang, Byungki, 200–201, 211, 214n24
Hwang Pyŏngju, 206
Hwasin (Hwashin) department store, 31, 32–33, 34, 35–36, 38n3, 77

identity. *See* national identity
Imch'ŏnggak, 96, **96**, 98
IMF Crisis, 48, 111
Im Kwon-taek, 201; *Sŏp'yŏnje*, 6–7, 15
industrial production: of *changsŭng*, 129, 130, 131, 135, 136–137; of kimchi, 151, 152–153, 157, 162–163
intangible cultural heritage assets, 4, 14, 100, 138, 168, 196, 202, 207
Internet, music downloads, 204. *See also* Backpacker.net
Ishii Baku, 170, 173–174, 175, 176, 191n12, 193n21

Jameson, Frederic, 39–40
Jang Sun Woo, 208–209
Japan: cultural relations with Korea, 160; dance, 173–174; department stores, 29, **30**, 75; diplomats, 68; guidebooks, 76; imperial tombs, 69; kimchi sales, 157–158, 159, 160–161, 163, 166nn12–13; Kimchi War, 158–161, 163; nostalgia in, 5–6, 83; proximity to Korea, 68; theme parks, 43; tourism industry, 71–73t, 73–75, 111–112; tourists from, 46, 47, 58–59; traditions, 5–6; world's fairs displays, 67. *See also* colonial period (1910–1945)
Japan Hot Springs Association, 74
Japan Imperial Railways (JIR), 69, 74, 78
Japan Tourist Bureau (JTB), 69, 74, 75, 76, 77–78, 85n4

Kang, Hojoong, 203
Kang Nae-hŭi, 39, 45–46, 51
Kang Sanae, 202
Kang Sŏk-kyŏng, "A Room in the Woods," 1–2
Kang Ŭnil, 205, 208
kayagŭm (zithers), 205, 206–207, 210
Keijō (Seoul): department stores, 31; districts, 32; elites, 24; hotels, 24–25; modernity, 3; restaurants in, 22–25; tourist guidebooks, 77. *See also* department store restaurants; Seoul
Keijō Chamber of Commerce, 22, 25
Keystone View Company, 136
Kihinkai (Society of VIPs), 73–74
Kim Dae Jung, 91
Kim, Eun Mee, 17
Kim Il-ryun, 205, 206–207
Kim Kisu, 198
Kim Kisun, 204–205
Kim Kyung A, 205
Kim Sang-sook, 59
Kim Sŏnghye, 198
Kim Soochul, 6, 15, 201

Kim Sugun, 12
Kim Tu-ha, 139
Kim Won Kil, 88–90, 94, 95–96, 97–98, 99, 100
Kim Yŏngjae, 202
Kim, Yong Woo, 203
Kim, Young Dong, 201, 205
Kim, Young-hoon, 189–190
Kim Young-sam, 158
kimchi: authenticity, 153, 155, 158–159, 161, 163, 164; Chinese production, 156, 161–163, 165n3, 166n16; as class indicator, 150, 155–156; commercial production, 151, 152–153, 157, 162–163; consumption, 149, 150, 153–154, 164n1; flavors, 157, 161; foreigners' views of, 157, 158, 165n9; global markets, 151, 157–158, 159–160, 163, 166n14; home preparation, 151–153, 155–156, 163, 164; imports, 156; ingredients, 149; marketing strategies, 154–155, 165n7; national identity and, 149, 157, 162, 164; prices, 165n8; safety issues, 161–162; social history, 149–151
kimchi networks, 151–153, 155–156
Kimchi Wars (kimchi chŏnjaeng), 7, 149, 158–164
kimuchi, 158–159, 160–161, 163, 164, 165n2
Kirshenblatt-Gimblett, Barbara, 4
kisaeng (court, then commercial entertainers), 78, 175
Ko Hŭnggon, 206
Koh, Kyeong-Hwa, 162
Kojong, King, 24
Konggan (Space), 12
Korea House, 129
Korean Culture and Arts Foundation, 197

Korean things, 12, 16, 92, 107, 158
Korean wave (hallyu), 17, 84, 100–101, 160
Kot'aek Munhwa Pojonhoe (Old House Culture Preservation Society), 97–98
kugak (traditional Korean music): broadcasts, 196–197, 198; concerts, 200, 210; instruments, 205, 206, 210; national identity and, 195; new compositions, 198–200, 202, 211; orchestras, 197–198, 205, 206; popularity, 5, 195, 196–197; preservation and promotion, 196, 199, 211; recordings, 204, 205, 210, 211; songs, 202–203; university programs, 197–198, 199; use of term, 213n1
Kugak Festival (Kugak ch'ukch'ŏn), 197, 202–203, 211
kugak fusion (kugak p'yusyŏn): audiences, 195; broadcasts, 197; concerts, 200; controversies, 210–211, 215n25; development, 200–203, 205–207, 209–210; film soundtracks, 6, 15, 208–209; instruments, 206–210; meaning, 195, 212; music industry and, 204–210, 211–213; recordings, 204–205, 208, 209, 211
Kungnip Kugagwŏn, 196
Kungnip Minsok Pangmulgwan (National Folklore Museum), 53, 138
kutkŏri ch'um, 172–173, 177
Kwang Soo Lee, 202
Kyŏnggi Province Peace Festival, 140
Kyŏngju: sites, 108–109, 111; tapsa in, 108–110, 109, 112, 116–119, 123

Leach, William R., 28
Lee, Chaesuk, 205–206
Lee Choon-ho, 56–57

Lee Doo-jae, 44, 53, 57, 58–59
Lee Garag (Yi Ka-rak), 132, 141–142
Lee Hye-Ku, 198
Lee Rang, 207
Lee Sanggyu, 201
Lee Yun'gyŏng, 197
leisure activities, 29, 33, 38, 81. *See also*
    entertainment; tourism
Lim, the, 210
lineage houses (*chongtaek*), 88, **89**, 92,
    94, 95, **96**, 97–99, 102
Lonely Planet, 105, 119
Lotte Group, 47–48, 59
Lotte World: amusement parks, 40–
    41, **40**, 43–45, 51, 61; architecture,
    50–51, 52–53; authenticity, 61; char-
    acteristics, 44–50; convenience,
    43, 49; description, 39–40; folklore
    museum, 47, 53–60; hidden areas,
    60–61; lack of unity, 44–46; loca-
    tion, 39, 48–49; logic of miniatur-
    ization and, 50–53; mascots, 44;
    number of visitors, 63n3; opening,
    48, 62n1; in Pusan, 44, 49; safety,
    62n2; scale, 52; shopping mall,
    40–41, 43–44, 45, 46, 61; social
    relations, 41–42; spatial differentia-
    tion, 46–47; success factors, 48–50;
    television programs filmed in, 52,
    61; visitors, 43, 46–47, 48, 49, 58–59

MacCannell, Dean, 2, 10, 48–49
Makerji, Chandra, 27
Mall of America, 40, 45, 48
malls. *See* Lotte World; shopping
    malls
Manchuria, tourism in, 74–75, 76,
    77. *See also* South Manchurian
    Railway
manners and customs, 67, 76, 78, **79**, 81

markets, 113, 114–115
marriages, 97, 104n15
Marx, Karl, 106
material culture: anthropology of,
    12–13, 128, 135; Korean things, 12,
    16, 92, 107, 158; objects, 128, 132–133,
    146; scholarship on, 137
materiality: of modern environment,
    27; of tradition, 12, 94, 97, 102, 129
Mauss, Marcel, 128
meals: side dishes, 150; traditional
    cooking, 93, 150–151. *See also* kim-
    chi; restaurants
mechanical reproduction, 12
Metropolitan Museum of Art, 107–
    108
middle class, 41–43, 46, 48, 49, 91–93,
    105–106. *See also* classes
Miller, Daniel, 1, 2, 106–107, 113, 114,
    123, 128
mimesis, 42, 55, 60, 144
Minakai department store, 26, 30–31,
    77, 78
miniaturization, 50–53, 54, 56–57, 60
Ministry of Culture and Tourism,
    Korean, 88, 91, 97, 196
Minjungmunhwaundong. *See* Popu-
    lar Culture Movement
Minsokch'on (Folk Village), Suwŏn,
    53, 55, 129–130
Minsok Pangmulgwan (Folklore Mu-
    seum), Lotte World, 53–60
Mitsukoshi department stores, 25, 26,
    29, **30**, 31, 33, 36, 75, 78
modern dance, 169, 174, 182
modernity: in colonial period, 3, 24;
    Confucian culture and, 91; con-
    sumption and, 1, 4; cultural, 169;
    department stores and, 36–38;
    experiences of, 2; gaze in, 20; Japa-

nese, 81, 82; materiality of, 27; as sensate experience, 20; tradition and, 4
Mogin Gallery, 131–132
Moon, Okpyo, 11
mothers, 153, 154–155, 164
Mun Chaesuk, 207
Murayama Chijun, 136
museums: *changsŭng* in, 129, 136–137, 147n2; in colonial period, 69, 79; criticism of, 112; in South Korea, 107–108. *See also* Folklore Museum
music: in colonial period, 6–7; jazz, 202; Korean wave, 17, 84; pop, 6–7, 202, 203, 205, 209; university programs, 197–198, 199; Western classical, 205–206, 207, 209, 212. See also *kugak*
Musicore, 210
Myers, Fred R., 128

National Center for Korean Traditional Performing Arts, 196
National Folklore Museum (Kungnip Minsok Pangmulgwan), 53, 138
national identity: Confucianism and, 91, 99, 101, 102; dance and, 176; of emigrants, 99; Japanese, 83; kimchi and, 149, 157, 162, 164; *kugak* and, 195; nostalgia for, 17; Popular Culture Movement and, 90; search for, 91; tradition and, 139
nationalism, 53
national symbols. *See* national identity
New Community Movement (Saemaŭl Undong), 138
"new dance." See *shinmuyong*
nobility. See *yangban*
North Korea: Ch'oe Sŭng-hŭi in, 172,

186, 191n10; family unification, 140; travel in, 107
Noryangjin, 138
nostalgia: in advertising, 154–155; of *han*, 58, 59; in Japan, 5–6, 83; for Korean things, 92; for national identity, 17; for rural life, 6; sensate experiences, 13; for tradition, 4, 6, 94

objects. *See* Korean things; material culture
Oh, Se-Mi, 3
oikotypes, 43–44
old house culture experiences (*kot'aek munhwa ch'ehŏm*), 92–93, 94, 98–99, 101, 102
Olympics, Seoul, 48, 90, 139, 157, 158
"Oriental" dance, 181–185
Osgood, Cornelius, 138
overflow, 115–116, 118, 120

Paekche kingdom, 80
paekhwajŏm. See department stores
Paek Hyang-ju, 186–187, 192n14
paenang yŏhaeng (backpack travel): in Europe, 111, 119; framing, 123; instructions, 121; motives, 119; narratives, 120, 121–122; participants, 105–106, 110, 111–113, 119; popularity, 105, 110; relationship to *tapsa*, 107, 110–111, 122–123; rhetoric of authenticity, 120
Paenang yŏhaeng magazine, 110, 111, 120, 121
Pak Hŭng-sik, 31, 32
Pak Kyŏnghun, 205
Pak Pŏmhun, 206
Pak Se Ri, 131
Pak Sŏnggi, 206

Park Bum-hoon, 202
Park Chan-ho, 131
Park Chung-hee, 5, 48, 58, 90
Park, Sang Mi, 185
Park Sŭngwŏn, 209
Peabody Essex Museum, 136
Pels, Peter, 135
performing arts, 14–15. *See also* dance;
    music
photography, 67, 78, 100, 120, 125n19.
    See also postcards
Poole, Janet, 23
popular culture, 17. *See also* Korean
    wave; music
Popular Culture Movement (Min-
    jungmunhwaundong), 5, 90, 139,
    140, 143, 144
postcards: of battle sites, 76, 86n9; of
    changsŭng, 136, 137, **137**, 141; in colo-
    nial period, 12, 76, 81
postmodernism, 4, 61, 110, 155
Pugachova, Alla, 210
Pusan: department stores, 31; pro-
    posed Lotte World, 44, 49
P'yŏngyang: Ch'oe Sŭng-hŭi in, 172,
    191n10; department stores, 30–31;
    School for Kisaeng, 78; tourism,
    79–80; tourist guidebooks, 77

radio stations. *See* GugakFM
railways, 68, 69, 70, 74, 76, 77, 78,
    86n10. *See also* Colonial Govern-
    ment Railways Company
Ranger, Terence, 4
restaurants: *changsŭng* at, 129, 131,
    144; cuisines, 22, 23–24, 25–26;
    hotel, 24–25; in Keijō, 22–25; kim-
    chi served in, 150. *See also* depart-
    ment store restaurants
rituals: ancestral, 88–90, 99–100,

101–102, 103n2, 104n18; *changsŭng*
    veneration, 133, 138, 145–146; folk
    museum representations, 55, **56**;
    music, 196; purification, 133
rural life: in colonial period, 37–38, 81;
    folk museum representations, 53,
    55, **56**, 60; images in guidebooks,
    81; marriages, 104n15; nostalgia for,
    6; peasants, 81, 90; positive views
    of, 90
Russo-Japanese War, 68, 74, 76, 86n9

Saeul Ensemble, 206
Sagye, 207
Sai Shōki. *See* Ch'oe Sŭng-hŭi
Salcedo, Rodrigo, 41, 44
Samsung, 204
School for Kisaeng (Kisaeng Hak-
    kyo), 78
School of Tradition and Modernity,
    103n5
Sejong Cultural Center, 132
Sekino Tadashi, 79
sensate experiences, 5, 13, 20. *See also*
    music
Seoul: apartment complexes, 41; Insa-
    dong District, 1, 130; theme parks,
    49; urban life, 41. *See also* Keijō;
    Lotte World
Seoul National University, 197, 198
Seoul Records, 197, 204, 205, 209
Seulgidoong, 203, 208
SG Wannabe, 202
Shankar, Uday, 182
shinmuyong (new dance), 169–170,
    183, 189
Shinsegye Department Store, 156
shopping, 28, 29, 33–34, 38, 41, 45, 84.
    See also consumption; department
    stores

shopping malls, 40–44, 45, 61. *See also* Lotte World

Silla Cultural Institute, 108, 109, 112, 116–119

Silla kingdom, 78, 82, 108

Simmel, Georg, 41

simulacra, 1, 4, 61–62

Sin Kyuk-ho, 47

skyscrapers, Lotte World and, 44, 49

Slater, Don, 114

Smith, Adam, 113

SMR. *See* South Manchurian Railway

soap operas, 17, 84, 100–101

soccer, 131, 202

Son Ch'in-t'ae, 135

Song Pangsong, 198

Sontag Hotel, 24, 38n2

Sookmyung Kayagŭm Ensemble, 205

Sŏp'yŏnje (Im), 6–7, 15

Sorea, 210

Soribada (Sea of Sound), 204

sottae poles, 131, 132, 145, 147n7

South Korea: ethnic and cultural diversity, 17; IMF Crisis, 48, 111; military dictatorship, 6

South Manchurian Railway (SMR), 68, 70, 76, 77

souvenirs: *changsŭng* as, 129, 130, 131, 135, 136–137; in colonial period, 12

spectacles, 3, 20, 36, 68

sports, 131, 139, 202. *See also* Olympics

Stewart, Susan, 50, 52, 54, 57, 130

stores. *See* department stores; shopping malls

Suzuki Kentaro, 135

Sydow, C. W. von, 43

Synnara, 204–205

Taiwan: national parks, 87n14; tourism, 75

tapsa yŏhaeng (field study travel): books on, 107; evolution, 108–109; in Kyŏngju, 108–110, **109**, 112, 116–119, 123; notebooks, 117; objectives, 113, 116; participants, 105–106, 117; popularity, 105, 107, 108; relationship to *paenang yŏhaeng*, 107, 110–111, 122–123; schedules, 117–119

television programs, 52, 61, 91–92, 197, 198. *See also* soap operas

theme parks: combined with shopping malls, 40–44; consumption and, 42; destination tourism, 48–49; Disney, 44, 48, 63n3; Everland, 44, 49; expansion, 49–50; foreign worlds imagined, 42; Japanese, 43; Korean Folk Village, 6; Mall of America, 40, 45; mascots, 44; scholarship on, 42–43; in Seoul area, 49. *See also* Lotte World

Third Generation, 201–202

Thomas, Nicholas, 114

Three Generations, 23

Tokyo: Ginza, 3; Imperial Hotel, 74

Tonga department store, 31. *See also* Hwasin department store

tourism: alternative, 91–93; archaeological sites, 69, 78–79, 80, 82–83; budget travel, 112; chronology, 71–73t; class distinctions, 106; in colonial period, 69, 71–73t, 74–81, **80**, 87n15, 137; contemporary, 83–84, 87n15; to department stores, 29; destination, 48–49; domestic, 91, 102; gaze of, 66; heritage, 6, 88–90, 99–101, 102, 105; international, 67; in Japan, 73–75, 83–84, 86n8; Korean wave and, 84; mass, 66, 67, 75; packaged tours, 75–76,

83–84, 85n1, 111–112, 115; photography, 120, 125n19; regions of Korea, 78–81; transactional view, 115; transportation for, 69, 76, 77. *See also* guidebooks; *paenang yŏhaeng*; *tapsa yŏhaeng*

tourists: backpackers as, 105–106, 110, 111–113, 119; domestic, 88–90, 93, 94, 101; foreign, 84; Japanese, 46, 47, 58–59, 83–84, 87nn15–16, 137; Western, 75, 79

traditions: functions, 4; invented, 4–5; Japanese, 5–6; sensate associations, 5

traditions, Korean (*chŏnt'ong*): clothing, 88, 109, 111, 177, 178–179; commodification of, 3, 16, 94, 99–102, 136, 170, 213; consumption of, 4–5, 7, 16–17, 109; contemporary attitudes, 1–2, 3–5, 144–145; cultural inventory, 54; dance, 169–170, 174, 176, 177, 180, 183, 187, 189; folk museum representations, 53–54; foods, 93, 150–151; materiality of, 12, 94, 97, 102, 129; modernity and, 4; national identity and, 139; nostalgia for, 4, 6, 94; old house experiences, 92–93, 94, 98–99, 101, 102

transportation, 67, 68, 69, **70**, 77. *See also* railways

travel. *See* guidebooks; tourism

Ŭisŏng Kim lineage, 88, **89**

UNESCO, 4, 168, 196

universities: *changsŭng* on campuses, 139–140, 148n16; music programs, 197–198, 199

University of British Columbia, Museum of Anthropology, 136–137

urban areas, 21–22, 24, 33–34, 41–42. *See also* Seoul

Urry, John, 10, 103n6, 106

Vinalog, 210, 214n23

visual clichés, 54, 55

Vlastos, Stephen, 5

Wang, Ning, 61

Warren, Stacy, 61

Weber, Karl, 24

websites. *See* Backpacker.net

Weiner, Annette, 128

Welcome Society of Japan, 73–74

West Edmonton Mall, 40, 41, 45

Williams, Rosalind H., 33

Wings (Yi), 21, 23

women: Confucian rituals and, 89–90, 101, 103n3, 104n18; consumer culture and, 33–36, **37**, 153; department store customers, 34–36, 46; domestic roles, 33, 96–97, 153; entertainers, 78, 175; images in tourism materials, 78, **79**, 81; kimchi networks, 151–153, 155–156; mothers, 153, 154–155, 164; peasants, 81; rights, 180; in urban culture, 33–34; in *yangban* families, 96–97. *See also* Ch'oe Sŭng-hŭi

Wŏn Il, 208–209, 210

World Cup, 131, 202

World Intangible Heritage designations, 4, 168

world's fairs, 42, 67

Yagi Shozaburo, 135

Yanagi Soetsu, 143–144

yangban (traditional nobility): ancestral rites, 88–90, 99–100, 101–102, 103n2, 104n18; clothing,

111; cultural reconstruction, 93–99;
lineage houses, 88, **89**, 92, 94, 95,
96, 97–99, 102; women in families,
96–97
Yeoul, 207
Yi Byung-wuk, 202, 214n23
Yi Haeshik, 205
Yi Kangsuk, 201
Yi Ka-rak. *See* Lee Garag
Yi Kŏnyong, 201
Yi Pilyŏng, 141
Yi Sang, *Wings*, 21, 23
Yi Sanggyu, 198–199
Yi Sang Ryong, 98
Yi Sŏngch'ŏn, 200, 206

Yi Sŭng-ŭn, 57–58
Yi Toegye, 94
Yŏlhwadang, 94
Yonsei University, 140, 148n16
Yoon Tohyun Band, 202
Yoshino, Kosaku, 4
Young, Louise, 29
Yu Hong-jun, 92, 107–108, 111, 112, 117,
124n2
Yun Chunggang, 211
Yun Miyong, 197, 212

zithers. See *kayagŭm*
Zozayong (Cho Cha-yong), 12

Production Notes for
Kendall / *Consuming Korean Tradition in Early and Late Modernity*

Jacket design by Julie Matsuo-Chun

Interior design and composition by April Leidig-Higgins

Text type in Arno Pro and display type in Myriad Pro

Printed by Edwards Brothers, Inc.

Printed on 60 lb. EB Opaque, 500 ppi